CONFIDENT

How to be confident using the
secrets and superpowers of neuroscience

*Best wishes
Caroline*

By

CAROLINE BREWIN

Grosvenor House
Publishing Limited

All rights reserved
Copyright © Caroline Brewin, 2025

The right of Caroline Brewin to be identified as the author of this
work has been asserted in accordance with Section 78
of the Copyright, Designs and Patents Act 1988

The book cover is copyright to Caroline Brewin

This book is published by
Grosvenor House Publishing Ltd
Link House
140 The Broadway, Tolworth, Surrey, KT6 7HT.
www.grosvenorhousepublishing.co.uk

This book is sold subject to the conditions that it shall not, by way of trade or otherwise, be lent, resold, hired out or otherwise circulated without the author's or publisher's prior consent in any form of binding or cover other than that in which it is published and without a similar condition including this condition being imposed on the subsequent purchaser.

A CIP record for this book
is available from the British Library

Paperback ISBN 978-1-83615-140-1
Hardback ISBN 978-1-83615-195-1
eBook ISBN 978-1-83615-141-8

TO MY PARENTS

For giving me confidence in every step of this journey

AND TO MY HUSBAND

For your love, laughter and support

CONTENTS

INTRODUCTION ix
The C.O.N.F.I.D.E.N.T. Framework xiv

Part 1: The C.O.N.F.I.D.E.N.T. Framework 1

C: CONFIDENT FOUNDATIONS 3
    What is Confidence? 3
    An Introduction to Your Brain 7
    The Impact of Lack of Confidence 11
    7 Confidence Myths 19
    Cheatsheet 22

Confidence Masterclass:
Kim Winser OBE – 4 Key Elements of Confidence 24

O: OWN YOUR JOURNEY 28
    Emotions and Negativity Bias 28
    The Power of Personal High-Fives 31
    Black Dot and Gratitude 37
    Cheatsheet 44

Confidence Masterclass: Ben Crowe – Rocket Scientist to Shaman 46

N: NORTH STAR LIVING 49
    Values: The Low Down 49
    Why are Values So Important? 51
    FInding Your Guiding Stars 56
    Cheatsheet 61

Confidence Masterclass: Nicola Bennett – Golf Winning Mindset 63

F: FIGHT THE GREMLIN 66
    Who is the Gremlin? 66
    Your Brain's Bouncer 70
    The Rumination Machine 76
    Perfectionism & Champagne Moments 80
    Cheatsheet 83

Confidence Masterclass: Phil Kearns – Wallaby Captain to CEO 85

I: IMPOSTER TO EMPOWERED 88
- The Imposter Breakdown 89
- 10 Ways to Smash the Imposter 93
- The Procrastination Problem 100
- Cheatsheet 105

Confidence Masterclass: Neelu Agarwal – Love Your Imposter 107

D: DANCE WITH STRESS, UNLEASH RESILIENCE 110
- The Burnout Breakdown 110
- 1. The Pleasure of Predictability 112
- 2. Avoiding the NRC Pathway (Negativity, Rumination and Catastrophisation) 117
- 3. The Power of Perspective 123
- 4. Set Up for Success 127
- Cheatsheet 131

Confidence Masterclass: NIcolina Andell – Rejections to Resilience 133

E: EMPOWERED BOUNDARIES 136
- The Dream of Work/Life Balance 136
- Boundaries – Your New Best Friend 138
- How to Say 'No' 140
- Energy Audit 145
- Cheatsheet 149

Confidence Masterclass:
Oli Spensley-Corfield – Navigating Through Challenges 151

N: NAVIGATING FEEDBACK AND FAILURE 154
- Tribes and Tribulations 154
- Getting Feedback 157
- Giving Feedback 159
- Fail Forward: Building Confidence Through Setbacks 168
- Cheatsheet 172

Confidence Masterclass: Rob Caine – The Fighter Pilot 174

T: TRIUMPH THROUGH CHANGE 177

   Motherhood 179
      Why the Drop in Confidence? 179
      Return to Work with Confidence 185
      Prosecco Time 187
      A Different Lens 187

   Confidence Masterclass: Amy Taylor-Kabbaz – Mamma Rising 189

   Redundancy 192
      The Neuroscience of Redundancy 192
      Managing Redundancy with Confidence 193

   Confidence Masterclass: Steve Preston – Redundancy is Opportunity 195

   Menopause 199
      Menopause Low-Down 199
      Managing Menopause with Confidence 201

   Confidence Masterclass:
   Claire Hattrick – Executive Menopause Coach 205

   The Divorce/Break Up 208
      How Breakups and Divorces Impact Confidence 210
      Managing Divorce with Confidence 213

   Confidence Masterclass: Sara Davison – Divorce Coach 215
      Cheatsheet 218

Part 2 221

Chapter 10: **BEYOND THE FRAMEWORK:**
                UNDERSTANDING GENDERED CONFIDENCE 223
      Where It All Starts 223
      The Brain-Body Confidence Connection 227
      Cultural Norms and Cognitive Biases 229
      Bridging the Confidence Gap in Organisations 230
      Cheatsheet 237

   Confidence Masterclass: Dr Sarah Mckay, the Neuroscientist's View 239

Chapter 11: QUIETLY BOLD: REDEFINING CONFIDENCE FOR INTROVERTS 242
- Quiet vs. Bold 242
- The Quiet Model 245

Chapter 12: A BLUEPRINT FOR LASTING CONFIDENCE 247
- Take That First Step Forward 247
- Embrace the Journey of Growth 248
- Your Next Steps: Moving from Knowing to Doing ... 249
- Believe in Your Ability to Figure it Out 251

DEAR READER 253

ABOUT THE AUTHOR 255

ACKNOWLEDGEMENTS 256

GLOSSARY 258

NOTES 265

REFERENCES 276

INTRODUCTION

I couldn't believe it – I had done it again! Another stupid mistake, this one sent to all of the Global Senior Leadership Team. I had checked the email so many times because I knew I couldn't make yet another error. How on earth could I have missed it?

I was a few weeks into the biggest role of my life – Chief of Staff to the Head of a twenty-five-thousand-person organisation. In all honesty, I was still trying to figure out what that actually meant, but I knew I had to take it – it would have been the first job title that anyone outside investment banking would have understood.

I had been in the investment banking industry since leaving university – rather more by mistake than by design. But over the years I had done well, primarily through pure determination, hard work and perhaps being a little different from many of the 'geeky finance people'. This opportunity had been offered after a gruelling (but ultimately rewarding) few years doing two jobs – standard for me – leading two global teams and fixing all sorts of broken people and processes. I was told that the new role would be an 'adventure' – working with an extraordinary leader whom I respected and could have fun with. It was the right step to take.

However, since I had started, I knew I had been 'winging' it. There wasn't a job specification, so I was trying to construct the roles and responsibilities from speaking to others in vaguely similar roles. It was a jack-of-all-trades job in some ways, with a focus on people, strategy, communications and engagement. Oh, and making sure the CEO was up to speed for all meetings and issues that popped up (which was an enormous task disguised as a footnote). There was so much to do. I was working fifteen-hour days, trying to get through it, but I was not even close to having my head above water. In fact, I felt six feet under.

But I was not getting any feedback on how it was going. My direct boss was a very high achiever – an incredibly bright man with the ability to process and recall information at a remarkable level. He loved the numbers and minutiae, as well as going at a thousand miles per hour. While I was used to a fast pace, this was something else. I was trying so hard to keep up with both his and my very high standards that my stress levels started to rocket. The only feedback on how I was doing were small eyebrow raises or, worse, silence on the mistakes that were growing.

In the absence of the feedback that I needed, I assumed the worst.

My mind felt wound up in a tight, clenched fist, unable to think clearly and use the skills that I knew I had. I was picturing being sat down and told 'It's not working out'. The humiliation! My head was whirring, my stomach was sinking, and I was hardly sleeping because of the worrying. It got to a point where I had to take action; it was do or die.

So, I asked my boss for a meeting. I told him how I was doing my best but that I was struggling with the volume and pace of work: "I feel like you are a Japanese high-speed train and I'm clinging on to the side for dear life."

The response was unexpected: "Caroline, you're doing an amazing job! We are so happy – keep it up." The relief was palpable, and it was as if a switch flicked in my mind.

From that point forward, I stopped making stupid mistakes. I could think clearly and creatively, problem solving with an attitude of 'let's give it a go'. My confidence was restored, and I was off and running.

What had happened in that scenario is part of the reason I am here today, and I'm going to be explaining this puzzle to you in the coming pages. The other reason is that I struggled with my confidence during so many different parts of my life. There were times at school when I was bullied (in the horrible, subtle way only girls can do) and it made me miserable, doubting myself and everything I did. In my teens, the wonder of hormones sent my skin on an angry journey, with horrible pimples a regular and uncontrollable occurrence. I tried to just 'carry on', but it was so disheartening when I knew people were talking about me behind my back. I couldn't even bear to look in the mirror because of what would be looking back at me each morning.

Then, throughout my career, I would have what I call 'Yo-Yo Confidence' – feeling like I was killing it one day and falling apart the next. I was being choked with anxiety. I often suffered from terrible imposter syndrome, which would completely strangle me from taking action and turned me into a perfectionist. I struggled so much with saying no that I ran myself into the ground, probably earning less than the minimum wage, with the hours I worked. My solution to hiding my fear of being found out was to work harder, have higher standards, and to never let them find out that you don't know. Don't get me wrong, there were times I knew I was doing really well, but when I look back, my life would have been so different had I understood what I do now.

What would I have done if I had understood the truth about confidence?

- *Taken control of my career.*
- *Believed in myself and my capabilities.*
- *Challenged personal and professional relationships that needed tough conversations to be better.*
- *Asked for the promotion, pay and roles I deserved.*
- *Asked for what I really needed in a relationship.*
- *Enjoyed my life more, rather than worrying about what I looked like or how much I weighed.*

Why didn't I do it?

- *Because I didn't know how.*
- *Because I doubted my capabilities.*
- *Because I hated conflict.*
- *Because I was frightened that I would be rejected.*
- *Because deep down, I felt like I didn't deserve them.*

But then I got to know myself, deeply. I 'did the work' with a coach and eventually decided to train as a professional coach myself, alongside my banking career. I decided to take it a step further, and I learned about applied neuroscience for coaching. Whilst this doesn't make me a neuroscientist, nor this book a medical guide; it was like everything just fell into place for me – so much of my life suddenly made sense. Neuroscience, the study of how our brains work, is the key to understanding why we sometimes doubt ourselves, don't think clearly, or hold back from grabbing life's biggest opportunities. It is the most incredible partner to coaching, understanding relationships, organisational strategy, leadership and so much more. When you understand the 'brain-why', it is a foundation from which you can create the 'how' to move forward effectively, and with really powerful outcomes. Understanding how my brain worked, was what drove me to have that conversation with my boss, and it is so important for you to know, as it enables you to be your best.

I know you too have dark thoughts that tell you that you aren't good enough. I know you feel total terror sometimes when you walk into a room and have to present. I know you've had that sick feeling when you feel like you've forgotten everything you learned. You feel like everyone else is confident, brilliant, shining ... why not me?

So, what can you do about it? Whatever stage of life you are at, you can learn to be more confident in a way that is totally authentic.

In fact, the goal of this book is to create empowered, positive, confident readers, maximising your incredible authentic potential for success in this world. You have so much more to give and I'm here to help you release your true potential.

However, I bet, like me, you've picked up many books full of promises of transformation but no tools; platitudes but no real punchy substance; or packed full of research but no application. I've felt the same way after years of reading hundreds of books and having some of the best training money could buy – so often I've been disappointed. The promises didn't materialise with anything *actually tangible* that could really help, or felt as useful as a chocolate fireguard – very nice, but not with any real substance or methodology for the 'how'. It's like finding yourself in a darkened room only to hear someone tell you to turn the light on without explaining how to find the light switch!

So, instead, this is what I bring you with 'Confident'. Throughout this book, we'll explore together the latest neuroscience insights and research and show you simple, practical ways to apply them to your daily life. I'm not just giving you statements, but tools, exercises, techniques and research that you can integrate and apply. You are going to have lots of different levers you can pull to shift your confidence and it's important that you try them and *keep using them*. That's because:

Confidence is a muscle – you have to keep exercising it if you want it to grow.

You'll discover how to quiet your inner critic, manage stress with greater ease, and respond to life's big challenges with a calm assurance. We will do this using our **9-step framework: C.O.N.F.I.D.E.N.T.**

THE C.O.N.F.I.D.E.N.T. FRAMEWORK

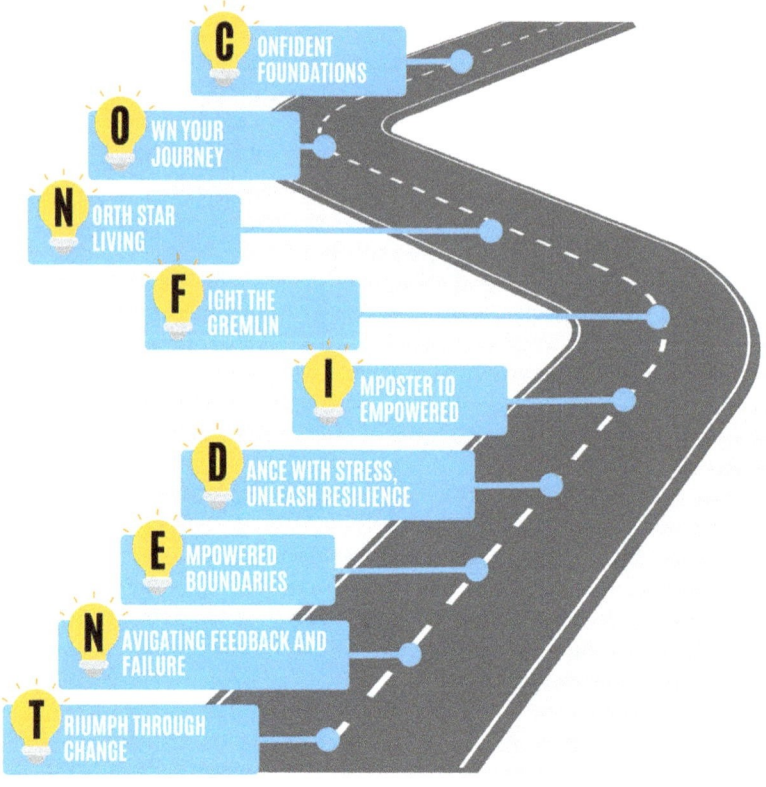

- C — CONFIDENT FOUNDATIONS
- O — OWN YOUR JOURNEY
- N — NORTH STAR LIVING
- F — FIGHT THE GREMLIN
- I — IMPOSTER TO EMPOWERED
- D — DANCE WITH STRESS, UNLEASH RESILIENCE
- E — EMPOWERED BOUNDARIES
- N — NAVIGATING FEEDBACK AND FAILURE
- T — TRIUMPH THROUGH CHANGE

As we go through the C.O.N.F.I.D.E.N.T. framework, first, I'll take you through some of the most critical concepts, exercises, research and tools about confidence and your brain. This information gives you the reason *why* you respond how you do. That's crucial, because when you understand why, you can break down the judgement of the behaviour itself, and from there move forward in an entirely different way.

Then, you will learn the fundamental building blocks for living your personal and professional lives in a way that bursts with YOU. Through working through the book and exercises, you'll have deeper trust in your skills and capabilities, with the confidence to step into new roles and stretch opportunities. You'll have a better understanding of the brain and emotions, reducing your stress levels and improving your overall wellbeing and mental health. We will address the biggest challenges that you face in life, explore the reality of how they show up, and then offer actionable steps to deal with them. These reflections and lessons will allow you to reframe failure so you can see opportunity and growth.

With more confidence in who you are and what you have to bring to the table, you will speak up more – raising the issues that need to be discussed at the right time, rather than allowing them to fester. You will not be pretending, not anxious about what people think, not judging yourself, but instead enjoying your life in a totally different, joyful, authentic way. With your brain in a positive state, you can drive innovation, perform better and create better outcomes in all of your life, because your brain is operating at its highest level.

This will all be blended with real-life stories, both of the ordinary and extraordinary, in our **Confidence Masterclasses**, as well as my experience from eighteen years of global corporate life. At the end of each chapter, you'll get a cheat sheet of the **Key Confidence Insights** and a **Time for Action** section, so you can easily reference the learnings and next steps from each. If you want to check up on a key term as you go, there's a glossary at the end of this book.

How do you know this stuff works?

For over a decade, I've dedicated my career to helping people build confidence that transforms their personal and professional lives. Through my company, Brain Powered Coaching, I've had the privilege of working with some of the world's most prestigious institutions – including Google and the Bank of England – to deliver workshops and courses that are grounded in neuroscience and designed for real-world impact. The results speak for themselves. Participants leave our programs ready to step boldly into the unknown – taking on challenges they once feared; from applying for new jobs to negotiating pay rises or even coaching a kids' football team. They start setting boundaries with confidence, saying 'no' without guilt, and discovering that the terrible consequences they once imagined simply don't materialize.

The change goes beyond the individual. One company we worked with reported a *22% rise in staff confidence and energy levels* and a *30% reduction in stress levels*. The ripple effects of this kind of transformation are profound, improving not only performance at work but also relationships at home.

Here's what some participants have shared about their journey (you can read lots more on my website at www.brainpoweredcoaching.com/testimonials):

"I've participated in other courses and read a few "life-changing" best-sellers, and not one has had such a profound positive impact."

"The program is amazing and has helped me develop healthy routines and habits to gain more control over my situation and surroundings."

"I feel privileged to be part of this group and wish more people could have the same opportunity. The world would be a happier place if all can have the opportunity."

This book brings together the lessons, tools, and insights from those programs, combined with exclusive research into the neuroscience of confidence and the stories of those who have successfully applied these concepts to their own lives.

We aren't here to change who you are. We are here to unlock the confident, resilient version *that's already within you*. Imagine having the tools to turn self-doubt into self-belief, to speak up and step boldly into new roles and opportunities. Imagine if you could approach every moment with genuine, grounded confidence.

With just a little bit of courage, and a sprinkling of trust, let me take you on a journey to unapologetic confidence.

A Quick Note

At Brain Powered Coaching, we believe that human experience is vast, complex, and beautifully diverse. While the content of this book often discusses men and women in a traditional sense, we fully acknowledge that gender is not binary and encompasses a spectrum beyond these categories. We recognize and celebrate individuals whose gender identities may not align with traditional labels, and we honour the richness they bring to the world. Additionally, though the tools and insights shared here are primarily designed with neurotypical individuals in mind, we wholeheartedly acknowledge the presence of neurodiversity in our world. We understand that individuals who are neurodivergent may experience life and learning differently, and we remain committed to employing an inclusive approach to coaching that values all minds.

Our aim is to provide insights that are accessible to many, but we also recognize that each individual brings a unique perspective, shaped by their own identity, experiences, and ways of processing information. We invite readers to adapt the ideas shared in this book to their own unique journey and embrace this content in a way that feels authentic to them.

PART 1

THE C.O.N.F.I.D.E.N.T. FRAMEWORK

CHAPTER ONE

CONFIDENT FOUNDATIONS

> "The privilege of a lifetime is to become who you truly are. Confidence follows when we let go of what we think we should be and embrace the strength of our true foundation."
>
> Carl Jung

WHAT IS CONFIDENCE?

Who do you think about when you think of confidence? Richard Branson, Elon Musk or Jordan Belfort (the Wolf of Wall Street) perhaps? Or is it more Christine Lagarde, with her effortless calm and understated wisdom? Or Barack Obama – articulate, considered and grounded? Confidence can sometimes have a bad rap as it is so often seen as arrogance; where interactions are win–lose rather than win–win. That's not what we are talking about here – we are looking for authentic confidence, where you are 100% YOU and happy in that.

Sadly though, it seems that the vast majority of people actually do lack confidence. In Brain Powered Coaching's 2024 research[1], we surveyed over seventeen thousand people about their confidence levels and found overwhelmingly that this was something people struggled with. In fact, seventy-seven percent of people struggle with confidence in some form. That's nearly *eight out of ten people* who are aren't meeting their full potential, frozen by a fear of failure and what might go wrong.

Here are some of the other high-level stats (we will go into these more later):

- **90%** of people question themselves and second-guess their decisions.
- **77%** of people don't always speak up in meetings because they doubt themselves.
- **82%** of people compare themselves to others, thinking they may be more intelligent or capable than themselves.
- **89%** of people worry about making mistakes.

Thought you were alone? Think again!

So, let's start from the beginning – what is confidence? Throughout this book, you are going to hear different ways that people describe it. We will start with five completely different perspectives, all of which are incredibly helpful when we want to figure out how to improve it.

Firstly, the good old Oxford English dictionary[2] defines it as:

"An appreciation of one's own abilities, qualities or judgement."

This is what we would traditionally expect to think about confidence – knowing our skills and capabilities. This is where we associate confidence with *competence*. A doctor is an expert in their field of medicine; a leader has lots of experience in running a business – we look at their knowledge and skills and think, yes, they demonstrate confidence.

Competence is also a critical part of us feeling confident. When I started in my Chief of Staff role, I didn't have a clue – my competence in the role wasn't high. But this grew over time, and so did my confidence levels. Unfortunately, though, just because we are *competent*, that doesn't mean we are totally *confident* – that comes from somewhere much deeper.

Let's look through a different lens. Psychologist Richard Petty[3] said:

"Confidence is the stuff that turns thoughts into action."

The key to this is that it is based on *action* and when you take action, you improve, which gives you the confidence to try something else. It is about having belief in your ability to put up a boundary, manage the unknown world whilst also knowing when to step out of your comfort zone and try something new.

Our third definition is from Brendon Burchard, motivational speaker and extraordinary entrepreneur:

"Confidence is belief in my ability to figure things out."

How often have you avoided doing something new because you were afraid of failure? How many times have you not put up your hand for fear of rejection? When you lack confidence, this powerful fear of failure can lead to complete inaction, thereby *guaranteeing failure.*

When I looked at our research, I found:

- **88%** of people might hold back from trying out a new task.
- **40%** of people would never apply for a more difficult job if they didn't have the qualifications.

These are the people who don't believe they will be able to figure it out, so they don't try. Failure is too scary. How much innovation and talent, how many challenges and improvements are organisations missing out on, just because their employees are afraid of taking a step into the unknown? This is a real challenge we need to solve.

Professor Ian Robertson is a clinical psychologist and neuroscientist. He speaks of this 'action' element in his book, How Confidence Works[4]:

"Confidence is made up of two parts. The first is the bet you make with yourself that you can do something. This is the 'can do' element. The second is the belief that if you do that thing, then the world will change a little. This is the 'can happen' part."

Combining this with the re-definition of Richard Petty's approach to turning thoughts into action, then we see that the more evidence you have of taking a step and the world not ending, the more you have confidence to try again. Please notice this:

Confidence isn't a destination. It's a journey, a muscle you need to exercise and grow as you move forward.

Finally, here's another way to think about it from my wonderful mindfulness teacher Jane Grafton:

"Confidence is grounding in your true self; integrating your internal and external authenticity and letting go of effort."

What do we need to let go of to allow our authentic confidence to surface? Maybe its over-analysing – turning things over and over in our minds, hoping that we will find anything that might trip us up (but invariably we just go over the same thing again and again). Perhaps we need to let go of trying to control everything as it only leads us to exhaustion and stress. Maybe we're terrified of failure, so we check, check and recheck again. We waste *so much time* going over things, just to try and stand on the head of failure; like a crazy game of whack-a-mole which never ends.

We've all seen the 'try-hards' bursting with bravado about how they've done this or that. Puffing out their chests and beating out their achievements. Imagine if they were to say "You know what? I'm exhausted. This isn't me. I'm actually really terrified."

Often, we are trying so hard to be everything to everyone, offering a false smile and a squeaky 'everything's fine'. It's the pressure we put on ourselves to be perfect – that's the killer – and it's something no-one else expects (nor really wants!). There is tremendous freedom in letting go of all these things and *just being yourself.*

Brendon Burchard puts it beautifully:

"The more you lie to yourself by not being authentic, the less confidence you have."

If we don't show up as our 'integrated' selves, *our brain knows.*

It knows that we are someone different in our mind, in our soul, to how we are seen from the outside, and it asks us, 'Why isn't that good enough to show people?'

It's crucial for us to be authentic, if we want our confidence to grow.

This was my big lightbulb. One day I realised that confidence isn't about being someone I'm NOT. It's about being unapologetically MYSELF. No-one... *no-one* can do that better than me! No-one can tell me I'm not doing that right, because that's true authenticity, and that shines with a glow that is grounding, secure and truly confident. I realised I didn't have to pretend anymore. It was like the pressure cooker was suddenly released and the weight of expectation was gone. **I just needed to be me.**

You may also be asking, but *how*? Especially if you aren't sure that you will actually like the *you* that will be 'exposed'. Stick with me – we will be building that capability through the book.

AN INTRODUCTION TO YOUR BRAIN

The brain is a beautifully intricate and interconnected system and we learn more about it every day! Here's a simple way to understand the key areas we are focusing on in this book:

Survival Systems: The Brain's Autopilot

At its core, the brainstem and hypothalamus handle the essentials – breathing, heart rate, and our fight-or-flight response. These areas act without conscious input, ensuring we survive even in moments of crisis. Imagine this as the **brain's autopilot**, always working in the background to keep your body running smoothly, no matter what. The autonomic nervous system (regulating involuntary functions like heartbeat and digestion) is closely linked to this area, primarily through structures like the brainstem. The nervous system will act as a dual control system, with two main branches: The parasympathetic nervous system which is the brake (a 'faint' or 'freeze' response) and sympathetic nervous system, which acts as an accelerator (a fight or flight response).

Emotional and Motivational Systems: Your Inner GPS

The limbic system, including the amygdala and hippocampus, is the emotional heart of the brain. It processes feelings, creates memories, and guides decisions based on past experiences. The amygdala works like a smoke alarm, instantly detecting threats and triggering emotional responses like fear or anger. The hippocampus, is your brain's memory organizer, cataloguing and retrieving experiences to help you learn and navigate life. Together, these systems are like a **GPS**, mapping out our emotional world and directing us toward what feels important or safe.

Executive Systems: The Brain's CEO

The neocortex, particularly the prefrontal cortex, is where the magic of advanced thinking happens. Here, we solve problems, plan for the future, and make decisions. The prefrontal cortex is especially important – it helps us regulate emotions, think rationally, and weigh long-term consequences. Think of this part as the **CEO of your brain**, bringing all the input from survival instincts and emotions into balance to make thoughtful, deliberate choices.

Note, while certain areas may have evolved earlier or perform specialised roles, most brain functions rely on collaboration across multiple regions.

With this basic knowledge, let's take a look at what is happening in our brains and how it relates to our confidence. I'm going to introduce you to four key Evolutionary Facts, which are the cornerstones of how your confidence works, so we will keep coming back to these throughout the book.

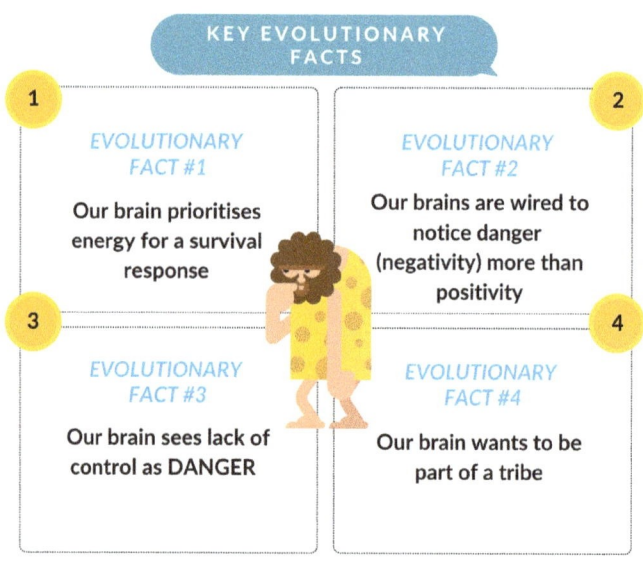

KEY EVOLUTIONARY FACTS

1. *EVOLUTIONARY FACT #1* — Our brain prioritises energy for a survival response
2. *EVOLUTIONARY FACT #2* — Our brains are wired to notice danger (negativity) more than positivity
3. *EVOLUTIONARY FACT #3* — Our brain sees lack of control as DANGER
4. *EVOLUTIONARY FACT #4* — Our brain wants to be part of a tribe

I will go through the rest in more detail later in the book, but let's start by looking at:

Evolutionary Fact 1: Our brain prioritises energy for a survival response.

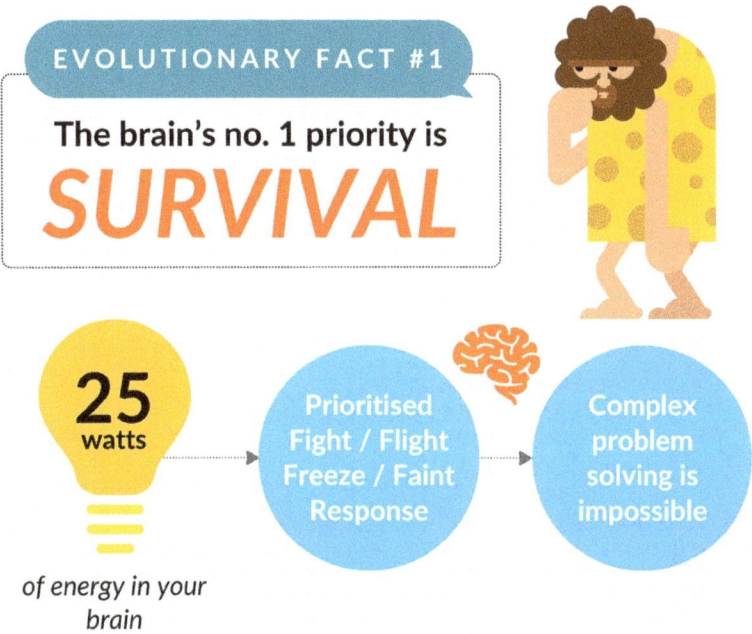

Let's see what this actually means from a brain science perspective. I'll give you the high-level workings, rather than too much technical information, but this is really important for you to understand in regard to its impact on confidence:

Our brain runs off around twenty-five watts of energy at any point in time (one weak lightbulb). It cannot 'power up' to forty watts if it is in a stressful situation: it would fry like an egg. So, well below the threshold of our consciousness, it manages its energy resources according to the perceived needs of that moment. If it feels something dangerous is happening, or 'threat' as the brain perceives it, this limited twenty-five watts of energy gets funnelled to the part of the brain that needs it most[5] – the brain's autopilot area.

This mechanism has kept us, and our ancestors, alive for many millions of years. In fact, the main survival components of the human brain are also found in the brain of the lamprey (a weird looking thing, a bit like an eel), which existed five hundred million years ago, albeit with many fewer nerve cells in each part. So, the origin of our brains and how they work stretches back quite some way!

This ancient brain hardware has us primed and ready to survive – which our caveman ancestors found very helpful when dealing with woolly mammoths, but we find problematic when trying to navigate office politics. The outcome of this energy shift is that our prefrontal cortex (PFC), the 'executive system' part of the brain, which developed much later in our evolution, is deemed less necessary at the point in time. **When we are under threat, we don't need to be thinking strategically for the future, we just need to survive!** This is when we get the 'rabbit in the headlights' effect, otherwise known as the 'Amygdala Hijack'. This is what was happening in my brain when I started my new job.

So, what is actually happening here? Let's look further inside the brain to find out.

The amygdala are two almond shaped parts of the brain which are part of your inner GPS, the 'Limbic system'. They are like your brain's smoke alarm, always scanning for danger. And if the brain perceives danger, BOOM! Then the amygdala hijack is off, with energy moving to your brain's autopilot area, powering up your body to respond chemically and physically. This may mean we can't think clearly, so are limited our ability to come up with any clever responses at the time (although we so often think of brilliant ones afterwards!). How many times have you had an argument, and then only afterwards had the *perfect* response that you wish you had said? Or only thought of that great answer to a senior manager's tough question after the meeting had finished. Dammit.

In my new job when I couldn't think straight, my fear was growing and, in the absence of any positive feedback to the contrary, my brain was going into survival mode. This was why I was making stupid mistakes, instead of being creatively adaptive as the job required of me. My brain was focusing on the threat and using all that energy for survival rather than problem solving, strategy and executive functioning.

Unchecked, this neurobiological response (and the physical stress) can completely erode confidence – shaking the foundations of years of experience, knowledge and talent, as it turns you into a nervous wreck. Running out of adaptive capacity, or having it blocked, is not fun.

So, *it's not just you*. In fact, having those moments isn't anything you need to judge yourself about – your old brain hardware is doing its job! You can take away the judgement of 'being emotional' or 'an idiot' or whatever you say to yourself. It's time to empower yourself to handle these situations more effectively by approaching them with confidence.

What's the bigger effect?

OK, so you know that your brain is operating on Microsoft 1.0. What's the impact apart from the 'freeze' or survival response?

You'll have higher stress levels. You'll innovate less. You will think short-term (who needs long-term thinking when you're just trying to stay alive?). You'll make more errors because you're not using your prefrontal cortex.

Needless to say, what we want to do is *create a space where our brains can operate in a state of thriving, not striving*. Shawn Achor found in his research referenced in The Happiness Advantage[6]:

> *"Your brain at positive is 31% more productive than your brain at negative, neutral or stressed."*

A whole THIRD more productive!! Just think what you could do with that extra brain capacity – whether it is your own, your family's or your team's.

THE IMPACT OF LACK OF CONFIDENCE

Where do you lack confidence? Perhaps it's public speaking – or even the thought of it – that makes you start to sweat? Or perhaps presenting in front of senior leaders, with their eyes boring into you as they ask a tricky question? Well, that is very common too – in our research we found that 85% of people get anxious about dealing with senior leaders (they really have some power over us, those grand fromages). Maybe you dread discussions about your salary, performance or asking for the promotion that you so desperately want. What about tough discussions with friends or family, asking for what you really need to stop you falling apart? Perhaps you're re-joining the workforce after a career break and are downright terrified as you feel you have forgotten everything. You may be going for interviews or new job opportunities, or even the dreaded networking, which the majority of us tend to visibly squirm about.

Just read that list again.

Look how many areas of your life can be impacted by confidence!

- Feeling self-doubt
- Fear of failing
- Struggling to have work-life balance
- Ability to speak up
- Not putting yourself forward for a new role or promotion
- Feeling Imposter Syndrome – like you are a fraud
- Returning after a career break
- Perfectionism
- Increased stress and anxiety
- Feeling guilty for not doing/being enough

When we zoom out, it is apparent that a lack of confidence has an impact on a wide variety of forms in real life, personally and professionally, and the numbers really prove it.

Lack of confidence can also have a fundamental impact on both an employee's professional progression and an organisation's performance. According to Bandura[7] and Pipeline[8]:

People with low self-confidence:

- Shy away from difficult tasks
- Have lower aspirations
- Focus on negative reinforcement
- Are slow to recover from setbacks
- Waste cognitive bandwidth

The impact on an organisation when its staff have low confidence is that there is:

- Less 'diversity of thought' – people aren't creative so don't bring up great ideas because of personal risk.
- A higher risk culture, as people don't speak up about their concerns.
- A 'broken rung' because people (particularly women) are left stuck at entry level as they don't put themselves forward for promotion early in their careers. The career ladder has a 'broken rung' that stops them from climbing up[9].

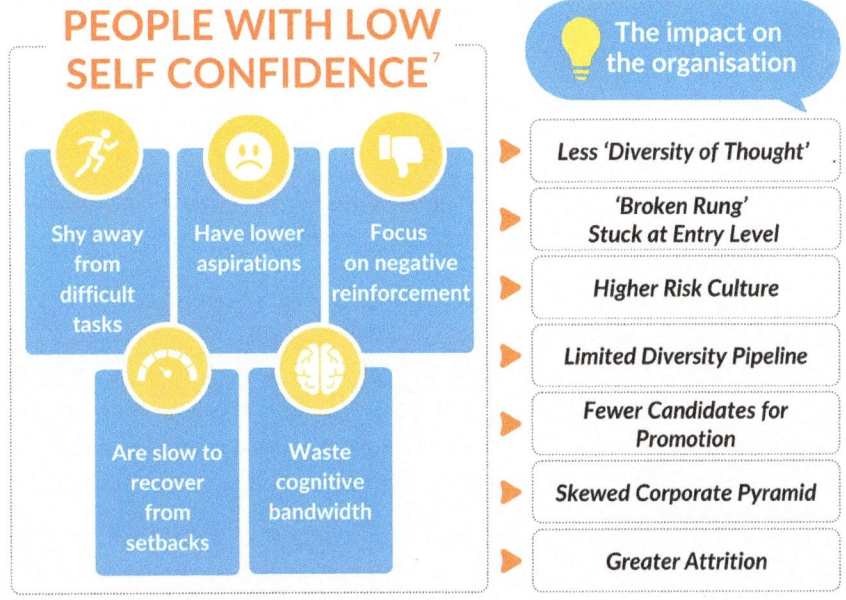

Where this is specifically associated with lack of confidence for diverse groups, it means:

- Greater attrition.
- Limited diversity pipeline for the senior roles.
- Fewer diverse candidates for promotions to senior levels.
- A skewed corporate pyramid (often with more men in senior roles).

From a regulatory perspective, lack of confidence is a real concern. Regulators, particularly in the troubled finance industry after the financial crisis, have been hugely focused on the importance of organisations creating a 'speak up' culture. However, people *need to feel confident enough to call out poor behaviour* or escalate the issue if they sense something strange happening. This could be the first thread of a major fraud; a Nick Leeson/Barings-type insider-trading incident, or the recent safety concerns with Boeing airlines. Regulators are reliant on confident people who challenge the status quo and, if needed, become whistle-blowers to avoid such major events occurring. A lack of confidence means that employees may back away from a situation, rather than take the personal risk, based on their trust in themselves and their intuition, to bring it up.

Within organisations, the broader impact of a lack of confidence is hugely under-valued. High-quality organisations are spending a significant amount of time trying to achieve gender balance, but what happens if women do not have the confidence to speak up when they are there? The excellent book The Confidence Code[10] explores research by Brigham Young University and Princeton that found that women speak 75% less than men when in the minority. You may be high fiving with a 50/50 representation around the table but, unless you can bring the joint contributions of the brains to the table, you are not maximising the cognitive capability of the group. I witnessed this far too often as brilliant, smart women were in a meeting but didn't speak up with their thoughts and ideas. What's the ultimate outcome of this lack of confidence? Lower performance of the company.

Lack of confidence can also mean staying in a toxic relationship because of fear of the unknown, which in itself further damages confidence. It can mean not bringing up that difficult discussion that really needs to take place, even though it is scary. Strong relationships are built on a foundation of communication – both positive and with the ability to pursue some of the harder messages. With my husband, we committed early in our relationship to the idea that we should communicate with each other, even if it was hard. There's been times where I've felt nervous to speak up, but I had to take a confident step forward so I could raise an issue that needed discussing. Without such communication, the core issues can turn into a pile of 'mental banana skins', just waiting for one of us to slip up.

Lack of confidence can also come in the form of procrastination ('If I don't start, then I can't fail') and can also lead to perfectionism, which means wasting precious time unnecessarily. I've spent many hundreds of hours servicing my perfectionist tendencies, just because I was scared of being found out. The result? Slow, or non-existent delivery, despite being perfectly capable!

What about the other way around, when people are too confident? Well, we've all been there, with the person trying to prove they are the best. They can be needy, committing to unrealistic goals whilst proving themselves incapable of making decisions (or only capable of making really poor ones). When we know that deep down, over-confidence is hiding real *lack of confidence*; deep insecurity – a big fear of being found out. Not only is that over-confidence annoying to experience, but it can be really damaging for people and organisations, as you try and operate in the carnage that they create.

What about you? Do you remember a time when you felt *really confident*? A time when you knew your stuff; you owned your space; you spoke up and did it from an authentic place, unapologetically being yourself. How did that show up? What did you achieve in that moment and beyond? How FREE did you feel?

Research by Bandura[7] shows that people with high self-confidence:

- Set higher goals.
- Perform better analysis and problem solving.
- Are more motivated.
- Cope better with change.
- Make decisions and don't let what others think influence their decision to take action.
- Don't mind trying new things, even if they've never done them before. They are happy to 'take a risk' (remember our definition 'belief in my ability to figure things out').
- Let go of their inhibitions and don't mind letting their guards down. They have the courage to be vulnerable – to say, 'I don't know, but let's figure it out together.'

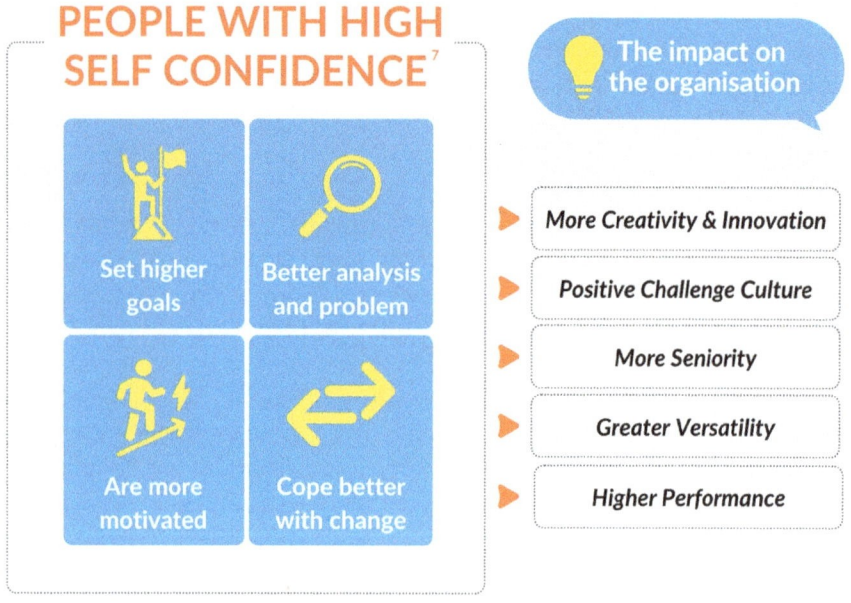

This is why you being here and reading this book is so important.

Life with authentic confidence is richer, deeper, more exciting and fulfilling. Authentic confidence allows us to flex, stretch and leap with joy into the unknown. We look at challenges with glee, knowing they make us better, shouting BRING IT ON!! And because of that attitude, we can ride the waves of change with a sense of authenticity that brings extraordinary FREEDOM.

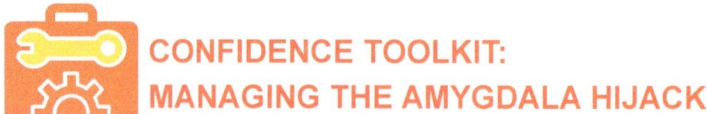

CONFIDENCE TOOLKIT: MANAGING THE AMYGDALA HIJACK

You're feeling stressed – that lack of confidence has reared its head and you can't think straight. Perhaps you've taken that wrong turn on the motorway and are zooming off in the wrong direction (again). Or perhaps you're about to step on stage and present, pitching for that business you want so dearly.

How can you calm yourself down quickly and operate at the level you know you deserve? Come to the rescue, what Dr Andrew Huberman calls the Physiological Sigh[11]. This is something we actually do naturally – particularly kids when they are upset. You know that point where a child has *completely lost their mind* in tears, and they start repeatedly taking quick breaths in through their nose? It's a clever way that nature gives them to calm themselves down.

Here's the process: two inhales through the nose, one long exhale through the mouth:

- Take a deep breath, then add another small breath, both through your nose, until you feel like your lungs are really full.
- Then exhale through your mouth.

How does it work? Inside your lungs, you have thousands of little balloons called alveoli that blow up with a breath in and pass oxygen to your blood through your blood vessels (whilst taking carbon dioxide with them on their way out). The issue is that we often don't use them fully – think of it like a balloon. When you first have to start blowing it up, you need two breaths to get it going. It's the same with your lungs – the double inhale pops open all the alveoli, so you're getting the maximum amount of oxygen and can balance the ratio of carbon dioxide and oxygen in your bloodstream and lungs. It also activates a circuit that goes from the diaphragm, sending signals back to the brainstem (called the phrenic nerve) and informing the brain about the status of the body: 'I am calm'. Just two to three of these will bring your autonomic nervous system baseline back down to a normal, relaxed level: it really does work!

During the pandemic, I was working with front-line workers in hospitals in South Africa, delivering my corporate confidence programme remotely via Zoom. They would join the training sessions online, having had people die *literally that morning*. They were scared, exhausted and so, so stressed. These doctors and nurses decided to implement the physiological sigh into their work.

They would huddle together and take those two breaths in, long breath out a few times as a team. They said it helped them so much that they were able to calm down, regroup and go to help the people who needed them on their game. They could use their fully functioning brains, feeling ready to do their best.

Another client, Catherine, used this tool with her daughter. She was just about to do her first show-jumping competition and was very nervous. Catherine and her daughter did three of these physiological sighs together and her daughter went out there and nailed it. I use it too when I get lost driving (a regular occurrence) or if I'm going to speak on stage; it's a brilliant way to be able to calm myself down quickly, so I can think more clearly and perform at my best.

So, add the physiological sigh to your toolbox; you'll be able to channel your inner hyper-chill and re-engage your fabulous prefrontal cortex. That will give you the confidence you need to face a variety of challenges as you'll know then that you will be able to cope with whatever comes up.

7 CONFIDENCE MYTHS

There are many myths about confidence that we will need to smash through at the start. Here are seven that I hear all the time:

1. Confidence = being extroverted
That person who is the life of the party is the confident one, right? Wrong. Confident people aren't always socially dominant and outgoing. It comes from within and can manifest in different ways, including being introverted. Often the loudest ones are hiding insecurity and cover it up with a facade of confidence. It's about believing in yourself, your skills and capabilities, not your volume (we will go into this more in Chapter 11).

2. You're born with it
Lots of people believe that confidence is innate. However, although you may have some genetic skews, personality traits or experiences that build your confidence, it's something that everyone has the power to develop and nurture over time. Remember, it's a muscle that we can build up over time as we take even just small steps outside our comfort zone.

3. It's a sign of your competence level
Whilst there is a relationship between confidence and competence, you may not even realise how competent (or incompetent) you really are. Someone who believes they are competent, but isn't, is at best irritating and at worst, downright dangerous (how hard can flying a plane really be?!!)

4. The more the better
OK true, as we've discussed, really lacking in confidence can significantly hold you back. But overconfidence can be damaging too. Imagine the people you will ignore, the lessons you won't learn, the blind spots you won't acknowledge, the caution you won't listen to and the risks you will take if you're overconfident.

The reality is somewhere in between, where you have the courage to step out and try new things and the humility to know you will always be learning.

5. Confidence is a destination

'When I'm confident I will...' How much have you held back because you were waiting for the day you felt confident enough to do it? This is the truth: confidence isn't an end game, it's part of the journey. Every time you move forward just a tiny bit, that builds your confidence. Plus, it's going to go up sometimes, and down at others, depending on your environment, situation, mood and people around you. Remember that confidence is having belief in your ability to figure things out; whatever comes up, I'll be able to work with it.

6. Confidence is arrogance

True confidence isn't about arrogance, it's about being truly *grounded in your own authenticity*. Some people mistake or mislabel the behaviours of a confident person for arrogance or being overly self-assured. Take care how you label people, because society has primed us to judge confidence in this way. However, real confidence has a different grounding from arrogance, which isn't focused on ego and insecurity, or needing approval, but being centred in who you really are. More on that in Chapter 10.

7. Confidence is based on looks

We're told that confidence belongs to people who fit a narrow ideal – slim, toned, flawless. But confidence doesn't come from how you look; it comes from how you feel about yourself.

You don't have to love every inch of your body to feel confident, but you do need to respect it. Your body carries you, supports you, and deserves kindness, not constant criticism. True body confidence isn't about meeting someone else's standards – it's about focusing on what your body does for you and shifting the way you speak to yourself. Confidence isn't granted by perfection; it's built through self-acceptance and compassion (how many examples of insecure models do we hear?). This is the reason we aren't focusing significantly on body confidence in this book. Of course, how we dress can impact how we feel, but you know this! What so many people miss is the internal confidence: our self-belief and identity, and that is where the real focus needs to be.

Final Word

With this chapter's deep dive on confidence, hopefully we have challenged your pre-conceptions and given you a new perspective on what true, authentic confidence really is. On this solid foundation, we are going to start laying the bricks of a new, confident you by looking at O – Own your journey.

KEY CONFIDENCE INSIGHTS

1. **The Neuroscience Behind Confidence:**
   Our brain's natural response to stress stops us from performing at our best. Your brain's survival mechanisms, like the 'Amygdala Hijack', can make you feel overwhelmed and paralysed under stress. This is because it's using that 25 watts of energy where it judges it needs it the most – your brain's autopilot area. This is something we all experience, and recognising it is the first step toward taking back control.

2. **Redefining Confidence:**
   Confidence isn't about being the loudest or most extroverted person in the room. It's about being authentically *you* and turning your thoughts and feelings into decisive actions. True confidence comes from within, not from external validation.

3. **It's Not Just You:**
   Research shows that confidence struggles are universal. Over **90%** of people question themselves, second-guess their decision making and worry about making mistakes.

4. **The Myths aren't true:**
   Confidence isn't about being naturally gifted, extroverted, or reaching a perfect state. It's a journey of continuous growth, rooted in being true to yourself and taking action.

5. **The Cost of Low Confidence:**
   A lack of confidence can hold you back from reaching your full potential, both personally and professionally. It's important to recognise this impact so you can take steps to overcome it (good thing you're here!)

TIME FOR ACTION

1. **Use the Physiological Sigh:**
   When stress hits, practice the 'Physiological Sigh' to quickly calm yourself and regain focus.

2. **Take Consistent Actions:**
   Regularly challenge yourself with tasks that push you out of your comfort zone. Each step you take will build your confidence.

3. **Be Authentic:**
   Stay true to who you are, rather than trying to meet others' expectations. Authenticity is the foundation of lasting confidence.

CONFIDENCE MASTERCLASS
KIM WINSER OBE – 4 KEY ELEMENTS OF CONFIDENCE

"You can be quietly or extrovertly confident. The richest depth of confidence comes from within."

Kim Winser, OBE, is a prominent British businesswoman known for founding and leading the womenswear label Winser London. She began her career at Marks & Spencer, rising to become their youngest divisional Board Director and led women into the commercial field. Winser later served as CEO at Pringle of Scotland and Aquascutum, where she revitalised these brands into global names. Recognised with an OBE for her contributions to the fashion industry, Winser has also advised firms like the private equity firm 3i and Net-a-Porter, the first luxury digital marketplace. She continues to contribute to business and charitable endeavours, including supporting youth enterprise with HRH King Charles.

For Kim, confidence is not just about outward appearance or being extraverted, it's deeply connected to positivity and energy. "If you're positively enthusiastic and full of energy and determination, you've made a good step towards your self-confidence," she told me. But beyond that, Kim sees confidence as something that comes from knowledge and ability. It's about being prepared, feeding your knowledge, and using your experience to foster a sense of security in yourself. This cycle of positivity, knowledge, and energy creates the 'confidence – competence loop', constantly fuelling and reinforcing itself.

> *"It's a continuous process. You build your confidence, feed it, allow it to breathe, and build it again."*

Kim believes that confidence doesn't have to be loud or extroverted. "You can be both quietly or extrovertly confident," she explained, the richest depth of confidence comes from within, and for her, it *should not be about how others perceive you, but how you feel inside*. She's also passionate about lifelong learning and stepping out of her comfort zone to grow. Kim chooses non-executive roles in industries outside of fashion, such as hospitality, science, or beauty – these challenges help in feeding and growing her knowledge. "You've got to want to feed your brain all your life," she said. For Kim, confidence comes not just from expertise, but from being willing to learn something new, even when stepping into unfamiliar territory.

Kim's sense of equality and confidence began at a young age, shaped by her upbringing in a family of four children. "We were always treated as equals," she recalled. Teamwork, particularly through sports, also played a crucial role in her development. Kim emphasised the value of recognising individual strengths within a team. "You don't all have to be the same. In fact, you shouldn't be," she said. She encourages everyone at the table to contribute, even if they don't feel like they are experts in the room. "Everyone brings something to the table, even if it doesn't seem obvious at the time," she reminded us, urging us not to stay silent out of fear.

As she has gained more experience, she's come to see confidence as multi-dimensional. She spoke about four key elements that contribute to confidence: **doing, feeling, being, and looking.**

- **Doing:** This is the 'ability' element of confidence – preparation and knowledge is key.
- **Feeling:** The importance of feeling optimistic and secure in yourself and your contributions.
- **Being:** How you project yourself as positive, energised and relevant.
- **Looking:** How you present yourself does matter – if you feel good, it will show.

Kim admitted, though, that there were moments in her career when she questioned herself. One such moment was when she was invited to speak at a prestigious International Herald Tribune (IHT) luxury conference, sharing the stage with impressive individuals like Ralph Lauren and Giorgio Armani. "I remember sitting backstage, seeing them all walk in to take their seats, and thinking, why am I here to present to such icons of the industry?" However, once on stage, Kim found her confidence by focusing on the reason she had been invited to talk to such a room – her experience in turning around heritage brands.

"I realised that I shouldn't have been concerned because I know my business," she said, emphasising that preparation and knowing your subject matter is key to overcoming moments of doubt. "The times where I have felt the least confident, I've just reflected on what I'm sharing; the reason why I've been invited into the room." For Kim, confidence comes from trusting her own knowledge and contributions, even when surrounded by industry giants.

One of Kim's most important lessons on confidence comes from her late mother. "My mum always said…"

> ***"Whatever you do, Kim, just always remember to be true to yourself."***

This advice has stayed with Kim throughout her life and career. For her, being authentic is key to building true confidence. "The more comfortable you become with who you are, the more confident you'll be," she explained.

Kim Winser's journey through the worlds of fashion, leadership, and business shows that confidence is not a one-time achievement but a continuous process of growth. Her advice is clear: be positive, stay curious, and trust in your own abilities. Whether you're speaking on a global stage or learning something new, confidence is about being prepared, embracing your individuality, and, most importantly, being yourself.

Kim's Top Tips for Confidence

1. Remember the four parts to confidence:
   - **Doing:** Prepare well and build your knowledge and ability.
   - **Feeling:** Remain optimistic and secure inside who you are.
   - **Being:** Project yourself as relevant, positive and energised.
   - **Looking:** Radiate confidence by looking the part.
2. Have a learning mentality – look to continuously feed your knowledge and know you are bringing your strengths to the table.
3. Don't feel you must always deliver 10/10 – you don't always have to be perfect. Sometimes it's fine to get 9 and then improve.
4. Don't try and be anyone else, just always remember to be true to yourself.

Want more wisdom from Kim? You can download the brilliant '**25 Lessons from an Exceptional CEO**' on the book website at: www.brainpoweredcoaching/book

CHAPTER TWO

" Knowing yourself is the beginning of all wisdom. "

Lao Tzu

EMOTIONS AND NEGATIVITY BIAS

Why do we have emotions? They actually exist to signal to us what is happening in our environment, to assimilate that and push us to take action. Feel frightened? Run away. Feel shame? Hide.

It's useful to think of the word 'emotion' as if it's hyphenated into 'e-motion' – energy in motion – which results in taking action. These emotions, can be distilled into eight core emotions[1] as you can see on the diagram:

- **Escape Emotions:** fear, anger, disgust, shame, sadness
- **Potentiator Emotions:** surprise/startle
- **Attachment Emotions:** love/trust, excitement/joy

The fact that we have such a wide range of 'escape' emotions means that the majority of the thoughts we have are negative. This is known as the 'Negativity Bias'. Evidence suggests that 60%-70% of the thoughts we have are those associated with 'escape' or 'survival' emotions[2]. If you want to dig deeper into this and hear from the creator of the model, Professor Paul Brown, you can see a fascinating interview I did with him on the book website: www.brainpoweredcoaching.com/book

The 8 Basic Emotions

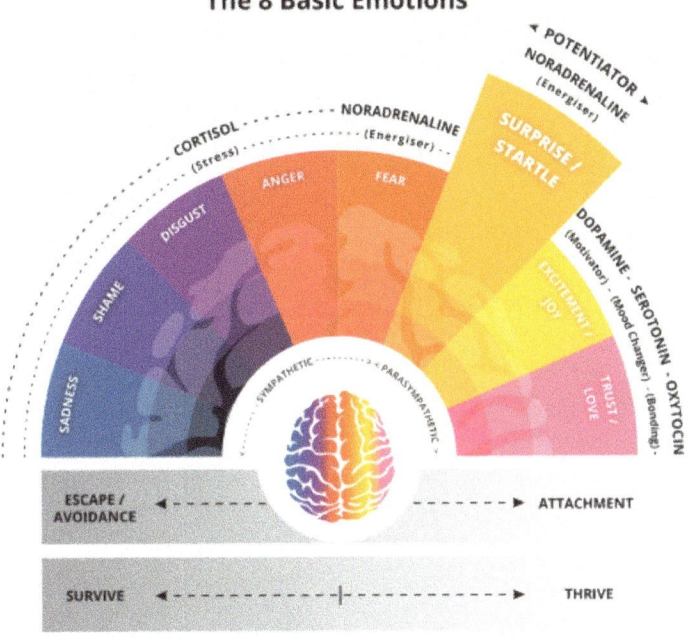

The London Protocol of the Emotions. ION Consulting International Pte Ltd 2023

Let's take a look at our second Evolutionary Fact which is relevant here:

Evolutionary Fact 2: Our brains are wired to notice danger (negativity) more than positivity.

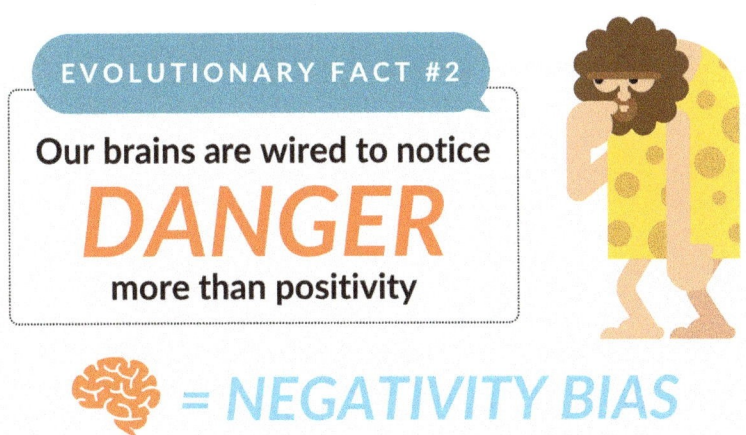

How often do you walk around judging people, worrying about what they think about you or thinking about that issue that's been bugging you for ages? What about that performance review you had, which was fifty-five minutes of telling you how brilliant you are. All the way through it you're thinking about the 'but' that's coming. Then it comes – the one development area – and what do you focus on afterwards? Only that. All the brilliant stuff you had done so well is forgotten, as you swear and curse for the injustice of that one small negative piece of feedback.

Functioning in this manner really does make perfect sense for us as a species – the more quickly we notice negativity or threat, the faster we are able to react and the safer we will be, thereby enabling us to continue to live longer and reproduce. The cavemen with rosy coloured spectacles on, sunbathing rather than running when the predator arrived, didn't last very long on the savannah. Our negativity bias allows us to see potential danger sooner and then have our survival response to fight / flight / freeze / faint / fawn as needed. However, there's a complication: the vast majority of situations we experience nowadays do not actually threaten our physical safety.

Office politics is a great example of this: how sick or angry do you become when you feel like you are being undermined, stabbed in the back at work? Is it threatening your life? No. But your brain does not know that and instead leaps into action, preparing you to survive. It is our 'self' that feels threatened and may not be able to cope. That's when we have our amygdala hijack, also known as brain freeze, and the whole thing falls apart.

Don't worry. It's perfectly natural. We just need to start managing it, if we are going to make lasting change to our confidence levels.

It is also the escape/avoidance/survival emotions that penetrate most strongly into our awareness. People tend to remember the bad more vividly, process it more efficiently and pay more attention to it (remember the performance review). Stereotypes and bad impressions form more quickly and the escape emotions produce longer-lasting effects, which is clever really, as if it's possible danger, we had better remember that for next time. But the impact on our confidence can be huge, if we are constantly allowing that negativity to shape how we see ourselves in the world.

The 'attachment' emotions, excitement/joy and love/trust, while important for social and parent-to-child connections, continuation of the species at a biological level are secondary. It really does make sense that our brains are more tuned to look for the things that may trigger escape emotions; this is your brain trying to protect you.

THE POWER OF PERSONAL HIGH-FIVES

Here's a question for you: *What did you do last weekend? How about the week before? Do you even remember what you wore yesterday?*

Chances are, if you're like most people, you'll have to think hard about it. Unless something went wrong. Maybe your car broke down, you had a big fight with your partner or a massive issue at work – those are the things that stick in our minds. As a result of our negativity bias, we are programmed much more effectively to remember the bad things that happen than the good.

So, let's extend the timeframe: *What are you most proud of in the last year? Last five years? Your whole life?* Have you ever actually asked yourself that question? When we all march on through life, *never actually celebrating the wins,* always focused on the negative, how on earth do we expect our brains to grow in confidence?

Let's go inside your brain for a minute and see what it might say: *'OK, we are going for a promotion! Great. I'm going to do everything I can to be successful. This is what I'll commit to for the next nine months:*

- *Working late*
- *Putting in extra effort*
- *Volunteering for extra projects*
- *Sacrificing time with my family*
- *Staying late in the (virtual) office*
- *Getting stressed*
- *Not eating properly*
- *Reluctantly dealing with idiots who we would normally tell to bugger off*
- *Not going to the gym*

…But it will all be worth it when I make it up that ladder!'

Then, it's the Big Day. You're nervous, not sure if all this will be worth it. You get called into the office and your boss shakes you by the hand, "Congratulations!" Woo hoo! You've got the promotion. You're happy and hugely relieved that you've finally made it. You might have a celebratory bottle of bubbles and a meal with friends. A day or so later, though, you're feeling a bit flat: what happens next?

Just compare the two. Look at ALL the effort you put into that promotion and the difference in terms of how much you actually acknowledged the brilliance of your achievement. Now, if you are your brain and you have lived and breathed all of that, why would you feel confident? Your brain says, 'I put in so much effort, but I was never rewarded. It must have not been enough. *Maybe I'm not enough.*' And your confidence drops.

So, what we can we do to acknowledge, celebrate and integrate these fantastic achievements, so our confidence grows? Here are two simple exercises you can work through which will have a big impact and be that personal high-five you need.

CONFIDENCE GYM: YOUR LIFE/CAREER TIMELINE

Until I really started to do some proper self-reflection, I kind of bumbled through life. Every year just zoomed past, and I struggled to remember the milestones I had experienced. The harder times, the negative memories, were definitely easier to bring to mind, but the achievements, highlights and things to be proud of, were a bit of a blur. When I actually took the time to reflect on my life, I realised it was a mixture of ups and downs, as with all of us, but there was so much to be proud of and to appreciate. My parents were (are) extraordinary, and they gave me and my siblings all the love in the world. We were listened to, heard, made to feel like we counted and had something to say. I grew up with lots of lovely friends (seven of which I'm still great friends with today) and we had all sorts of adventures over the years.

But, as I mentioned in the introduction, I was bullied a bit at school and the corporate world presented a whole lot of stress and challenges – some small, but some hugely impactful and devastating on my happiness and confidence levels. The biggest low light was a horrible break up, aged thirty-two, which tore me apart. Now, having spent the time reflecting, I know it was also my biggest lesson. It taught me resilience and a whole lot of emotional depth that I would never have understood otherwise. It's only when you really hit your rock bottom that you can then understand how tough that place is, and how much it takes to come back from it. I also see, looking back at it, how proud I should be of what I have achieved over the years. Whether it was having the courage to move abroad, to heal from the grief of my relationship breakdown or be the leader I was at work – there has been a lot to be proud of. The problem was, although my career had been accelerated, with fast promotions initially and being part of the 'top talent' group, I always just moved onto the next target, the next level or pay rise. I compared myself to others and felt like it wasn't good enough.

I never took the time to say, "Well done, me." No wonder I was always looking for more.

It was only once I drew up my life timeline, and took that time to reflect, that I could acknowledge the journey and give myself a big pat on the back. Had I not actually taken the time to really review my life in detail, it would be easy for me to miss the learnings, the growth and see all I have to be proud of. In fact, a big part of better confidence, leadership, self-assurance and feeling empowered is understanding yourself, reflecting on your past achievements and challenges and congratulating yourself. It's time to compare *you to you* – not to others who have all had different starting points!

So, this is what you're going to do too – your life or career timeline. Start with it as a one-off exercise, then I recommend you do it every year, just to keep it current. Here's the process and I've also given you an example what it could look like:

Step 1: Write

Spend some time reflecting on the **key events in your career or life**, from birth or when you started your first job (doing the whole lot is better, but only do that if you're comfortable to do so). If you're more comfortable focusing on your **professional life** that's totally fine, it is your choice. *No one else will see your timeline unless you want them to;* you will just use it for your own reflections.

The highlights or low lights might include:

- First day at school
- Being bullied
- A wonderful summer camp you went on
- First boyfriend/girlfriend
- Losing a loved one

Do it in whatever form you like – Microsoft PowerPoint®, back of a piece of paper, vision board, spreadsheet – whatever works for you.

Step 2: Reflect

- What do you notice when you look at what you have drawn up? Is there a pattern? What surprised you?
- How have your experiences shaped you as a person, colleague or leader?
- What can you learn from doing this exercise? What do you know is true about yourself?
- What might change for you having done this? What are your actions from the exercise?

Step 3: Integrate

Remember Brendon Burchard's definition 'Confidence is my ability to figure things out'? Look at your timeline and see how much you have figured out! See how you have the *power to choose how you interpret these experiences*. You can see them as problems that were unfair, and you wish hadn't happened, or challenges that made you stronger. Look how much you have to be proud of! Take a step back and really breathe that in. Put your hand on your heart and say out loud "I'm proud of myself" (and repeat it!). Then, write a letter to yourself reflecting on what you're proud of: 'Dear Caroline, I'm so proud of you for...' Dr Ivan Joseph, internationally renowned speaker, bestselling author and coach calls this a 'Brag Letter'[3] – he recommends you use it when you're feeling down and to shift negative thinking into positivity and performance.

Remember, you deserve to be confident, because you are resourceful, resilient and strong.

EXAMPLE: YOUR LIFE TIMELINE

Left	Year	Right
Born, healthy baby with loving family	1995	
Won first school science fair	2003	
Made the school soccer team	2007	Moved to a new city, left old friends behind
Graduated middle school with honours	2010	Experienced bullying at the new school
Started high school, met life-long friends	2012	Parents' divorce
Discovered passion for photography	2014	Struggled with self-esteem issues
Graduated high school, received scholarship to college	2016	Battled with anxiety during senior year
Studied abroad in Italy, gained new cultural experiences	2018	Lost a close family member
Interned at dream company	2019	Ended a long-term relationship
Graduated college with a degree in Graphic Design	2020	Pandemic disrupted job search
Landed first full-time job in the desired field	2021	Dealt with burnout and work stress
Promoted to a team leader position	2022	Had to relocate for work, left support system
Started a side business and reached first sales milestone	2023	Faced financial difficulties starting the business
Travelled to dream destination, Japan	2025	Experienced health issues, required surgery

CONFIDENCE GYM: CELEBRATE YOUR SUCCESSES

Just like the big picture, it's easy to forget the little bricks in our confidence wall that are built up every day. Spoke up in a meeting – one brick. Said no to someone – another brick. Had a conversation I've been avoiding – one more brick. The crucial thing is not to skip over these but to instead acknowledge them – then your confidence will grow.

So, once a week, spend time writing down what you are proud of from the week before – I do mine every Monday morning. What am I celebrating? What am I proud of? It doesn't matter if it's turning up every day when I don't feel like it or landing that big deal. I just remind myself of the week by looking at my calendar and then I start to write. I then discuss this with my assistant, and she does hers too – team high fives! It's amazing how, once I start, I realise how many things I've forgotten – hidden away in the confidence graveyard by my brain.

Why is this important? **Each time we acknowledge ourselves for the amazing work we have done, our confidence wall gets taller.**

Once you put in the hard work, improve, acknowledge and celebrate that, you learn that you can do the hard things in life and then you gain the credibility to believe in yourself.

I feel it with every achievement I write – I have a little fist pump 'yes!' and it spurs me to keep going. Why don't you start too?

BLACK DOT AND GRATITUDE

In February 2023 my father was diagnosed with Motor Neurone Disease (MND). This terrible disease had first affected his speech, making him slur, and over the next few months his swallowing was affected too, making talking and eating impossible. Soon after, he was fitted with a tube in his stomach for him to get the food he needed to stay alive.

Dad had always been the life of the party. Not in a 'look at me' way, but always bringing great conversation, joy and laughter. It was never a dull moment. So, this was a huge blow to him and all of us around him. Thanks to technology, we still get his wonderful spark and wit via his iPad, which he types into so that it can speak for him. It's an absolute godsend, given the circumstances.

One morning, a few months after the diagnosis, we were sitting having tea – Mum and Dad tucked up in bed, me sitting on the end. Dad was feeling down. 'I don't feel like I want to get up in the morning like I used to,' he typed. 'It feels a bit pointless.' (Your energy levels go down a lot with MND as the neurones are working so much harder to get things done).

I drew a small black dot in the corner of a big white piece of paper. "This is what we focus on," I said, pointing to the dot. "We focus on the black spots in our lives, because of our natural negativity bias, but the reality is, there is SO much we can be grateful for – that's the white piece of paper."

This is true for all of us. How easy is it to focus on that one argument, that small piece of negative feedback or issue? We focus on these black spots rather than all the incredible gifts, experiences, relationships and circumstances in our lives.

We agreed that Dad would start adding a gratitude practise to his daily reflection time in the morning. Every day, he started writing down a few things that he's grateful for; from the love of the family, to playing his violin or being able to work on his vegetable patch. And he found it really started to help. Even with the cruel disease that he is dealing with, he has a choice in terms on how he shows up every day: *poor me* or *lucky me.* A strong faith has also always been the foundation of Dad and Mum's marriage. Before they were married, they read 'Letters to Karen: A Father's Advice On Keeping Love in Marriage' By Charlie W. Shedd (1965). This classic book speaks of trying to think of ten positives each day to say to each other and only one negative – a rule they have tried to keep to all their time together (fifty-five years and counting!) and which is clearly helping them with these challenges today.

So, how does this personal anecdote relate to confidence? Meta research has found huge science-based benefits of *gratitude*[4].

People with a regular gratitude practise reported 23% less stress and more energy and vitality in their lives.[5] They also had better cognitive processing due to more grey matter in their brains.[6] Yes, it actually changes how your brain is structured!

A study on chronic pain sufferers found that when they had a regular gratitude practise, they had 19% lower depression versus a control, and 10% improvement in sleep.[7]

Gratitude also helps fight what's called familiarity dissatisfaction, technically called Hedonic Adaptation. This is important, so listen close.

Let's say (God forbid) you have a car crash and its life changing: you end up in a wheelchair. Now, first up, this would be incredibly shocking and so much would change in your life. But the research shows that, even with these life changing events, our happiness levels tend to go back to a 'baseline level'.[8] Although we have the initial drop, we then return to this 'normal' level – our brain adapts to its new circumstances. Interestingly, this happens whether the change is negative or positive. Lottery winners have the same thing – a spike, then a drop back down to around your base level.

Now, you may not have experienced those extremes, but this happens on a simple day-to-day level. You buy a new car and you are super excited about driving it each day for a few weeks. Then the 'novelty wears off' and it's just your car to get you from A to B. Same with a new watch, new house, even a new relationship; after a while, your partner is just there (and maybe even slightly irritating). This is hedonic adaptation and we have to beat it if we want to maximise happiness and set ourselves up for a confident life.

This is where gratitude comes in.

Most mornings when I wake up, my first thought is 'urgh, I've not slept enough.' Then all the things I need to do and how I'm so behind. What a way to start the day! Gratitude reminds us of the good things that are already in our lives. It refocuses the mind on the whole big white piece of paper that we have, rather than the tiny black dot on the page. And we have SO much to be grateful for; it's just that our negativity bias makes us forget the good things.

It also increases the level of serotonin in the brain. Serotonin is the neurotransmitter which psychiatrist and author Daniel Z. Lieberman calls the 'here and now' chemical.[9] It's what makes us feel good, as it promotes feelings of wellbeing and happiness. Dopamine is what he calls 'the Molecule of More'[9] – pushing us to pursue more rewards. Imagine a see saw: one side is dopamine, the other is serotonin. They work together to keep us motivated (dopamine) and happy (serotonin). If we don't focus on being grateful for the present; if we skip over these happy feelings, we don't replenish our serotonin and can end up feeling empty and discontented (remember the power of doing your timeline). It also means we will struggle to keep going in the long term, as we aren't replenishing our dopamine levels, which drives us to keep moving forward, motivating us to achieve our goals.

Please read this next line carefully.

If all you do in your life is strive for MORE, it will never, ever, ever be enough.

How many of you have got that promotion you've been fighting for, then simply look up at the next one? Or bought that bag you've wanted for so long, then feel a bit 'meh' once you've got it? What have you wanted more of?

- More Money
- More Promotions
- More Stuff
- More Clothes
- More Recognition

The problem is that *all that happens when we get it, is that we want MORE*. That's why Lieberman describes dopamine, what drives us, as 'the Molecule of More' in the book by the same name.[9]

Gratitude, and the serotonin it produces, rebalances that dopamine drive. It means you see the sparkle in your child's eye; the brightness of the sun shining through the leaves, the gift of having a roof over your head or the rubbish men who collect your rubbish each week. Life becomes like you've painted it with glitter: everything sparkles with joy, warms your soul and leaves you with a smile on your face. That gratitude powers you to keep going, even when it's hard work.

High-performance groups like SAS, special forces, know this link and so practice gratitude too. They know that being grateful that they're waking up (serotonin) actually puts them in forward motion (dopamine).

Work by Martin Seligman, the father of Positive Psychology, found that the gratitude 'high' is even greater when you give gratitude to others, for both giver and receiver. A study published in the Journal of Personality and Social Psychology found that individuals who wrote a letter of gratitude reported greater levels of happiness and decreased symptoms of depression compared to those who did not.[10] So, writing a letter of thanks to that old teacher or your parents, leaving a bottle of wine for a kind neighbour, or just sending a card to say how much you appreciate someone really can change your happiness levels.

The happier you are, the more confident you will feel as you'll be more optimistic about life and its outcomes.

For the leaders out there, research from Grant and Gino found that just by saying 'thank you' people worked harder.[11] They found that fundraisers who were thanked for their work did 50% more calls than the control group. Being nice really pays off from a performance perspective too. This isn't about 'toxic positivity', where people should always be positive and smiling, even when they are experiencing pain or hardship. It is about acknowledging that life is both dark and light, but we should appreciate that lightness because of the opportunities it brings.

And this brings me onto an important equation, from Buddhist teacher Shinzen Young, which I drew with my parents as we sat and drank our tea:

Suffering = Pain x Resistance

I talked them through the concept. The pain is the disease, the MND. That is a fact. The suffering is driven by *how much resistance you have*, the self-pity, poor me, why me, how could this happen - the victim mentality. Now, I'm not minimising the pain - not at all. But *know that we all have a choice*, in terms of how much suffering we create for ourselves. What is the antidote? Acceptance.

Dad paused. 'A very deep thing that I need to consider,' he typed. A week later he sent me an email.

> *'Darling, I was thinking about your equation, suffering pain and resistance. I listed the positives and negatives of my MND at present. Would you believe there are more positives than negatives. Quite a sobering lesson, and good to keep recalling.'*

He could be miserable; thinking he was so unlucky, angry and feeling really sorry for himself – that would be the resistance (and totally understandable!). But he has made a choice, not to take the victim approach, but to accept the situation and make the best possible life of what he has. It doesn't mean he isn't fighting to survive the disease, but he isn't wallowing with all the sorrow and suffering that brings. Dad highlighted this when he preached a sermon, shortly after getting his diagnosis, enumerating six positives and only four negatives of his situation.

So, why is this all so important in a book about confidence? This is because confidence and happiness are inextricably linked. Having a deep level of contentment, joy, life satisfaction and a positive outlook are such fundamental parts of true *authentic* confidence.

When you approach life with this outlook, you're not coming from a place of lack, insecurity and neediness. You've got a really strong foundation, which enables you to deal with the inevitable challenges of life. You're more optimistic, so you will try bigger, better, harder things (because you think they will probably work out). You're happier deeper down, so won't let that challenge stop you from moving forward. You really do believe you have the ability to figure things out. That's real confidence.

So, gratitude is the first new daily habit I want to you to implement in your confidence journey, starting today.

CONFIDENCE TOOLKIT: GRATITUDE PRACTICE

When you wake up in the morning, before you do anything else, start by taking three grateful breaths. Really appreciate that moment – it gives you such a wonderful start to each day. Then, as part of your morning routine, spend a few minutes each day writing down five things you're grateful for. Really enjoy writing them, feel the appreciation you have for each of them and breathe in that joy.

Success Tips for your Gratitude Practice

What can you be grateful for? You could focus on:

- WHO is in your life... partner, kids, colleagues, family.
- What THINGS you have... dog, bed, coffee, warm clothes.
- What ACTION you have taken... quitting my job, speaking up.
- Your CHARACTER traits... tenacity, courage, kindness.
- Your ENVIRONMENT... safe home, nice neighbourhood, garden.
- Your HEALTH... legs to walk with, good general health.

A great way for habits to stick is by having these three steps, as detailed in the amazing book Atomic Habits by James Clear[12]:

- Anchor Moment – After I... (Brush my teeth, wake up, get into bed).
- Tiny Habit – I will... (do my gratitude practice).
- Celebration – Then celebrate by... (having a nice coffee, herbal tea or whatever brings you joy!).

If you have kids in your life, in whatever form that is, get them thinking about what they are grateful for. Maybe it's at the dinner table, or before bed, but it's such an incredible gift to shape their mindset that early in their life to see the positives in life. If you're at work, try using it as the first thing in a weekly team meeting – what are you celebrating as a team? Or perhaps with your partner as you take a nice walk – surprise them with a few things about them that you're grateful for. You'll be amazed at the impact on you both.

Final Word

This chapter is all about owning who you are, warts and all, because that's where true confidence begins. Once you're the proud captain of your own ship, you can set sail in any direction. Next, we'll discover our 'North Star' (N) to make sure we're heading where we really want to go.

KEY CONFIDENCE INSIGHTS

1. **Evolutionary Fact 2:**
   Our brains are wired to notice danger (negativity) more than positivity.

2. **Understanding Negativity Bias:**
   Our brains are naturally wired to remember negative experiences more vividly than positive ones. This is an evolutionary trait designed to keep us safe, but in today's world, it can diminish our confidence. It's time to start challenging that instinct.

3. **The Importance of Celebrating Achievements:**
   If we don't acknowledge our successes, our brains might conclude that our efforts aren't good enough, which chips away at our self-worth and confidence. Regularly celebrating your achievements, big or small, builds that essential belief in yourself.

4. **The 8 Primary Colours of Emotions:**
   Our 'survival' emotions are: fear, anger, shame, disgust and sadness. Our 'attachment' emotions are love/trust and excitement/joy. The 'potentiators' which move us towards survival or attachment emotions are surprise/startle. If you want to learn more about this model, you can go to the book website to see a really helpful interview I did with the creator, Professor Paul Brown. www.brainpoweredcoaching.com/book

5. **The Power of Gratitude:**
   Gratitude shifts your focus from what's lacking in your life (the black dot) to what's present and positive (the white paper). It's a powerful tool that not only boosts your mood but also builds your confidence by reminding you of all the good things you already have.

TIME FOR ACTION

1. **Create Your Life/Career Timeline:**
   Spend some time reflecting on the significant events in your life or career. Map them out in a way that works for you – whether it's writing, a visual timeline, or even just some notes on your phone. As you do this, think about what you've learned from these experiences and how they've shaped you. You'll be amazed at how much resilience and strength you've built.

2. **Celebrate Your Successes:**
   Every week, write about what you're proud of from the past week. It doesn't matter if it's something as simple as showing up on a tough day or landing that big deal, celebrate it. Trust me, every time you do this, your confidence will grow.

3. **Start a Gratitude Practice:**
   Start each day with three grateful breaths, then write down five things you're grateful for. Doing this daily will help shift your focus from negativity to positivity, making you feel more content and confident as you go about your day.

4. **Incorporate Gratitude with Others:**
   Why not take this gratitude practice a step further? Share your gratitude with those around you, your family, colleagues, or friends. Not only will this boost your own happiness, but it will also create a positive environment that's contagious. Plus, it's a great way to strengthen your relationships.

CONFIDENCE MASTERCLASS
BEN CROWE – ROCKET SCIENTIST TO SHAMAN

"Dare to embrace all the incredible gifts that you have within you."

Ben Crowe is a modern-day shaman, who was once a rocket scientist. As a system engineer in the aerospace sector, he specialised in the design, construction, testing and performance analysis of the satellite rocket engines. Ben is an ordinary guy with an extraordinary story: his journey toward self-discovery and confidence. Ben's story is a powerful example of how embracing one's true self can lead to profound transformation and inner peace.

Ben's childhood was marked by emotional hardship. With both of his parents being caught up in other parts of their lives, there was, he felt, an absence of the love and support that he deeply craved. This experience shaped his belief that 'achieving would bring love', leading him to relentlessly pursue academic and personal success. He described this period of his life as living with a 'mask' that hid his inner turmoil: "I was dead on the inside, and in life – obviously, the universe knew that," he told me.

However, this facade began to crack after a series of personal crises. These included a miscarriage with his (then) girlfriend and struggles at work, where he felt hugely unappreciated. He reached a breaking point that forced him to confront his own self-hatred and acknowledge a truth he had long suppressed – that he was gay. This was a realisation he had been avoiding due to self-created, societal and familial expectations: he didn't want to 'disappoint' the world. He decided he wanted to end it all, to step outside in front of a bus into a road and leave his life to fate. Ben said, "I made a deal with the universe... If the bus hits me, great. If it misses, I promise to do everything I can to find happiness." As he took his step into the road, the bus swerved by a long way. He survived; the Universe had answered clearly. Ben started his long journey towards finding true happiness.

Coming out to his family was emotionally painful, but ultimately liberating. He quickly realised that the barriers and fears that he had been expecting were all mental constructs of his own. Ben made the decision to stop fighting and embrace his true self: "The whole journey has been an incredibly long journey of accepting myself for who I am." It was this acceptance that allowed him to cultivate a deeper, more authentic confidence, one no longer dependent on external validation or societal approval.

Shamanism, a spiritual practice centred on finding inner strength, was a huge step in his journey. He explained, "Shamanism is about remembering who you truly are on the inside. It's about healing and embracing all parts of yourself, especially the parts of you that you have avoided most of your life, and daring to embrace all the incredible gifts that you have within you."

"When you suddenly start knowing yourself, trusting yourself and, dare I say it, loving yourself, you realise that you are all you need to overcome any challenges in life."

Through this practice, Ben learned to see every challenge as an opportunity for growth, shifting his perspective from victimhood to gratitude. He now performs healings alongside his corporate career and knows that shamanism is as much about who he is as it is about what he believes.

How does Ben define confidence? He differentiates between ego-driven confidence and a more authentic, self-rooted version.

"Confidence comes from your heart... When you love yourself, you've got nothing to prove, nothing to hide."

Ben sees that true confidence is built on a foundation of self-worth, where one's integrity and values become non-negotiable boundaries.

Ben's Top Tips for Confidence

- **Start small, with simple, actionable steps.** Do one thing that makes you happy... If you can listen to your heart and do just that one thing, you will begin to understand who you are.
- **Set boundaries and take time for self-care** – real confidence grows from a place of inner fulfilment.

Ben acknowledges that fear still exists in certain areas of his life, but he approaches it differently now, viewing fear as a challenge rather than a barrier. "I've been through quite a few challenges... I've realised, okay, well, I came out the other side, and amazing things happened because of that," he reflected. This mindset has enabled him to continually grow and evolve, maintaining a sense of calm and resilience in the face of life's inevitable challenges. He says:

"Your integrity to yourself gives you confidence, because when you have your own red line that you won't cross; people know you won't cross it. And that's who you are."

You can find a wonderful heart meditation that Ben runs in the resources section at www.brainpoweredcoaching.com/book.

Want more? Ben runs incredible workshops, shamanic healings and individual coaching sessions. If you'd like more information about the work Ben does, you can contact him at bcimperious@gmail.com.

CHAPTER THREE

*" When you know yourself,
you can trust yourself. "*

Anon

VALUES: THE LOW DOWN

How can you really understand yourself? The guiding north star for who you really are comes from your values.

Values are traits or qualities that represent our highest priorities, deeply held beliefs and core, fundamental driving forces.[1]

They are key building blocks that define how we see and experience the world. Once we are conscious of them, they enable us to understand our reactions, make the best possible decisions and live a life better aligned with our purpose. A meaningful and fulfilling life with confidence is one in which our most important values are honoured daily; it's how you show up every day to this world. When they get stomped on, we *feel* it. Our body screams THIS ISN'T RIGHT and tells us with physical responses, our body's own red flags being waved furiously.

They aren't something we actively choose; they come from our background, parents, cultures and experiences. However, with self-awareness, we can choose how we show up and act on our value system. I remember clearly my father saying, "Caroline, never *ever* compromise your integrity." They will be different for you, as they are for us all, and they will change over time, as your life and what's important to you changes. There are some core values that seem to be consistent across humans, like honesty, trust and kindness. It makes sense as they are the key approaches we can take to building trust between ourselves and our tribe (which is vital for our survival). I'm sure, if you thought about it now, you would be able to remember some of the similar messages you've been given from your caregivers as you grew up. Just think about those core statements and how they shape how you work, deal with friends or family today:

- Always work hard (discipline, determination, hard work)
- Never lie (honesty, integrity, trust)
- Go out and explore (adventure, freedom)
- Just be you (authenticity, sincerity, worthiness)
- Be better every day (growth, learning)

Values can, when taken to the extreme, be damaging (some, at worst, even dangerous). If you have been told that 'we don't quit', perhaps it shows up as loyalty in your life. That can be a great thing, but it can also be a hindrance. That quality of loyalty may keep you in a job that actually you should have left a long time ago. Your need for security may mean you're terrified to leave a relationship that no longer serves you. Your value of decisiveness may mean you don't consider all the options properly and bulldoze people trying to raise an issue. However, many people go through their lives with no conscious awareness of what theirs are, which really impacts their confidence levels because they are lacking a firm anchor in their lives.

I was working with a client on their values analysis a few years ago. She had been in the same job for years and had not felt good enough to try for the next level. Once she understood more about her values, her life journey and her resilience, she grew in confidence and decided to apply for a new role. She said that she had performed the best she had ever done in an interview, remaining calm and articulate, because she *was not trying to be someone else; she was just authentically herself,* in line with her values. She just let go of fear and trusted that what was within her control was how she showed up. What she could not control were the other people in the process and other considerations in the interviewers. That gave her tremendous personal power. She didn't actually get the job, but she was delighted all the same: "I had my best interview ever!!" She had been 100% herself, aligned with her core north star. She may not have won that promotion that time but, with her new confidence, it was certainly a 'not yet' rather than 'never'.

WHY ARE VALUES SO IMPORTANT?

"Your whole life improves when you begin living your life by the values that you most admire."

Brian Tracy

I was sitting opposite my manager in total disbelief. As he was talking, I couldn't decide whether I wanted to burst into tears or just throw up on the spot. I felt rage, total indignation and, frankly, wanted to punch him in the face. It was a totally visceral reaction.

He had decided my life for me.

"Caroline, you are going to move up to Singapore. You will be the APAC Head and run the region from here." Excuse me? Were you even going to *ask*?

The reality was that I was in a very happy relationship at the time, and I couldn't move to Singapore. I loved where I lived and I didn't want the job he had decided for me. It would have been a massive change for me at that time and it just wasn't possible. But what was really going on with my reaction? Why was it so visceral? It was all about my values.

What this man had done was completely ignore anything important to me (lack of respect). It was, in fact, totally self-serving (selfish, zero empathy) and he didn't even ask what I wanted (family, security, love). Once I realised that this was what was happening, I understood why I had had such a physical reaction.

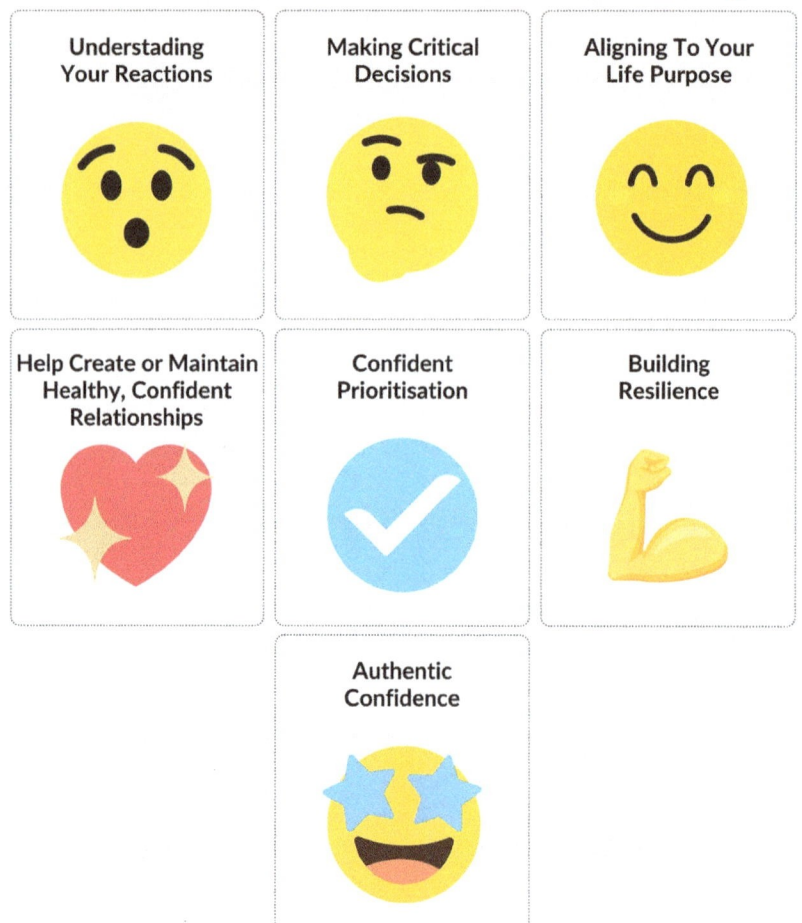

Here are the most important reasons to understand your values:

To understand your reactions.

Let's say integrity is a core value for you, and you work with people who are outright liars, manipulative, with lots of office politics. In that situation, you are going to find it incredibly difficult to stay long-term as you will feel real dissonance. What about if fairness is a core value, but you get served a smaller glass of wine than anyone else? You may well feel very triggered, because that just isn't fair (and I would sympathise as I would do the same!). Having our values trampled on feels a bit like feeling poked in the stomach. It's uncomfortable and it can make us angry or frustrated, just as I was when my manager decided my life. But, if we don't know that's what's happening, we can misjudge situations and people.

Here's another personal example.

One of my core values is efficiency. I just LOVE things working smoothly, like a well-oiled machine – with zero wastage. Yes, I'm the person carrying huge piles of books and papers, whilst balancing a cup of tea, my water bottle, iPad, phone and box of tissues up the stairs so as to avoid doing two trips (what a waste of time that is!).

All of this can be linked to my other value, respect; when we go out, I want to be on time (or early), with no faffing, taking the most efficient route and getting a pace on. However, my husband really values calmness, which shows up as taking his own time, doing things at his pace. When that is linked with his other value of optimism, then he will squeeze in doing those extra three tasks before we leave the house, all whilst I have steam coming out of my ears as I stand outside tapping my watch.

Now, if I didn't understand the values piece of this, I would just think it was really annoying, or that he was being thoughtless (yes, I admit I thought this at the start!). When I realign that understanding, it means I respect his values and just plan more time for us to leave, so we are both happy.

Making critical decisions with confidence

How many times have you made a decision that you thought was right but, once you put your foot on the path, it was so terribly wrong? Perhaps it was a change in job – when you chose the shiny one that paid more, but it ended up giving you no balance and left you unable to see your family. Or was it an exciting new relationship with someone a bit 'edgy' and exciting, who ended up out all the time, giving you no security? Perhaps you like change and creativity – you really don't want to move to a company that is traditional and static; stuck in its old ways.

Knowing our values allow us to make the right decisions, based on what is most important to us at our core.

They clarify our goals, creating more success as we become aligned with our passions and purpose. We then have more confidence in ourselves and our direction, so we're more discerning with our decisions. When we ask, 'Am I on the right track?' The response is: abso-bloody-lutely!

The lesson here is that if your core values are not allowed to be expressed in your life, dissonance will show up. What does that mean? Dissonance is that discomfort in your body. It might show up as anxiety, a sick feeling, anger, frustration; a churning or butterflies in your stomach. Please *trust it* – your body is a very well-tuned messenger. In fact, we have over 500 million neurons in our gut[2], which is about the same as a dog's brain! It's telling you from a place of *intelligence* about what's important to you, even if we don't quite understand how that is all connected (yet). We are the only mammals who ignore our instincts; override them with our societal conformities. Trust it. Listen to it. And inform it with deep self-knowledge. That's true confidence.

Values help create (or maintain) healthy, confident relationships

If you're dating, you can waste a lot of time meeting people who just aren't right – it can be so terribly disheartening. Let's be honest, your time is precious, so if you are giving anyone an IRL (in real life) moment, you want it to be worthwhile! Once you're really clear on your own values, you can start to listen for those of potential partners and where they will conflict. You'll be able to quickly say "thanks, but no thanks" and date with confidence, knowing your core criteria. Beware of the person who sees duty and frugality as paramount, if you are footloose and fancy free (side note: make sure you're aligned on your values around money as that can be a really tough one if not).

Once you're with a partner, finding out their values could save your relationship longer term, once you are past that shiny fun bit at the start. One of my relationships was ruined because my partner had a core value around stability and security, whereas I was much more driven by adventure and change. My 'scary' approach totally freaked him out, but I didn't see that until it was too late.

Even if you've been with your partner a while and were aligned on values before, the reality is that our values can shift over time. Things can come into focus later in life that weren't so important in the past. Perhaps now that the kids have finally flown the nest, the value of adventure that your partner has always had, is bursting to come out. Don't let ignorance ruin your connection. Spend the time to check back in and see what's really driving them now.

Confident Prioritisation

Self-awareness of our values helps ensure our energy, resources and time are directed in the best possible way. We can focus on the activities and relationships that bring us the most fulfilment and joy, whilst letting go of those that are dragging us down. Let's say you've signed up to be on the PTA (Parent Teacher Association). You did it with a sense of duty, and now it's just a drain – their approach on rules and rigidity are totally against your creative and flexible values. *You can say no* (yes, really). Let someone else take part who loves all that stuff! Then you can apply your time to your joys – your family, love of travel and art.

When we run through that prioritised filter of values to make the right decision, we save so much time as we don't take wrong turns. We avoid figuring out later on that the alternative was much more aligned to our deepest desires and needs.

Building Resilience

Life can be hard. You are going to have ups and downs, it's just the way it is, but knowing your values is like having anchors on a boat in stormy seas. They steady you, balance you, help you to see beyond the storm and focus on what's most important. From that place, you can lean into your experiences, knowing that whatever the weather brings, you can trust yourself and your capabilities.

Authentic Confidence

We've all felt pressured by what we feel we 'should' do. What a parent thinks is best for us, or the judgement of changing jobs. But knowing your values gives you a level of confidence that is authentic. It's knowing deeply *who you are,* so no-one can knock that. Think back to one of our definitions of confidence: 'integrating your internal and external authenticity, letting go of effort.' Your values are those Lego pieces that create the real you, no pretence, no bravado, just you, unapologetically yourself.

FINDING YOUR GUIDING STARS

CONFIDENCE GYM: VALUES IDENTIFICATION

I've worked with lots of people who I ask, "Do you know your values?" Often, I get, "Of course", and then a slightly nervous response giving one or two examples that sound like they are taken from a company website. So, let's do it properly. It won't take long and, remember, this is the foundation for building your confidence, so don't skip it!

There are three parts:

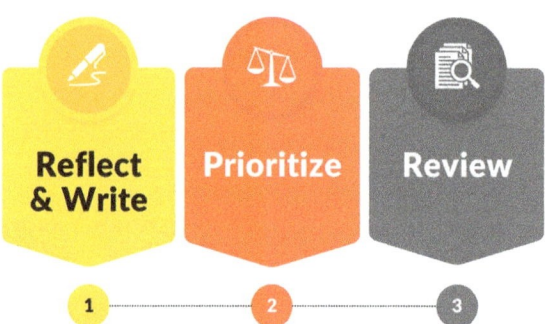

1. Reflect and Write:

Answer the questions below. Write down the words that matter most to you in big capital letters, underline them or circle them. Some may resonate with you more than others, but don't judge and just allow the words to pop up in your head. You will have repeats (that's meant to happen and will help us later on):

a) What qualities do you look for in friends or a partner?
b) Think about where you were angry or frustrated. What was causing it? What value was being squashed?
c) Identify three role models: what qualities in them do you find inspirational?

2. Prioritise:

Finding True North, by Michael Henderson[3], has this great exercise to really sharpen up how you see and prioritise these values. Firstly, get out your sticky notes! Then make three columns: Most Important, Very Important and Important. Then write each of your values on the notes and for each one, compare it to another. Which is more important? If you really can't decide, they are both in the 'most important' column. But going through this process should allow you to rate them against each other. If there are some that are very similar, group them into themes, seeing if there is a values description that summaries them.

MOST IMPORTANT	VERY IMPORTANT	IMPORTANT

3. Review:

In front of you is what's really important to you. What do you notice? How is your life aligned to these values right now? What needs to change? What could you do to integrate these qualities into your life to be more authentically confident? If we can be intentional in terms of how we are showing up, staying aligned with our values, then we can better walk through the world with agency and confidence.

Important! Take a photo of these and save it to your favourites. Print it out, stick it on the wall. Use it regularly when you are making decisions, feel discomfort, choosing a partner; whatever the life moment is, these should guide you.

CONFIDENCE TOOLBOX: MICRO CONFIDENCE CHALLENGE

We know that your confidence muscle needs to have a bit of a stretch if it's going to grow. Just like our own fitness levels, we aren't going to be more confident from just sitting on the sofa! This is where Micro Confidence Challenges come in. So, where are you lacking in confidence? What are you wanting to target so you can grow in confidence levels, personally or professionally? What would be a small step (even if it's really tiny) that you could take to improve it?

The key is that every single time you try something new, just a little bit harder than normal, your confidence grows.

Maybe it's:

- Asking questions when you wouldn't normally
- Speaking up in a meeting
- Saying no to something or someone
- Saying yes to something you wouldn't normally
- Empowering someone to do something so you don't have to

I bet you it won't be as bad as you thought, probably a whole lot better. However, if you do fail, remember what Dr Henry Cloud said:

"Failure is the critical partner to confidence."

Take a Micro Confidence Challenge today. However small, just try one thing, then really be proud of yourself for trying it out. Post it on social media and tag me at @brainpoweredcoaching and get some support from other people doing the same thing!

Final Word

When you're aligned with your values, you'll always know which way is true North. It's time to trust yourself and navigate your life with purpose. Remember, confidence isn't about being perfect. It's about being real, being you, and standing tall in your truth.

As we move to F of our C.O.N.F.I.D.E.N.T. framework, get ready to confront those inner critics in 'Fight the Gremlin', because nothing holds us back like our own doubts.

KEY CONFIDENCE INSIGHTS

1. **Let Go of the Façade:**
Confidence isn't about putting on a show. It's about stripping away the layers of bravado, pretension, and the exhausting need to prove something to everyone around you. Instead, focus on what makes you unique, and own it. Your strengths, your quirks, your values – that's where your real power lies.

2. **Anchor in Self-Knowledge:**
Knowing who you are is the foundation of true confidence. Remember that life journey: the ups, the downs, the lessons learned. When you truly understand yourself, you can trust yourself. And trust me, when you trust yourself, the world can't shake you.

3. **Values as Your North Star:**
Your values are the core of who you are. They guide your decisions, influence your relationships, and shape how you see the world. When you're clear on your values, everything else falls into place as you:

   — Understand your reactions
   — Make aligned decisions
   — Build strong relationships
   — Prioritise what matters
   — Stay resilient
   — Embrace authentic confidence

4. **Beware of Misalignment:**
When your life or work doesn't align with your values, it creates this internal tension, a feeling that something's just not right. Pay attention to those feelings. They're your body's way of telling you that you need to make a change. Don't ignore it. Your body is wise; listen to it.

TIME FOR ACTION

1. **Identify Your Core Values:**
   Sit down with the exercise in this chapter and really dig into what matters most to you. How does your current life reflect these values? What needs to change?

2. **Release the Need for Approval:**
   Stop trying to meet everyone else's expectations. You're here to live your life, not theirs. Let go of the pressure to conform and embrace who you truly are.

3. **Listen to Your Body:**
   Pay attention to feelings of discomfort or unease; they're your body's way of signalling that something's off. Trust those signals and make the necessary adjustments.

4. **Use Your Values as a Compass:**
   When you're faced with a decision, check in with your values. Are you staying true to yourself? If the answer is yes, you're on the right track.

5. **Take Micro Steps Toward Confidence:**
   Find an area where you're feeling a bit shaky and take a small, bold step. Each step builds on the last, creating a stronger, more confident you.

CONFIDENCE MASTERCLASS
NICOLA BENNETT – GOLF WINNING MINDSET

"If you can think it, you can achieve it."

Nicola Bennett is a professional golfer, motivational speaker and advocate for diversity in sports. Starting golf at age ten, she quickly excelled, becoming one of the few Black female professionals in the sport.

Nicola is passionate about helping young girls and women build their own confidence. She firmly believes that confidence is not a destination but a continuous journey. "I've seen women who are twenty-four, and I've seen women who are eighty-two still lack confidence," she noted. Her goal is to plant seeds of self-belief and resilience early, giving others the tools they need to handle life's challenges with strength and grace.

In our discussion, Nicola shared her unique perspective on confidence and how it has shaped her life and career. She believes confidence is something you create rather than inherit. From her perspective, it's a skill that can be developed through practice and intention. She told me, "If you're lacking it, I would really recommend *acting* confident." Nicola uses the concept of a persona or alter ego to embody qualities like assertiveness, clarity, and a strong sense of purpose – stuff you really need when you're a professional golfer.

Nicola is also great at reflection and self-awareness; she knows her values and has that rock-solid foundation. "I went on a spiritual journey in 2015, and I learned how to live life from the inside out." She treats every experience as an opportunity to grow. She frequently reflects on her actions, asking herself, "How did I handle that in comparison to the previous encounter? Did I come across more confident?" This ongoing process of mindful self-reflection, she says, is central to her growth.

Nicola has had doubt, particularly during her teenage years in the golf industry. She recalled an incident when she was just 14, playing in a semi-final match. Despite making an incredible fifty-foot putt, the crowd remained silent, while her opponent's small putt was met with applause. "I doubted in that moment... I doubted my ability," she confessed. However, rather than letting that doubt define her, she chose to view it as an opportunity to build her 'adversity muscles'.

> *"It's about overcoming these hindrances and seeing them as opportunities to actually grow."*

Her journey was also shaped by her cultural background. As a young Black woman in a predominantly white sport, Nicola faced many challenges, both overt and subtle. She speaks openly about the discomfort and scrutiny she experienced, but she has come to see these experiences as a source of strength. They have made her "a stronger, better, more advanced person." Now, Nicola is dedicated to creating a more inclusive space in golf so that "young females from all different ethnic backgrounds can come into the game and feel more comfortable."

What is most compelling about Nicola's perspective is her commitment to authenticity. For her, confidence is about being comfortable in her own skin, no matter what others might think. Nicola believes that true confidence comes from accepting that people will have different perceptions and being okay with that:

> *"Confidence for me is being so comfortable with yourself, despite what anyone could ever think. You have to accept that some people are going to like you, some people aren't... but ultimately, be yourself."*

Nicola's Top Tips for Confidence:

- **'Act like her,'** meaning that you should act like the best version of yourself (even if you don't feel like it).
- Surround yourself with people who **elevate and support** you.
- **Avoid being too attached and over investing**. There's a healthy level where you can let go, accept what has happened and just focus on the next thing you can control.
- **Be your own best friend** and champion yourself like you would to others.

"Be authentic, be true despite what is around you, and more than anything, be comfortable with your truth, and you will radiate confidence."

Nicola's journey is a powerful reminder that confidence is built through discipline, resilience, self-awareness, and a deep commitment to authenticity. She believes wholeheartedly, "If you can think it, you can achieve it." Her mission is to help others find their own path to confidence, whether through golf, speaking, or simply through the way she lives her life.

Want more? Find out about the amazing work Nicola does at www.nicolabennettofficial.com/

CHAPTER FOUR

> "You have been criticising yourself for years and it hasn't worked.
> Try approving of yourself and see what happens."
>
> Louise Hay

WHO IS THE GREMLIN?

I was once at home watching *Charlies Angels*. What an empowering film; awesome, fun, smart women owning their space and taking on the world. I watched them doing karate in cracking tight jumpsuits and totally kicking arse. When the film finished, I was off to a sailing club next door, but the gate was locked. Rather than doing the long walk round, I climbed up onto some bins and jumped off a ten-foot wall, landing perfectly and strolling off to my evening. It was only then that I realised something: I don't jump off ten-foot walls!! I looked back and saw the height I had jumped, without even thinking twice, just through channelling my inner Charlie's Angel. All I was missing was the leather jumpsuit…

It was SUCH a great example to me of the limitations of my mindset and the opportunities that would exist if I thought differently. In this case, I saw the world through the lens of a strong crime-fighting woman! Now, I can't say this has continued (in fact, it really gave me quite a shock that I had done it!) BUT, let me ask you this:

What would you do if you weren't afraid?

What would you do if you deeply believed in your capabilities, if you saw success in your outcomes, or learnt from the process, just like Nicola Bennett? What would it be like if you felt truly grounded in your authentic self?

If our foundation is fear, my goodness, it holds us back. How we shape, control and manage our mindset is a fundamental part of how confident we are. This is where the inner critic and its cousin, 'imposter syndrome', come into the confidence story.

The inner critic, sometimes called the 'saboteur' or A.N.T. (Automatic Negative Thoughts), is that little (sometimes big) voice that judges, threatens, commands and monitors weaknesses or mistakes[1]. The language usually comes from your childhood, maybe a parent, teacher, sibling, or school experience. Everyone's developmental experiences and societal standards are different, so it is different for us all – louder for some and quieter for others. However, in our research[2] we found that 90% of people question themselves and second-guess their decisions. That's the critic saying 'Do you really know? Do you? Or are you going to look like a fool?'

Whatever the volume of this for you, these figures show clearly it is experienced by nearly *everyone.* And, without question, the critic can be very nasty and so very damaging to our confidence levels.

Now, here's the vulnerable moment. Let's have a look at mine, who I call the Gremlin, and some to the things it has said to me over the years.

- *God, you're stupid. Everyone else is smarter than you. You don't belong here.*
- *Look how disgusting you look! Urgh. I can't even look at you.*
- *You are so WEIRD. Look at your troll feet and weird skin – no-one will ever love you if they figure out the real you.*
- *You don't belong here. They are all going to find out you're a total fraud and have been blagging it. Just imagine when they do – you'll be so ashamed.*
- *Look how much weight you've put on! That cellulite is disgusting. You need to hide yourself away.*

What does yours say to you?

Let's be honest here: it's really *really* mean!! It says things to us we would never DREAM of saying to anyone else. It creates 'cognitive distortions' and says things like 'You look really fat in that outfit!' or 'Stop acting like a complete idiot!' or 'You screwed this up again!' or 'If you don't work harder, you'll get sacked and be out on the streets!'

Reflecting, though, on how our brain works, this horrible character is most likely here for a reason: to keep us safe. It's protecting us, whether from taking risks, by avoiding rejection or failure, loss of security or just simply from the unknown (even if it doesn't really feel like that at the time).

The result of the inner critic saying these horrible comments can itself create a very real physical stress response: the 'survival' sympathetic nervous system (the accelerator) is activated, with cortisol and adrenaline pumping, causing sweaty palms, heart racing, shortness of breath and the other fight/flight survival responses. Then a kind of self-fulfilling prophecy can occur, as the stress responses reduce the effectiveness of our performance. The critic can say, 'See? I knew you would mess it up.' When this continues at a low, constant level, the outcome can be a persistent background of anxiety and total loss of confidence, which then has the potential to become chronic stress and eventually burnout.

So, how can we manage this critter, who holds back our confidence levels and stops us achieving our fabulous potential? Here are the three steps:

1. The first key step is the simplest: naming it.

By naming it, we are able to *observe* it, rather than have it like ivy wrapped tightly around us, burrowing into our being. Giving it a name (the sillier the better, and don't be afraid to swear) allows you to say: I see you gremlin and you don't have control over me.

2. Noticing it.

When you really start to tune into your mind chatter and messages, the level of negativity can be a bit of a shock. It is incredible how harsh and judgemental you can be to yourself, in a way that you would never dream of being to anyone else. So, write down what your critic is saying to you. Just do the brain download of it and then look at what you've written. Pretty confronting, isn't it?

3. Channelling your Champion

I want you to think about your Champion. The superpowered character who is going to crush that critic with its bare hands. They are like your best friend who is cheering you on, telling you all the fantastic skills, capabilities and attributes you have. Reshaping those negative thoughts in a way that you would say to other people can start to shift the radio channel in your mind to build, rather than destroy, your confidence.

Here's what mine says:

'You can do this!! You've done it before. You'll figure it out again.'

'You are a bloody ROCKSTAR! Commeeee onnnnn!!!' (*Insert fist pumping and furious clapping*)

'You have nothing to lose and everything to gain!'

'No regrets – just get out there."

'Enjoy this challenge – you're learning and growing so much!'

Now it's your turn. Please go through those steps and see if you can rephrase and write down your comments as if your champion was talking to you, just like a great mate would as they stepped in to pump you up.

- Was it surprising what it said to you?
- Would you ever say anything like that to anyone else?
- Any thoughts on what came up?

Incorporating this process of challenging your critic and channelling the champion is a crucial part of building up your confidence levels. There are some more brain principles, though, that can add to your confidence superpowers, so let's dig into those...

YOUR BRAIN'S BOUNCER

Have you ever noticed how, when you start searching for something on your phone – a new house, car, computer – you get served up that item, time and time again, whether on ads, searches, new articles or YouTube videos? This is the computer algorithm doubling down on what you want, like or see, with a view to 'sell' you more of it. The more you like articles about loving or hating beach holidays, the more of them you will see. The same happens with your brain.

Look around the room now and look for anything you see that is red (yes, actually do it!).

Now, write down all the blue things you saw (I bet you are looking back around the room!). This is your brain's filter, called the Reticular Activating System (RAS), cleverly helping you sieve through the millions of inputs it has at any point in time. Why does this happen?

We are designed to filter these inputs to our brains, because otherwise there is no way we could consciously process all the constant stimuli and activity in our environment. Imagine being aware of your heart beating, blood flowing, breathing, the person shouting at their children next door, blinking and your performance on a Zoom call all at once – it really would be mind-blowing! The RAS is like a bouncer on the door of your brain, deciding what gets to come in. The good news is that survival information gets straight through and remains unfiltered (very important for our ongoing species). Otherwise, the brain flags up only the 'essentials' that are deemed important to your conscious mind. This is extremely important, because these essentials are defined by:

- the **thoughts** we focus on (like our red and blue exercise)
- our **beliefs**; and
- what we **identify** with.

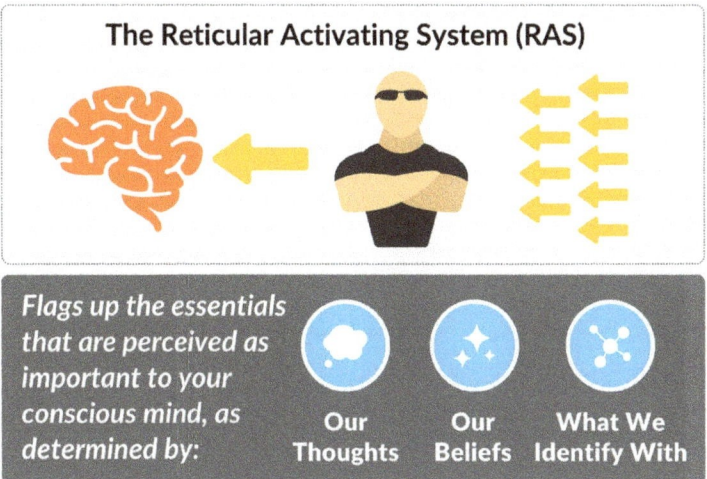

A great example of this is a dentist. They will see wonky teeth everywhere because that's what's important to them. Bought a white car recently? You will notice white cars everywhere.

This relates to a concept in psychology called 'confirmation bias', which is defined by the *Cambridge Dictionary* as '*the fact that people are more likely to accept or notice information if it appears to support what they already believe or expect.*' We subconsciously select to retain only the information that confirms what we already believe (this is why biases are so hard to shift).

Why does this matter with confidence? If we tell ourselves that we are bad at presenting, *we will look for evidence to reinforce that* we are a terrible presenter. If we tell ourselves we are an imposter, *our brain will search for examples as to why that is true*. This means, **the messages we tell ourselves are crucially important in how we see and operate in the world.**

So, to improve our confidence levels, we need to start changing the messaging, so our filter looks for the good stuff, not the bad. A great way to start shifting this filter is through the power of positive affirmations.

CONFIDENCE GYM: POWER UP WITH POSITIVE AFFIRMATIONS

So, let's recap. Your confidence is shaped by the language you tell yourself. Your brain's bouncer is trained to let in what resonates with your thoughts, beliefs and what it identifies with. If the things you say to yourself on repeat are:

- *You're a loser*
- *You're fat*
- *You don't have any confidence*

…Then guess what? Your brain bouncer (the RAS) is going to look around for evidence to reinforce that point, strangling your confidence. So, how can we manage it so that our confidence has a chance to grow? Change the language!

Coming up with language that lifts us, excites and propels us forward each day can be a very powerful way to increase our confidence levels. It's looking for evidence of our champion, cheering us on and affirming the deep sense of who we really are (and that's bloody fantastic, by the way).

We can do this by using positive affirmations. You may well have heard of these – social media is loaded with statements of positivity (hurrah, we can at least celebrate that part of it!). But did you know, research from Harvard researcher Shawn Achor[3] showed that just three statements of positive affirmations per day builds your happiness levels, with the studies showing:

- 19% more productivity
- 29% increase ability in analytic problem solving
- Increased revenue by 38% for sales people

As we've discussed, happiness and confidence are so closely linked. If you feel happier and more competent, then your confidence will grow. Remember too **Evolutionary Fact 1: Our brain prioritises energy for a survival response.** So, your brain *functions much better in a positive environment* (thrive), rather than negative (threat), because the 25 watts of energy in it is freed up. If you can create a 'thrive' environment in your mind with your words, then you will free up cognitive bandwidth for better creativity, performance and problem solving. Your confidence will grow every time that you reiterate those words.

What should positive affirmations look like? Here are a few examples from people you may well know:

- "I am the greatest." – *Muhammad Ali*
- "I am a powerful creator. I create the life I want." – *Oprah Winfrey*
- "I am a person who has a lot of confidence, and I have a lot of faith in myself." – *Beyoncé*
- "I am my own sanctuary and I can be reborn as many times as I choose." – *Lady Gaga*
- "I am motivated by fear. Fear of fear." – *Will Smith*
- "I am lucky that whatever fear I have inside me, my desire to win is always stronger." – *Serena Williams*
- "I am who I am today because of the choices I made yesterday." – *Eleanor Roosevelt*
- "I am destined for great things." – *Jim Carrey*
- "I am youthful and timeless at every age." – *Jennifer Lopez*
- "I am enough." – *Iyanla Vanzant*

There are few guidelines to follow with affirmations, which are important in making sure they work best:

- Make them **present tense**, as that's what your brain responds best to. 'I am' rather than 'I will be' is bedding the belief of your identity into your brain.
- They should **reflect your core personal values**, rather than some arbitrary sentence you don't connect with. If it really doesn't connect with your core, fundamental driving forces (values), the affirmations can end up backfiring (your brain says 'that's nonsense' and pushes further in the opposite direction)[4]. So rather than focusing on the *outcome*, focus on the *attributes you have to get there*. ('I am a supermodel' changes to 'I work hard to stay fit and strong').
- Your affirmations should be **positively focused** and **spoken as facts**. Avoid negative statements like might / could / don't / won't. Your brain will find it much easier to action them, versus having to translate them first from negative to positive.
- Make sure they are reinforcing your deep sense of self-identity with **targeted action**. 'I am positive' shifts you to look at the world from that perspective.

Look at your life timeline and identify your strengths that have got you where you are today. Are you strong, resilient, tenacious, disciplined? Say those things. If you still struggle, ask your friends or family three things they love about you. You'll be amazed what comes back.

A hot tip for you is to enlist your body. We all know what people who are depressed look like: hunched over, arms crossed, maybe the foetal position. What about someone who is confident? Arms out wide, or on their hips, perhaps a bit of jazz hands...? The point here is **embodiment works**. Internalising our words and showing them in our body positions makes a big difference to the impact on our minds.

The work of social psychologist and author, Amy Cuddy on 'power poses' is a great example of this[5]. They got people to assume a position of a power pose, like having their hands on their hips, arms raised in the air or taking up more space at a desk. They compared them to people who crossed their arms, touched their necks; made themselves small. It turned out that 86% of the power posers were up for taking a risk, while 60% of the low-power posers were a bit more hesitant. They also checked their saliva and found the high-power posers had a boost in testosterone by about 8%, while the low-power posers saw a drop of 10%. And when it came to stress, those in the power poses had a 25% dip in cortisol, but the low-power crew had a 15% increase in stress levels. Now, some of this research has been challenged, but I can tell you from personal experience: this stuff works!! So many of the people I've worked with use this before a meeting, pitch or interview and they feel calmer and more confident.

I did it the day of my director interview. Wow, I was nervous, because I wanted it so much. So, I got to the video conference early and, whilst I waited, I was in the meeting room next door with my arms in the air saying, *"You are a f'ing rockstar, and you're going to nail this!"* over and over again. Thank goodness no-one came in. But when it was time for my interview and that video switched on, I performed at my best. I wasn't overtaken by nerves; I was articulate and well-structured in my responses. The feedback was it was the best interview of the lot. If only they knew why!

So, for your affirmations, use your body too – have your arms up in the air and say I AM STRONG, I CAN DO THIS. Your brain listens to your body mentally and emotionally, so tell it that you mean it!

When, how and where should you do them? In the words of Shakira, *"Wherever, whenever."* You can do your affirmations wherever works for you best. Here are some of my favourite spots:

- The shower – private and totally realistic and appropriate for jazz hands and other power poses.
- Cycling on my way to boot camp, saying, "I am positive, resilient and strong!"
- Morning walk – there's something special about being *in action* while you do them. I use my pre-recorded ones Successful Entrepreneurs (you can find these in the resources area for the book at www.brainpoweredcoaching.com/book) and repeat them as I pace the streets. It's a great way to power up for the day.
- In front of the mirror – I even had them written on my mirror in lipstick for a while… goodness knows what the cleaner thought of me (but who cares right?!)
- Whilst exercising – my favourite one for this is "I burn fat easily and quickly." However, I also use "I am powerful and healthy" and "I am stronger every day." Boom. Watch out world!

THE RUMINATION MACHINE

You're sitting and contemplating a difficult conversation you need to have. (Inside your head): I would say, "You need to change", then they will probably say, "Screw you. I'm not changing! It's your fault." Then I'll get angry and shout, "You never change! Why is it always me?" You visualise the fight that ensues and you feel yourself getting more wound up (and so it goes on). Or perhaps you've got a big presentation coming up. You imagine yourself flushing as you start to talk; you forget what you're saying and fluff the answer to a question. You start to feel queasy at the *mere prospect of it* and your confidence takes a nose-dive.

What's going on here? Welcome to your default mode network (DMN). This is defined by the American Psychological Association (APA) as 'a specific, anatomically defined brain system preferentially active when individuals are not focused on the external environment.' What does that mean? It means that when we are not focused on a task, it hums away like a generator, thinking about the past or the future. Often it comes up with all sorts of stories or scenarios that did not, or will not, ever exist (it does a whole lot else, but we are focusing on this part for now).

There may be little or no value in this process of rumination, but it can take over and cause *actual physical anxiety* in the body, even though it is completely fabricated. The APA goes on to say that "ongoing unconstrained self-reflective thought might be the natural (default) state of the mind when individuals are not otherwise engaged." This means, if we don't focus on the present moment, our brain is naturally thinking forward or back, testing out mental scenarios and replaying old ones. This is also evidenced by functional magnetic resonance images (fMRI) of the brain showing the same areas being activated when thinking about the past or future as when the DMN is active.

Now, this is quite a clever approach; it's part of what makes us human, with an ability to process scenarios and understand consequences. It's important that we are able to think through something that has happened and how we could do better, or the impact of our actions going forward. However, it shouldn't be all the time, uncontrolled like a malfunctioning robot.

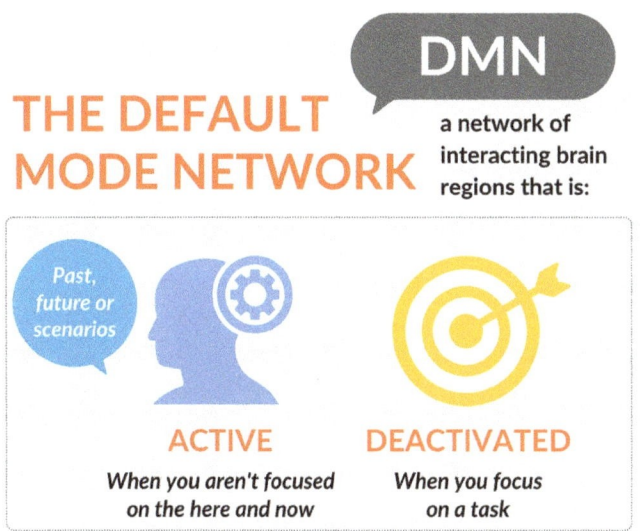

Why does this have an impact on confidence?

It has an impact on confidence because of the mind's natural negativity bias (our second Evolutionary Fact). Our tendency is to focus on the emotions associated with 'escape', which equates to keeping you safe. If we don't regulate our thoughts, this will be the 'default mode' for them. Over time, that negative anticipation of the future, or judge of the past, grinds down our confidence levels and we hold ourselves back.

How can we manage our DMN? The best way to manage it is with mindfulness. That means being really *really* present in the moment. Here are a few very simple ways:

- Feel your feet on the floor. Feel where you are sitting. Notice the weight of your body on the seat and the presence of you being in the room.
- Feel the water on your skin as you're in the shower, or the feeling of your fingers typing on a keyboard.
- Go for a walk in nature and really notice the sun shining through the trees, the wind in your hair, and the noise of the birds.
- Be really WITH someone as they talk to you, focusing on what they say, not what you will say next. They will feel heard and seen and you'll feel the joy of the moment so much more.

CONFIDENCE TOOLBOX: BRAIN HACKS

So, how can we stop the 3am mind racing or that critic saying, "You're overweight, you're lazy, you're ugly... you're not enough"? Use a brain hack. These brain hacks include Cognitive Behavioural Therapy (CBT) techniques, which act as circuit breakers for your negative mindset. They stop the critic or catatrophisation in its tracks, allowing your brain to free up for positive, creative thought (or just plain old sleep). You can use one of them, all, or a combination of them. Try them out, get creative and see which one works for you:

- **Picture a big red STOP sign** in your mind. You can even say "STOP". Use your body, stand up and put your hand out like someone in the police (the mental version of this is advisable for maintaining social etiquette in a meeting though...).
- **Imagine you are writing STOP on a whiteboard,** or spray painting it on a wall. Put that full stop at the end of the word firmly too. Own the stop and deliberately change your mental direction.

- **Put on some cheerful / powerful music** to shift your mindset. It's very hard to be angry or upset if you're listening to 'We are the Champions' by Queen or your favourite Backstreet Boys tune (whatever floats your boat).
- **Sing the words of your inner critic** – As this is a book, you thankfully are saved my screeching impression of this, but imagine, 'Heaven is a place on Earth' tune to 'Oooh you're a lazy cow.' The singing makes it ridiculous, so it just doesn't have the same power over your mind and emotions.
- **The Explosion** – Give it a 5-4-3-2-1 count down and imagine that critic exploding – no power left there.
- You can also **mix them up** – Emma, one of my previous clients, decided to do a blend of a few of these and sings 'Stop' by the Spice Girls when her critic pops up. Add one of their outfits to your critic and hey presto! A gremlin in a rubber Union Jack jumpsuit is something I cannot take seriously.

Want to supercharge it?

Combine these with our other tools of positive affirmations and gratitude, and you're building up that mental strength. You are gaining the self-belief that will ensure that: you are confident, you can do it, and you will take on that challenge and thrive.

PERFECTIONISM & CHAMPAGNE MOMENTS

One of the outcomes of a strong inner critic is perfectionism. At times, when I felt under huge pressure in terms of performing, the tendency to attempt perfectionism was extreme and almost crippling. My critic would be obsessed with making *everything absolutely flawless*. It would often show up as my total emersion, bordering on obsession, in sharpening up PowerPoint® slides – perfect alignment, page to page consistency and flow. Time wasted: hours.

Even today, as a recovering perfectionist, I will sometimes read an email ten times to make sure it is *just so*. Time wasted: five minutes per email. These things all add up. The lack of confidence in my ability means that I'm spending more time on perfection than getting out there and progressing.

How would my time have been better spent? In so many other ways! Including taking a step back and figuring out what would have the most impact longer term. That's how you progress. Sheryl Sandberg, American technology executive, philanthropist, and writer puts it beautifully in her book *Lean In*[6]:

> *"Done is better than perfect."*

A great friend in a *Financial Times* Stock Exchange Index (FTSE 100) company was also a Chief of Staff, albeit on a much larger scale. She was very clear: "80% of the work I do doesn't need to be perfect. But I know that 20% does and that's what I focus on when I need to." That attitude and self-confidence meant that she was able to cover more, better and faster, and then focus on the strategic, high-impact issues when she needed to. She called these her 'Champagne Moments'. They were the ones that really mattered, where people would need to see her at her very best. The rest of the time? Prosecco (or even just a nice Sauvignon Blanc) would be fine.

Where do you need to accept that done is better than perfect? Where do you need to back yourself and know that you are all good? Where do you

3 PERFECTIONISM EXERCISES

Permission to press send   **Practice Messy**   **Be more authentically YOU**

have to feel confident that you have got this, trusting your judgement and capabilities to get the important things right?

If you are a perfectionist, you can try out a few different stretches (Micro Confidence Challenges) to break down that fear of it not being perfect.

Try writing an email, re-read it once, then press send. You are allowed to re-read it twice if it's to royalty, the CEO or your top client. Then press send and notice how free you feel not spending twenty minutes checking, checking and checking again.

Try being messy and, for your next big proposal/report/meeting, set your stopwatch for twenty minutes to do a full brain download of ideas (whiteboard or large blank piece of paper is my preference, but do whatever works for you). Then use this to put together the high-level outline report. *You don't need another two hours to stew over the details and bits you could possibly add.* As always, with good old Pareto principle – you've done 80% of the work in 20% of the time. Just roll with it. If you feel uncomfortable, just caveat your submission with, 'these are my initial thoughts – happy to discuss'. I promise that you'll be amazed at the quality you can produce in those short bursts; it will feel messy, but in fact, you're delivering at your best. Then go for lunch, grab a coffee or get some exercise with the extra time you've created. As John Wooden, the legendary basketball coach, says:

"Don't worry about perfect, just get in the game."

Maybe it's as simple as you wear less make up (or none at all). Perhaps its ditching the heels or fancy shoes and donning those trainers you feel comfier in. Maybe you could open up and talk about your family, hobbies or that secret love of subterranean structures you have (yes, that's a real thing someone shared with me recently). Embrace the imperfect bits and celebrate them. It is so damn tiring being *perfect,* isn't it? Why not be real when you show up and see the difference it makes with those around you. Because aren't we all just holding up that perfection filter, when all we want to do is say, "I'm having a shit day, and I need some support."

Final Word

So, you've met and started to manage your critic. Know that the muscles it has are strong and they will take time to unwind, but they *will start to release their hold on you* if you stay with it. Keep coming back to the tools we have discussed and you'll be amazed at how your inner dialogue can change for good. Remember, **confidence is a muscle: you need to work on it consistently.** Keep returning to these tools, and over time, you'll find that your inner dialogue shifts, empowering you to step into your full potential with confidence and clarity.

The next step on our journey is a look at the cousin of the inner critic: imposter syndrome (I) – something I touched on earlier. It's got a bit of a different vibe, as it isn't always around, but it can rear its head when you least expect it. So, let's arm you with the knowledge and tools to kick it into oblivion when it comes up.

CHEATSHEET

KEY CONFIDENCE INSIGHTS

1. **Mindset Shapes Your Reality:**
   Remember the incredible power of our mindset: how we perceive the world directly impacts what we believe we can achieve. When we shift our mindset, we unlock new possibilities.

2. **The Inner Critic: Your Unwelcome Companion:**
   We all have that pesky inner critic – an unwelcome voice that sows seeds of doubt and undermines our confidence. Research shows that nearly everyone struggles with this inner voice to some degree, and it can be incredibly damaging if left unchecked.

3. **Your Brain's Filter: The Reticular Activating System (RAS):**
   Your brain's bouncer is The Reticular Activating System (RAS). It filters how you see the world based on your thoughts, beliefs and what you identify with. You can influence this with simple things like gratitude, positive affirmations and shifting your perspective from critic to champion. The more you take control of this, the more capability you have to grow your confidence.

4. **Perfectionism: The Productivity Killer:**
   Perfectionism might seem like a noble pursuit, but in reality, it often hinders progress and productivity. Instead, embrace the mantra, 'Done is better than perfect'. Let go of the need for perfection. Instead, focus on progress and taking action. Remember, champagne moments are the key – that's when you will shine.

5. **The Default Mode Network (DMN): Your Mind's Wanderer:**
   When your mind isn't focused on a task, the DMN kicks in, often leading to unproductive rumination about the past or future. This can cause anxiety and sap your confidence. Practicing mindfulness and staying present can help you to manage this natural tendency, keeping your confidence intact.

TIME FOR ACTION

1. **Name and Tame Your Inner Critic:**
   Identify your inner critic by giving it a name. Notice when it starts chattering and counter its negativity by calling on your inner champion. Remember, you have the power to shift that internal dialogue. Keep going back to it and, over time, it will shift.

2. **Stay Present with Mindfulness:**
   Combat the anxiety-inducing effects of the Default Mode Network by grounding yourself in the present moment. Practice simple mindfulness exercises, like feeling the weight of your body in the chair or the sensation of your feet on the ground. This helps keep your mind focused and your confidence steady.

3. **Train Your Brain with Positive Affirmations:**
   Develop affirmations that truly resonate with your core values and identity. Make them present tense and positive, such as 'I am resilient' or 'I am enough'. Repeating these regularly will help retrain your Reticular Activating System to focus on the positives, boosting your confidence from within.

4. **Leverage Physical Cues for Confidence:**
   Use your body to reinforce confidence. Whether it's striking a power pose or walking with purpose, your physical posture can greatly influence your mental state. Before big moments, try out these poses to boost your confidence and calm your nerves.

5. **Brain Hacks to Crush that Critic:**
   - Stop Sign
   - Whiteboard of STOP
   - Your favourite music
   - Sing it
   - Positive feedback folder
   - The Explosion
   - Mix them up.

CONFIDENCE MASTERCLASS
PHIL KEARNS – WALLABY CAPTAIN TO CEO

"Back your judgment, even though you're not always going to get it right."

Phil Kearns is a highly respected leader with a diverse and impressive career. Best known for his time as the captain of the Australian national rugby team, the Wallabies, Phil has also made a significant impact in the corporate world. He has served as CEO of multiple companies across various industries, including wealth management, insurance, and property development. Despite his broad-ranging expertise, Phil is particularly renowned for his leadership skills and his ability to build strong, effective teams. His journey from sports to business has provided him with unique insights into confidence, leadership, and personal growth.

I chatted with Phil about confidence through his remarkable career. He told me about when he became captain of the Wallabies after the team's captain, Michael Lynagh, was injured. The then coach, Bob Dwyer, called Phil into his room and told him he wanted him to lead the team. Phil asked, "What do you want me to do?!" Dwyer's response was simple yet powerful: "Just be yourself. I've picked you because of the way that you train, because of the way you play, because of the way you interact with the rest of the team, so just do more of that." This simple advice became a cornerstone of Phil's leadership philosophy and a key lesson he carries with him to this day. "When you lead as *your true self*, you naturally build confidence and trust with others."

Phil candidly shared that even he, despite his extensive experience as a CEO and leader, frequently experiences self-doubt. The key, he emphasised, is to learn from the past and focus on your strengths.

> **"You always have self-doubt… but I get over it by relying on the things I've done in the past and what I know I'm good at."**

When he was up for his first CEO role, despite being technically the least qualified candidate, he got the job because of his strengths – his leadership skills. He recalled, "I came last on every single [skills matrix] metric that the recruiters had for the role… But the key thing was around leadership, and that's what Dave [Shein, The Chairman] saw." It's a reminder that self-doubt is normal (even for a CEO!) and can be managed by staying grounded in what you do well.

Many people, especially in professional settings, struggle with feeling like they don't belong or aren't as competent as their peers, which is known as imposter syndrome. Phil acknowledged these feelings but suggests a powerful approach: be upfront about your limitations and focus on what you *can* contribute.

"I tend to put those [limitations] on the table pretty early in a meeting… It shows a little bit of vulnerability but also a bit of reality. No one in any scenario is perfect and it's better to admit that than try to 'bullshit' through the bits you don't know. If you do 'bullshit' and get 'found out' you have lost all cred."

How did he define confidence? Phil underscored that confidence is closely tied to trusting your own judgment. He explained that good judgment, which develops over time, is just about *making more right decisions than wrong ones*. This skill is essential for leadership and can be cultivated through experience and reflection.

> **"Trusting yourself is the simplest way I can define confidence. You need to back your judgment, even though you're not always going to get it right. Good judgement is a top three attribute in picking good potential leaders."**

Phil is all about embracing failure along the way too; he actively encourages his staff to take measured risks and not be afraid of making mistakes. He sees failure as being inevitable, and also a crucial part of personal and professional growth. He shared that while critics may judge, what truly matters is the *effort* you put into achieving your goals and how you learnt from any setbacks. "If you can reflect upon your own efforts and say you've given everything you possibly can... If you failed, that's okay," he said.

Phil's Top Tips for Confidence

- **Be yourself, trust yourself, back yourself;** it's easy being you (and people can easily identify fakes).
- **Stay grounded in what you do well.**
- **Keep pushing yourself.** It's through experience that you gain confidence. The more you face challenges and get out of your comfort zone, the better you get at handling them.
- **Don't be afraid to make mistakes** – learn from them. Never stop learning.
- **Surround yourself with people who are better than you,** and always be learning from them too. "You're an apprentice until you die."

CHAPTER FIVE

> "No one can make you feel inferior without your consent."
>
> Eleanor Roosevelt

I was sitting in my first interview in the City after university, at Global Investment bank. "Why do you want to work in banking, Caroline?" the lovely German lady asked.

"Well," I said, "I don't actually know what an investment bank is, but I bought a book yesterday and I'll learn."

Somehow, I got the job!

When I started in banking, I went in 100% me. I didn't pretend. I didn't know a single sausage about it. It was brilliant for me; I got to ask all the questions with no fear of judgement. Unfortunately for those I worked in a team with, eager future traders (or so they hoped) who read the Financial Times every day, the painfulness of my total incompetence was palpable, with rolling eyes at each question.

Caroline: "What's BO?"

Trainer: "Back Office."

Caroline: "What's Back Office?"

Trainer: "They work with MO."

Caroline: "Who is MO?"

Trainer: "Middle Office, they work with FO."

Caroline: "What's FO?"

Trainer: "Front office."

Caroline: "What do Back Office, Middle Office and Front Office all do?" … and so it continued at a snail's pace.

But, over time, my (perhaps slightly misplaced) initial confidence waned, and the Imposter Syndrome started to creep in. Yes, I learned a whole lot that I didn't give myself credit for, but there was a lot of 'technical' stuff (also known as finance 'geek speak') that I didn't really understand (or have the time or inclination to learn). So, I would sit in some meetings, *totally overcome with fear* that I would get found out; they would realise I was a total fraud and the game would be up.

That fear crept up for me throughout my 18-year finance career. This is what is called Imposter Syndrome. It's something you *experience*, not something you *have* and, even though it's called a 'syndrome', it's not an actual medical diagnosis.

THE IMPOSTER BREAKDOWN

Take a guess, what do all these people have in common?

- Tom Hanks
- Lady Gaga
- Maya Angelou
- David Bowie

They have all admitted to experiencing imposter syndrome. Even Einstein (yes, really). He said:

> *"The exaggerated esteem in which my life work is held makes me feel very ill at ease. I feel compelled to think of myself as an involuntary swindler."*

So, if you feel imposter syndrome, you are in the best of company!

As I have already said, imposter syndrome can be seen as the cousin of the inner critic – they are related, but not quite the same. The term was first introduced in an article published in 1978[1] where they defined it as:

"A psychological pattern in which an individual doubts their skills, talents, or accomplishments and has a persistent, internalised fear of being exposed as a 'fraud'."

The key point about the syndrome is that there is external evidence that the person *has* the skills, but they believe they have got there with luck and do not deserve to be where they are now. The kind of internal language we use is:

- *I'm a fraud.*
- *I just got lucky.*
- *Anyone could have done it.*
- *They didn't have anyone else to do the job.*
- *I don't belong here, and someone is going to find out.*

What is that fear stopping you from trying? What is that judgement holding you back from?

The true impact of imposter syndrome

Brain Powered's research[2] found that 53% of people experience imposter syndrome at some point, with 19% saying they *always* do. A 2019 study[3] of around 1800 people found 52% of female and 49% of males experience imposter syndrome daily or regularly.

So, if you look around the room in a meeting, it's possible that half of the people in the meeting are also experiencing imposter syndrome too!

There are also 5 really important features to note about imposter syndrome:

Firstly, it is different from self-doubt, although they can both be present. Self-doubt is about what you can *do* (the skills you have), whereas imposter syndrome is at an identity level; it is about who you think you *are*. Clare Josa, writes about it beautifully in her book, *Ditching Imposter Syndrome*[3]. Importantly, *you have the skills,* but you still tell yourself the story that you can't do it.

Second is the deep fear of failure. The sense that 'I might be exposed as a fraud' can be totally overwhelming, which can lead to procrastination, perfectionism and even avoiding challenges at all. I often felt like this, which is where my perfectionism (and hence massive time wasting) came from.

Thirdly, those experiencing imposter syndrome tend to overlook or ignore their achievements. They feel like they don't deserve the complements; they put the success down to luck or coincidence rather than their actual intelligence, skills and capabilities. This was something I would do all the time in my investment banking career. I would look up to a big role, and then, whenever I got promoted and ended up there, I would think: 'Oh, they just couldn't find anyone else.' Familiar?

Fourthly, imposter syndrome is context dependent. Let's say you've been in your role for a long time and you know your stuff – no imposter syndrome. Then, you changed your role, stepping out of your comfort zone towards something bigger, better or different. All of a sudden you find yourself thinking, 'Oh God, *why am I here?* They will find out I don't know what I'm talking about!' This is why it is often experienced by top talent; they may be comfortable in one role but then, if asked, for example, to join a board, they feel they don't deserve to be there.

Fifthly, we tend to make blind social comparisons, like 'they know it all and I'm the only one who doesn't.' How many times have you looked around a room and thought that? That everyone else has it figured out, and you're the odd one out? Well, that's a classic for people experiencing imposter syndrome. Our assumption is that we know less than everyone else. We found from our research of over 17,000 people that over 82% of people negatively compare themselves to others, believing that they were less intelligent or capable.

The reality? Each of us is bringing our own great stuff to the table. We aren't meant to know all the same things!

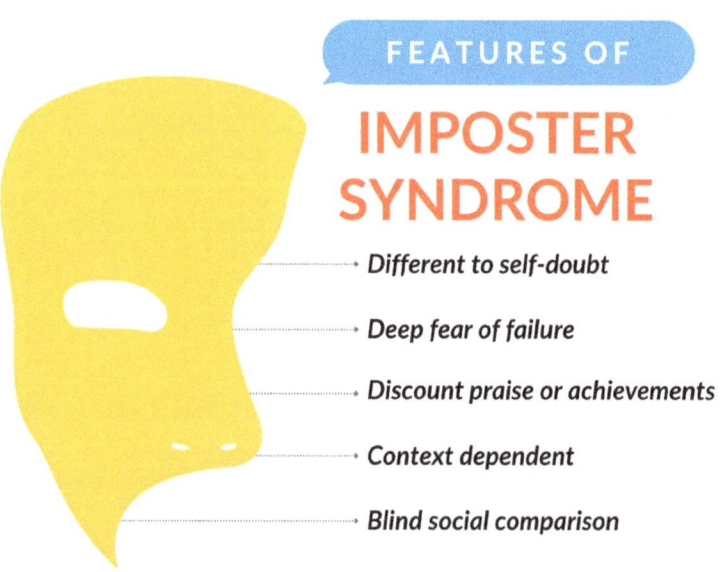

FEATURES OF IMPOSTER SYNDROME
- *Different to self-doubt*
- *Deep fear of failure*
- *Discount praise or achievements*
- *Context dependent*
- *Blind social comparison*

Back to Kim Winser OBE, who had and continues to have huge success in business:

> *"You're not the same as the person over the other side of the table. Well, you shouldn't be. The idea is to respect them for what they contribute, but you bring your own position to the table and build your confidence from there."*

But we end up judging ourselves, allowing the inner critic to tell us we aren't good enough. We have all these negative subconscious beliefs about ourselves, all of which holds us back. Then, no-one talks about it, and we assume we are the only ones. It's a cold, dark desert out there, feeling you're alone in the world of being a fraud. When we don't talk about it, it makes us feel *shame*. In her book *Daring Greatly*[5], Brené Brown talks about shame 'hiding in the dark'. When we don't talk about it, it only grows like mould. She says:

> *"If you put shame in a petri dish, it needs three ingredients to grow exponentially: secrecy, silence, and judgment."*

If only we looked around us and realised that we stand together with so many, in this tumultuous sea of imposters. The light would shine on it and the mould would disappear. Who is to say who belongs anyway?!

The outcomes of imposter syndrome can show up in different ways: deep anxiety, fear of failure, people pleasing, perfectionism (where we are having a 'fight' response) and procrastination (where we are effectively having a 'freeze' response). Perhaps you are constantly looking for validation as proof that you do belong. However it shows up for you, imagine it's like having your foot on an accelerator of a car continuously as you screech round the racetrack: there's no let up. The stress response of your nervous system is constantly being pressed, slowly eroding your energy and confidence with every turn. For organisations, that is so much brain space wasted that could be focused on helping them succeed.

10 WAYS TO SMASH THE IMPOSTER

Imposter syndrome is something that can be eradicated, managed, or even celebrated! Try out these steps and you will be amazed how your confidence levels can change.

1. Identify Your Values.

A great way to manage that imposter is by getting to know your values – let me tell you a story why.

It was the day of my interview to be promoted to Director and I was in floods of tears on the phone to my coach. I was sobbing uncontrollably.

"I'm so, so scared!" I said.

"What's the biggest thing you're frightened of?" she asked.

"Being asked a technical question I should know the answer to, but don't."

It was tapping right into that huge fear from my imposter syndrome; it was a situation I couldn't control, and I would *finally* get found out that I was a fraud. She asked me my core values.

"Integrity, respect, honesty, positivity," I replied.

"OK," she said, *"So, if you get asked a question you don't know the answer to, lean into those. Your response could be: 'I don't know the answer to that, but because my core values are about integrity and honesty, I'm not going to make it up, but I'll find out.'"*

Boom.

The point is this: **You may not have all the answers, but you bring SO much to the table and that's why you have been invited there. Bring all that brilliance and share it, from a place of integrity, aligned with who you really are. Own your space.**

This is how these things link together. Knowing and leaning into your values can really help you to eliminate that imposter syndrome. You aren't pretending, you're being authentic and *that's the magic*.

2. Manage the Judgement Saboteur.

Stop and close your eyes for a minute and step into that feeling of imposter syndrome. Just hear what it says to you.

- You shouldn't be here.
- You're a fraud.
- You don't know what you're doing.
- They will find out.

Even writing those things stirs up old fears and anxieties in me! It's time to ditch the judge (who is wrong, misinformed and frankly a complete idiot). Let's start looking at the facts. Clare Josa talks about this in her book *Ditching Imposter Syndrome*[3] – we need to shift from judgment to a fair evaluation of our performance.

- Judging is about identity: it focuses on who someone IS.
- Evaluation is about behaviour: it examines what someone DOES.

This is where enlisting a friend or trusted colleague can really help. Tell them you're feeling imposter syndrome, get out a pen and paper and go through the facts:

a) What is true? What are the **facts** of the situation? What are you bringing to the table? Think about your strengths, experience, values and unique perspective that others might not have. Lucky for them they have got you to come and bring new light on the situation!

b) Where is **negativity bias** colouring your perspective?

c) What is the chance you could produce even a **moderately** good outcome? There are plenty of people who are playing in mediocre every day! I know you are better than that. You will bring your best and that's what matters.

3. Pose Questions with Confidence.

That's the approach of Brendon Burchard who is often brought in as an advisor to a room of incredible people, from presidents to film stars, to help solve issues. But he openly says that he knows *nothing* about the subject they are discussing! His advice? Ask them, **"Where do you think I can be helpful here?"** Isn't that magic? Flip it over to them. *They have invited you,* so see if they have a need you can help with, given the experience you have. Have confidence in what you are bringing to the table and bring curiosity and excitement to the solution you can build together.

4. Own the Shared Experience.

Remember those statistics: half of people may be experiencing imposter syndrome daily or regularly. That means, when you look around a meeting, potentially *half the people there* (men and women) could well have the same fears, doubts and voices saying they don't belong. It's totally normal!

So here is a **Micro Confidence Challenge** for you: why not mention it to someone? Step out of the box and talk to someone about it to reassure your value. I bet you they will say it's come up for them too. If you are a leader, this could be exactly what your team needs!

5. Step Into 'The Learner' Persona.

Lisa Bilyeu, the legendary businesswoman with a huge focus on empowering women, takes this on too. She spent many years in boardrooms, meetings and situations where she says she felt massively out of her depth. As Lisa, and her husband, Tom Bilyeu, built their multi-million-dollar business, they were surrounded by experts, advisors and potential investors speaking a language she often didn't understand. How did she deal with it? Rather than berate herself for not being good enough, she says, "Amazing. I don't know this stuff and I'm going to learn it and grow." She relabelled herself as 'The Learner'. How good is that? This is what the experts call a 'growth mindset': she has belief in her capability to grow and learn. We are going to dig more into that later as there's some fascinating science behind it and why it's so powerful.

Imagine if you were to take on those new opportunities, getting excited about learning about any gaps in knowledge, rather than beating yourself up? Bring curiosity to the table and excitement about all that you are going to learn!

Just imagine what else you would take on and try?

6. Trust The Process (Be Patient).

Yes, I know, you feel you should know it all *now* and you aren't good enough, but really, how long have you been in the role? Have you even given yourself a chance to learn?! It is totally normal to feel like you are not competent when you are new in an endeavour. **Don't judge yourself against other people when their starting point has been completely** *different.* Whether it's in time, or direction, **you are not them and that is your gift.** So be patient, play the long game, turn up with integrity and a willingness to learn and you will rock it in no time.

7. Embrace Authenticity and Humility.

Remember, no one likes a know-it-all when they have just showed up. We all know the annoying graduates who have arrived from university, feeling like they are the Yodas of their field (yawn). The 'fraud' feeling we have is validated when we lie, make false claims about our capabilities or try to fit in, when right now, we don't! **Authenticity and humility in not-knowing is actually your superpower.** Those who have been in their roles for a while will be appreciative of you being honest, listening, respecting them, understanding and doing the work to be better each day. Believe in you and that value of hard work you have, knowing you will show up every day to grow.

8. Reframe and Love Your Imposter.

It's showing you where your gaps are, both in terms of your self-belief and how much more other people think about you. Use it as fuel to drive your self-reflection and growth (see how in our next Confidence Masterclass, from Neelu Agarwal).

9. Stop Overestimating Everyone Else.

A friend of mine who is very successful in her field was asked if she experienced imposter syndrome. "Absolutely not. There are so many average people around the table, why shouldn't I be there?!" I love this and it's so true. Why is it that we assume people are so much better than us? We tend to make false comparisons, believing that they know more and have better, more applicable experience than us. The gap is caused by our inner critic's negative voice about our abilities, our subconscious beliefs and what people share about themselves.

Why should we be there? Why the hell not?! Channel some of that screw-you attitude, show up and own your space.

10. Turn Discomfort into Triumph.

The reality is that if you're experiencing imposter syndrome, you are pushing yourself. Bloody well done you. You haven't stayed in the safe zone. Instead, you have gone beyond, taking on something you don't know, and that takes courage. *Be proud of yourself!* Channel that champion and when the imposter pops up say, "YES!!! There you are!! Welcome. I'm here nailing it. Want to watch?"

Let's Recap

You have been invited to the table, interview or meeting. They have asked you because of the skills and experience you uniquely have. No-one else. OWN IT. Celebrate the insecurity and show them how bloody brilliant you are!

You may not have the smartest response to every point, but you are, together, *building a solution.* Your comment or question may be the thought spark that someone else uses as a foundation for another thought – and that's teamwork! So, ditch the judgement and get out there; you have every right to show up as your authentic, brilliant self.

CONFIDENCE GYM: THE BRAVE FRAMEWORK

Here is my five-step B.R.A.V.E. framework you can use to beat that critic or imposter, channel your inner champion and step out there with confidence. We will start with the framework then go through an example:

B.R.A.V.E. FRAMEWORK *the*

We can manage our inner critic and imposter syndrome through using this step-by-step process. Get out your journal and work through these questions.

You can use this all the time to stay rational, positive and on track with your goals.

1.  BREATHE
2. RECOGNISE
3. ACKNOWLEDGE & ASSESS
4. VALIDATE & VERIFY
5. EMPOWER

BREATHE
Pause and take a deep physiological sigh (two breaths in, one breath out) to calm your nervous system, shifting from survival mode to clear, rational thinking.

RECOGNISE
Recognise the voice of your Inner Critic, give it a name and notice and what it's saying to you.

ACKNOWLEDGE & ASSESS
Acknowledge its presence without judgment. What is it trying to protect you from? Write it down and thank it for surfacing.

VALIDATE & VERIFY
What evidence is there? Is it 100% right? What's the truth vs negativity bias? Find an experience that disproves it.

EMPOWER
What's a different perspective? Rephrase it positively (like you would say to a friend in the same situation) What positive action can you take?

Here's an example with my critic:

Breathe: *Deep double breath in through the nose, long breath out.*

Recognise it: *Hello Gremlin, there you are. I see you and hear that you're a bit concerned.*

Acknowledge & Assess: *It's saying I'm out of my depth. I shouldn't be here. I don't know what I'm talking about. Everyone will laugh at me when I say something stupid.*

(Now here, if you are finding you can't shift the thought pattern, try using one of our Brain Hacks, like the 'stop' sign or playing music or similar as a circuit breaker).

Validate & Verify: *It's trying to protect me from making a fool of myself. That could happen if I haven't prepped properly, but I've worked so hard. I couldn't have done any more. The evidence that I'll make a fool of myself is zero, aside from when I was at school and couldn't spell!*

The reality is that now I make sure I've done the background research. There may be a question I don't know the answer to, but I can just say, "I'll check and get back to you." That's what I did last time.

Empower: *You have done this so many times. You're going to NAIL IT! You know your stuff, that's why they have asked you! I know you'll do well, so just go out there and show them how fab you are. (Really visualise your champion saying this, clapping and cheering you on). I'm going to go in with my head held high, trusting in my abilities and knowing I'm bringing my best.*

THE PROCRASTINATION PROBLEM

When we lack confidence, procrastination is a really common avoidance strategy and it's a very normal part of imposter syndrome. It may be that really important piece of work you know you have to do but keep avoiding, or that call you need to make. It's hanging around, sitting on your shoulder, tapping the back of your head incessantly: 'I'm still here', tap, tap, tap. And it's making you feel a bit sick too. Urgh, when will I get it done? How will I even start? This is me (and I think most people) every year with my tax return! We know it will need to get done, and there's no avoiding it, but we do everything else instead. Never has housework seemed so appealing as when we are trying to avoid something!

So, why do we wait?

- **Fear of Failure** – maybe I don't have the skills to do this. If I don't start, then I can't get it wrong.
- **Fear of Judgement** – what will people think of me when I do it or muck it up? I'm just going to freeze and hope it gets better.
- **Lack of control** – I don't think I can control the outcome of this, so I'm not going to start.
- **Inability to create a mental map** – I can't see the pathway to success, so how am I even going to get going?
- **Lack of Social Commitment** – Who cares if I don't do it? No one will know if I don't…
- **High Stress** – My brain just can't deal with it. I can't think straight.

Stress was a big issue through the pandemic; our brains were exhausted having to deal with uncertainty and change. They essentially ran out of juice (that twenty-five watts of energy) for the executive decisions, because they were operating on the survival side (in many cases, quite literally). Research by The Harris Poll[6] found that almost one-third of adults (32%) said sometimes they were so stressed about the ongoing Covid-19 pandemic that they struggled to make basic decisions, with millennials at

48%. Over a third said it has been more stressful to make day-to-day decisions (36%) and major life decisions (35%) compared with before the pandemic.

Remember the amygdala? The smoke alarm in your brain that is looking for danger and controls motivation. A study in *Psychological Science* in 2014 found the amygdala was actually larger in procrastinators[7]. It also found weaker connections between the connections between the amygdala and a part of the brain called the dorsal anterior cingulate cortex (DACC). The DACC takes information from the amygdala and makes a decision around what action the body will take. It also blocks competing emotions and distractions, keeping you on the right path. So, if that connection isn't working as well AND we have more activity in the amygdala, our decision-making process and task management capabilities aren't as good. The outcome? We put off that task and procrastination wins the day.

The good news is that there are some great brain–based principles we can use to overcome procrastination and take on tasks with confidence:

- **Start with the hardest task first, in the morning** – Earlier in the day works well (0-8 hours from waking up) as we have greater levels of chemicals in our brain that will drive better habit uptake (noradrenaline and adrenaline, dopamine and cortisol are elevated during this time).
- **Take one step** – Even if it is a REALLY TINY step. Reward yourself after completing it to release dopamine and reinforce positive behaviour – coffee is my favourite reward! But don't reward yourself every time; intermittent rewards work best as they aren't expected, so your dopamine levels rise more (just like a surprise gift).
- **Visualise it** – How will it feel after completing it? What will you be proud of?
- **Decrease the 'Activation Energy'** – Activation energy is the energy it takes to start the task. For example, if I want to go to the gym, I make it easy by getting my stuff ready the night before, and then don't even allow myself to think of reasons I won't do it!
- **Create a project plan, to-do list and set specific milestones and deadlines** – Make it something you'll really enjoy working

on! If you're visual like me, get it up on the wall with Post-its and colours. I get so much joy from all those Post-its! Or, if you love Excel, get tapping and produce the dream spreadsheet tracker.

- **Use time blocking** – I've started this one and it really works. When I plan my day, I write out blocks of time I'll be spending on specific tasks. Sales pipeline: Thursdays for one hour. Social media reels: Tuesday afternoons. Then I *actually do those things*, no compromise. It's amazing how things I thought would be hard just get crossed off the list!! Overcome the negativity bias of how hard it will be and just start ('Eat the frog' as Brian Tracy would say).
- **Eliminate distractions** – Pop your phone on 'focus' or airplane mode; close all the other tabs on your computer, clear your desk. Allow your brain as little cognitive friction as you can, so it can focus on the matter at hand.
- **Increase your energy** by, for example, taking necessary breaks. Brendon Burchard uses the 'release' process, where he repeats the word 'release' over and over every hour. I like to do a walk around the block or a few stretches. For those overachievers amongst you, you are not wasting time! You will be more effective by having a rest. In fact, research from Microsoft from 2021[8] showed that short breaks (ten mins) in between the countless meetings meant less stress, less exhaustion and actually improved their ability to focus.
- **Use social techniques** – Commit to an accountability buddy and tell them your goals. I have a mastermind group where we share our goals – no getting out of them after that.
- **Find something you like doing even less!** Oh yes. We as humans are *wired to avoid pain*, so if you have something else that you like even *less* than the item on your list, you will *want* to do the real thing you need to get done! In fact, the research shows, if we go and do something else that is more effortful than what we need to do, we can wait until motivation comes back, and use that dopamine rebound to fuel your motivation. This could be a cold shower or something else you're not a big fan of! Clever, isn't it? If you want to learn all the technicalities of this, Dr Andrew Huberman explains this beautifully in his 2023 podcast on dopamine[9].

CONFIDENCE TOOLBOX: 54321

Mel Robbins is a podcast host, motivational speaker and bestselling author. She recommends using the simple 5,4,3,2,1 method[10] for kicking that procrastination into touch. When you're faced with a task or a decision you've been putting off, you count down 5,4,3,2,1 in your mind or out loud. Then, as soon as you reach '1', take *immediate action without giving yourself time to overthink or hesitate.* The idea is that you can interrupt your brain's usual habit of self-doubt and overthinking. It's a way to activate your prefrontal cortex, the executive functioning part, and override the impulses of your pesky amygdala, which may be flagging up concerns, leading to procrastination or avoidance.

Final Word

Feeling like a fraud just means you're growing into bigger shoes. By now, you should be stepping into them with style. By embracing these strategies, you'll not only dismantle imposter syndrome but also step into your full power, bringing your unique brilliance to every room you enter.

Next up, we'll focus on **D** - dancing with life's stress and boosting resilience – because the stronger we are, the more unstoppable we become.

KEY CONFIDENCE INSIGHTS

1. **Imposter Syndrome is More Common Than You Think:**
   Even successful figures, like Tom Hanks, Lady Gaga, and Einstein, have admitted to feeling like imposters. This isn't about actual incompetence; it's a psychological experience many people face.

2. **Understanding the Beast:**
   - **Identity vs. Skills:** Imposter syndrome strikes at the core of your identity, making you doubt whether you truly belong, even when your skills are undeniable.
   - **The Fear Factor:** It's not just about the fear of failure; it's the terror of being exposed as a fraud, leading to procrastination, perfectionism, or avoidance of new challenges.
   - **Discounting Success:** Those with imposter syndrome often attribute their achievements to luck rather than their abilities.
   - **Context Matters:** You might feel confident in one area, but stepping into new territory can reignite those imposter feelings.
   - **Blind Social Comparison:** Stop assuming everyone else has it all figured out. Chances are, many are feeling just as unsure as you.

3. **Ten Ways to Smash Imposter Syndrome:**
   1. Identify Your Values
   2. Manage the Judgment Saboteur
   3. Pose Questions with Confidence
   4. Own The Shared Experience
   5. Step Into 'The Learner' Persona
   6. Trust The Process (Be Patient)
   7. Embrace Authenticity and Humility
   8. Reframe And Love Your Imposter
   9. Stop Overestimating Everyone Else
   10. Turn Discomfort into Triumph

TIME FOR ACTION

1. **Own Your Values:**
   When imposter syndrome creeps in, remind yourself of your core values and let them guide your actions. Staying true to who you are will help you navigate any challenge with integrity.

2. **Reframe the Inner Critic and Imposter:**
   Use the B.R.A.V.E. framework to shift from self-judgement to self-evaluation. Focus on your strengths, achievements, and what you bring to the table.

3. **Normalise the Experience:**
   Open up about your imposter syndrome with others. You'll find that many people share the same feelings, and talking about it can reduce the power it holds over you.

4. **Adopt a Growth Mindset:**
   Embrace challenges as opportunities to learn and grow. See every new experience as a chance to develop your skills and expand your knowledge.

5. **Tackle Procrastination with Brain-Based Strategies:**
   Use practical tools, like time-blocking, starting with the toughest tasks first, and visualising your success, to overcome procrastination and keep moving forward.

Remember: You have been invited to the table, interview or meeting because of who you are. OWN YOUR SPACE.

CONFIDENCE MASTERCLASS
NEELU AGARWAL – LOVE YOUR IMPOSTER

"I'm uncomfortable not having imposter syndrome, as it's a sign I'm complacent."

Neelu Agarwal is the Head of Diversity, Equity and Inclusion for the Prudential Regulatory Authority, part of the Bank of England. She is also a Happiness Coach, Public Speaker, Board Member and Asian Woman of Achievement.

Neelu overcame deep-seated insecurities to get where she is now. In her early years, she grew up as the less favoured sibling compared to her academically and physically admired sister. From a cultural perspective, Neelu experienced the pressure of growing up in an Asian household, where the focus was often on what was *lacking*. These feelings of being invisible and unworthy led to a lack of self-confidence. As a mother, Neelu consciously strives to avoid replicating these patterns with her own son.

When her sister left for college, Neelu experienced a shift. The focus of her family turned towards her, which helped her begin to feel valued and seen, sparking her journey toward self-awareness and confidence.

One of her earliest challenges was overcoming her concerns about her appearance, particularly her orthodontic issues. At 23, she took the bold step of undergoing a five-year dental treatment, which significantly boosted her self-confidence and allowed her to feel more comfortable with herself. *She took action* to make changes, which is such an important lesson. However, Neelu still felt like she lacked confidence due to her lack of hobbies and interests, which made social interaction difficult. However, she gradually pushed herself to build knowledge and step out of her comfort zone, forcing herself to speak up in meetings despite fumbling or feeling inadequate. In our discussion she shared with me:

> *"Externally, people saw someone confident to put their opinion forward, but internally, I was focusing on all the ways I might have failed."*

But over time she learned the truth is that the world often sees us differently from how we perceive ourselves.

What tools does she use to build confidence? She credited surrounding herself with supportive people who believed in her, even when she doubted herself. She learned from mentors and public figures, actively reaching out to those she admired to seek guidance. "You need people around you who genuinely want you to win," she stated. Neelu also emphasised the importance of taking small, manageable steps toward self-improvement, celebrating the actions rather than the outcomes.

Imposter syndrome? Neelu spoke with a big smile: "I love imposter syndrome!" She even welcomes imposter syndrome when it comes up:

> *"I love imposter syndrome, because it means that people believe in you more than you believe in yourself. Then, it's about assessing, what's the gap? Why don't I believe in myself and how can I fix the deficit of self-belief?"*

She believes that once you've fixed the deficit, the actions you take don't just fix the gap in belief, but they also *make you better at your job*, which you're already good at! So, if you're able to fix the gaps and satisfy the intrinsic belief system, it's only a massive win-win for the person who trusted you, because you'll be growing. Once you stop feeling that imposter syndrome, you need to beware; she says you need to look for a new challenge or upgrade your environment as you aren't growing.

> *"I'm uncomfortable not having imposter syndrome, as it's a sign I'm complacent."*

Neelu knows that having imposter syndrome along the way is a really important part of the journey: "It builds your resilience and confidence to climb that next mountain, and the next – each one helps you to grow and take on a bigger challenge again." Isn't that just a great way of knocking that imposter on its head?

Neelu's Top Tips for Confidence

1. **Challenge Yourself** – Step outside your comfort zone regularly, starting with small actions like speaking up.
2. **Build a Support Network** – Surround yourself with people who uplift and encourage your growth.
3. **Take Small Steps** – Break goals into small tasks and celebrate each achievement.
4. **Reframe Setbacks** – View failures as learning opportunities instead of dwelling on them.
5. **Embrace Imposter Syndrome** – See it as a sign of growth and use it to push yourself forward.

CHAPTER SIX

> "The purpose of pain is to move us into action. It is not to make us suffer."
>
> Tony Robbins

THE BURNOUT BREAKDOWN

That morning was the final straw for my brain. As I looked at my enormous list of things to do, the page went blurry, and it felt like my mind had short circuited: the screen was glitching and the transmission was lost. The reality was that this had been bubbling for months.

I had been given seven different teams to manage (around fifty people in total), all with their own different stakeholders, goals, challenges and needs. Every meeting my mind was having to change gear entirely, trying to stay on top of all the pressures and requirements for that particular part. Call. Video call. Email. Meeting. Message. Call. Meeting. Meeting. Meeting. Video call. Message. Email. Email. Email. It never ended. I was working fifteen-hour days and it still wasn't enough. And every one of my seven managers wanted priority, half my time, with little consideration for the other pressures I was under.

Then my brain stepped in and said, no more.

I stood up and went to a meeting room and cried. A lot. I then breathed. And breathed. I used my meditation 'count to ten' over and over and slowly started to calm down.

I felt so fragile, exhausted and drained. Like I would shatter if touched. My breath shallow and chest contorted. I knew I had to wind it back or else I would fall off that mental cliff, out on stress leave with true burnout. If you have been there, then you know exactly what I mean.

So, what does this have to do with confidence? Everything.

I wish I had had the confidence to say no. To stand up for myself and create proper boundaries. I wish I had taken more care of myself, rather than having to get to the point where my body had to step in because my mind wasn't disciplined enough to do it earlier.

Unfortunately, this isn't an uncommon story. In fact, it's more common to hear of people being burnt out than ever before; with the world speeding up every second, it's hard not to feel like we are spinning out of control. The pressures that people have in their lives, particularly those who are parents or carers, is extraordinary. But you're meant to do it with a smile on your face, whilst looking like the supermodel Gisele Bündchen, dressed immaculately in your Lululemon or stylish Louis Vuitton cream trousers, calmly picking up the children having bossed it at work that day. What a load of bollocks.

Let's be honest here:

- If your kids are still alive, loved and you manage to get them to school each day, you're doing a bloody fantastic job.
- If your elderly parents, or just the one left, feels safe and loved and knows you're there for them, you're doing a bloody fantastic job.
- If you manage to get yourself up each day, after another awful online date evening, where you've numbed the boring chat with three G and Ts, you're doing a bloody fantastic job.

Life isn't easy, and yet we all know we set the bar so high, based on unrealistic comparisons, and proceed to waste each day judging ourselves against the ridiculous fake bar.

We create so much additional stress trying to be the perfect parent / child / Sex in the City-style singleton, at some point we just want to curl up and get someone to pat our heads as we gently sob, "Arrgghhhhh."

If the bar is so high, we can't even dream of reaching it, so no wonder we lack confidence! If every day, our gremlin is telling us we are a loser, a bad parent, and not enough, the stress builds up and chips away at our confidence levels.

In fact, our research[1] found that 84% of people are stressed from taking on too much and 72% of people have feelings of being a failure. When you combine that with all the other statistics around self-doubt and imposter syndrome, no wonder we are all struggling with our confidence!

So, let's look at the connection between stress and confidence, what's happening in our brains and some awesome research-based tools we can use to minimise it.

FOUR MAJOR STRESS TRIGGERS (AND HOW TO DEFEAT THEM)

OK, so you may think you can skip this part as you've heard it all before, but here we are going to look at this stress from four unique perspectives, all which impact confidence:

1. **The Pleasure of Predictability**
2. **Avoiding the NRC pathway (Negativity, Rumination and Catastrophisation)**
3. **The Power of Perspective**
4. **Set up for Success**

1. THE PLEASURE OF PREDICTABILITY

How much stress do we cause in our lives from these challenges which come up day after day? And why is it so stressful? This brings us to our third Evolutionary Fact:

> **EVOLUTIONARY FACT #3**
>
> The brain sees lack of control as
> # DANGER

Evolutionary Fact 3:
Our brain sees lack of control as danger

For our brain, lack of familiarity and control of any situation equates to danger (I haven't been down this path before; therefore, it may not be safe). Why does it happen? It's because the brain has an *inability to create a complete map of a situation.* Remember, our brain's number one priority is survival, so if it can't create a plan of how to deal with something, then it is really scary. Control = Safety. Lack of control may look like redundancies at work, becoming a new parent, driving to work in traffic each day or a global pandemic. What's the constant with all of these? Change. A 2005 study found that even just a little ambiguity on its own lights up the amygdala, our brain's smoke alarm. The more ambiguity, the more threat response[2].

Anytime we encounter a change in our environment, that lack of control over what happens next can feel anything from exciting to uncomfortable, to unpleasant, to downright terrifying. Our confidence can be shattered as we are asked to step into the unknown and try that new role, that secondment or start at a new unknown company. This depends on the person and our level of comfort with change, which comes from our background and experiences over the years.

Psychologists call our comfort with what we know, the 'Pleasure of Predictability' as it's warm and fuzzy when we have seen it before. 'Phew,' it says. 'I was safe and in control last time, I'll be fine if I do the same thing again.' Its neural pathway has been established, like a track in the woods, and down it we walk each time, as we feel safe doing it.

However, when things are new, we are totally out of control. Our brain can't see that pathway through, and it panics. 'Arggh! Which way?' And we have that threat response from our Evolutionary Fact One – our brain prioritises its limited energy for survival.

Change is tough, as you need to create a new pathway, like knocking down branches in a forest. Once your brain has learned it was OK and survived last time, it will use that pathway again. Adding strong emotions to a thought, creates an even stronger path and sears it into our memory like a fire trail.

Why does this impact confidence? If you spend time, energy and emotions on thinking 'I am bad at presenting', your brain will default to that strong pathway. It will *look for evidence of that in your world which will reinforce it.*

The impact of this on confidence levels is important. If someone is feeling threatened by their circumstances being out of their control, this can elicit that same survival response in their brain and body, further sending them spiralling down into feelings of low confidence. COVID-19 was a very interesting example of this: we saw an almost primal response from people, particularly at the start when people were sadly dying and we did not have a vaccine to protect us.

We saw people hoarding, fighting, showing aggression and being fearful. They were trying to control whatever could be controlled but, paradoxically, showing behaviours of being out of control because of their fear. However, once we were able to get to grips with what was within, or beyond, our control around the pandemic, the situation calmed. People could get masks, stay at home, wash their hands and sanitise. These were all choices, and a level of control we had, to reduce the stress of the situation and so grow in confidence.

The cognitive bandwidth that we use up, trying to control things outside our control, is often huge. We are snatching at feathers, never grasping them, despite furious effort. The outcome? **Our confidence is reduced, because we aren't getting the results we feel we 'should' do: 'I'm a failure' we say. We judge ourselves on targets and expectations that are completely unrealistic, leading to further negative thoughts and rumination**. The Brain's Bouncer, the RAS will be conditioned to look for (perceived) failure, with the Default Mode Network steaming away on what should or could have been.

So, in order to increase our confidence levels through change, we need to focus on what we can control.

CONFIDENCE TOOLBOX: CIRCLE OF CONTROL

"God, grant me the serenity to accept the things I cannot change, the courage to change the things I can, and the wisdom to know the difference." (Serenity Prayer)

In his book, *The 7 Habits of Highly Effective People*[3], Stephen Covey articulates the Serenity Prayer beautifully by distinguishing between our Circle of Concern (things we care about but cannot control) and the Circle of Influence (things we care about and can have an impact on). This was developed to include the Circle of Control, things that are directly in our control to change.

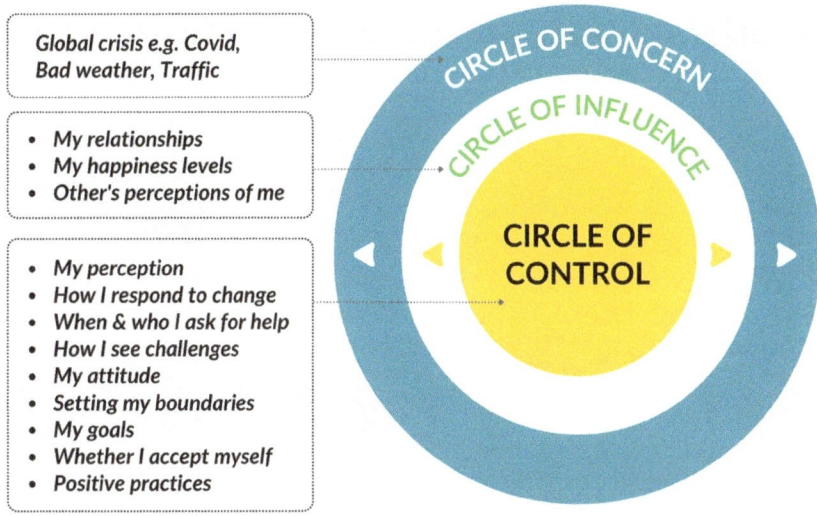

Adapted from Covey, S. (1989) The 7 Habits Of Highly Effective People. Simon and Schuster, New York.

1st Circle: Control
We need to understand what is inside our control (inner circle), that's where we can place our energy. Examples of this might be: our perspectives, how we respond to change, our attitude, setting boundaries and goals.

2nd Circle: Influence
This is the next circle out – we can't directly change it, but we can try to influence the outcomes. For example, a relationship: we can't control how that person feels about us, but we can *influence* it by our behaviour. Same goes for networking, connecting and taking action; we are influencing outcomes but not necessarily controlling them.

3rd Circle: Concern
It concerns us, but we can't do anything about it, for example the weather, traffic or a global pandemic. This is where we risk wasting cognitive energy on things that are outside our control, which only leads to high stress.

So, what does this mean practically? Lock in here, as this is really important!

Please, please, please, stop trying to focus on things you cannot control. It will only lead to stress and frustration.

Stop getting angry about traffic; about that horrible person at work; that weather forecast that you cannot change. Always think:

"What do I have control over in this situation?"

Not only will you be less stressed, but *your confidence will grow as you're taking on things you can actually influence.* You are much more likely to demonstrate success to your brain, if you're focusing on things within your control. You don't have a hope in hell if it's in the circle of concern, and that will only chip away at your confidence levels.

Here are parts of our lives where we usually have control:

- Personal habits and routines
- Goal setting and planning
- What perspective we take on situations (is it a disaster or an opportunity?)
- Our words and actions

What we can influence, but not control:

- Others' perceptions and actions
- Organizational culture and dynamics

What do you need to let go of?

- Past mistakes and regrets
- External circumstances (for example, the weather or traffic)
- Unrealistic expectations of perfection
- Trying to please everyone

How much brain energy would you free up by not worrying about things you can't control? By releasing concerns about uncontrollable factors, you can potentially free up a significant amount of mental energy, allowing for greater focus and productivity.

This thought process was helpful for a pitch that I had performed recently to a potentially hugely significant client for my business. This had required thorough preparation, the support of my amazing mentors and a deep knowledge of my subject. I was grilled by the client but managed the questions and walked away from it knowing I could not have done better. Did I get the client? No, they didn't feel it was the right fit for them. But did it knock my confidence? Absolutely not, because *I had controlled everything that I could within my power*. I had taken a step, tried it and performed at my best. I could not control what the client saw as 'a good fit for the organisation', but I could control how I showed up to that discussion, with all the preparation and hard work behind it. Focusing on what I could control was the key and hence my confidence wasn't damaged, despite the knock back.

2. AVOIDING THE NRC PATHWAY (NEGATIVITY, RUMINATION AND CATASTROPHISATION)

Take a minute – I want you to draw a quick pie chart with me. Draw a circle and split it into how much of your stress is real versus *imagined*. And really think carefully about this. Absolutely real stress exists. Events, circumstances and people can create stress, but *how much of it is our interpretation and internalisation of that stress versus the actual stressor itself?*

Remember our second Evolutionary Fact. We naturally have a negativity bias. We often assume the worst like:

- They are looking at me funny.
- They are judging me.
- He's going to be angry.
- She's going to be so upset.
- It's going to be a disaster.
- This is the worst thing that's ever happened.

How much cognitive bandwidth are you using about things that haven't even happened? How much time is being spent, with your imagination running wild, going from rumination to the full catatrophisation of a situation? What do you think is happening to your confidence as you think and experience that stress in your mind and body? If we are going to be able to manage our confidence, we have to take control of this NRC pathway in any way we can. Remember the Default Mode Network (DMN), which is an area of interactive brain regions that is active 'by default'. It is what makes us think through these scenarios, good or bad, and is deactivated when we focus on a task. There are some simple but very effective tools we can use to quiet this feverish engine of imaginary scenarios and apply some calmness and logic to it all.

CONFIDENCE TOOLBOX: AWAKEN YOUR INNER YODA

Mindfulness and meditation are both wonderful ways for managing that NRC pathway to prevent high stress. They are also great to have an emergency tool for moments when the mind is racing down a path of negative thinking. Making these parts of your armoury will create further anchors for deep confidence, along with your ability to manage stress and anxiety. ***If you know you can handle stress well, you are much more likely to feel confident about taking on bigger, better projects or walking into a big meeting.*** It's like a big squashy puffer jacket for your brain, absorbing pressure like a sponge and allowing that confidence to overflow.

Imagine we have a spring in our mind and over time all the stresses of life make it tighter and tighter. Our frequency is higher – people will even feel it.

We snap at people at the smallest thing; that feeling of 'I'm going to blow' is a reality, whether the person deserves it or not.

Meditation and mindfulness unwind our brain spring. They reduce the time between a stimulus and our response. Rather than just losing our mind, we have time for our executive functioning part of our brain to step in and say 'Hmm, what might be going on here? What's not being said? What's my best response?'

What exactly is mindfulness? Well, simply put, mindfulness is a practice of turning your attention away from distracting thoughts towards a single point of reference (e.g., breath, bodily sensations, compassion). When you are being actively mindful, you are noticing and paying attention to your thoughts, feelings, behaviours, and movements at that moment, as well as to the effects you have on those around you. Meditation is a type of mindfulness, often where people focus on the breath as an anchor point, but it could be a candle, mantra or body scan (amongst many others).

What are the benefits? Significant research shows that those who meditate regularly are more positive and less stressed.[4] Neuroimaging studies show that, after eight weeks of meditation, a meditator has actually increased grey matter density in their brain with better cognitive functioning[5]. It literally changes the make-up of your brain... extraordinary. The research showed activity in the meditators' amygdala (the smoke alarm) was lower, which means *less susceptibility to stress and anxiety.* It's like it turns down the sensitivity dial – I find I'm much more like Teflon to pressure and confrontation with regular meditation. There is also more activity in the hippocampus, the part of the brain associated with memory and learning.

Meditation also increases your capacity for compassion, decreases chronic pain and has been shown to decrease racial bias and impulsive behaviour. Two recent studies[6] with oncology and paediatric nurses indicated that nurses who had a mindfulness-based stress reduction practice reported significant decreases in compassion fatigue, burnout, stress and experiential avoidance as well as increases in life satisfaction, mindfulness and self-compassion. Here are some other benefits[7]:

- Builds focus and concentration
- Reduces depression
- Less stress, anxiety & burnout

- Boosts immune system
- Helps improve sleep
- Reduces heart risk through lower blood pressure
- Decreases pain sensitivity
- Slowing of cellular aging (so yes, makes you look younger – no face-lift required!)
- Builds self-awareness
- Helps overall life & relationship satisfaction
- Improves empathy
- Cuts emotional reactivity because your amygdala is less sensitive
- And even enhances self-confidence!

Imagine a FREE pill that did ALL of this: would you take it?

I used my meditation practise when I was accused by a particularly aggressive and toxic individual at work of lying to audit. This is a sackable offence, so not to be taken lightly at all, but it was totally untrue and entirely uncalled for. Not only had they sent me the note saying I was lying, but they had also cc'd my global head and their own global head as well. I was furious.

With integrity and honesty being two of my core values, the fact that I was accused of lying was a big trigger for me. I had always held my head up high, knowing I didn't play those games nor expect anyone else to. The rage was deep, visceral and burning from my stomach.

So, I meditated. I did my breathing and counted from one to ten, over and over again. My mind raced off repeatedly during it, darting this way and that about how angry I was and what a total bastard he was for accusing me. "How dare he?" (And breathe...) "I'm so angry!" (And breathe...) I just kept bringing it back to my breath. Needless to say, the mind-racing was extreme, but the ebb and flow of the breathing enabled me to calm down and think more clearly about my approach.

During the follow-up meeting with him, I had to really tap into my mindfulness training to reduce my anxiety and avoid the red mist of an amygdala hijack. I tuned into the feeling of my feet on the floor, my breath passing in and out of my nostrils; I pictured my breathing in as a cool blue mist, my breathing out as fiery orange. It really worked and enabled me to manage the situation to the best of my ability, rather than being clouded by anger and fear. The outcome was that I was able to be concise, speak with precision and push back on the lies with deep calmness, which made me look like the bigger person. My pre-frontal cortex was fully engaged, finely tuned to the moment and the facts it needed to recall so I was able to dismiss his ridiculous claim. He looked like a childish idiot.

This was huge for me. It provided another brick in my confidence path, as I knew I had the capability to show up when it mattered. This can be you too. Start today; your confidence will grow because you know you can really deal with pressure when you need to.

So, how do we do it? As with all habits, START SMALL!

There are so many apps now that you can download on this, but you can start very easily.

CONFIDENCE GYM: SUPER SIMPLE MEDITATION

Start by doing one minute of breathing each day. Close your eyes and focus on your breath going in and out of your nostrils. For each exhale, mentally count 'one', 'two', 'three' all the way up to ten. Then start again. If you notice your thoughts going elsewhere (which is entirely normal), just refocus on your breath and start from one again.

"But I've tried it and I'm not good at it," I hear you say... Well, read this paragraph closely: this bit is important. The neuroscience research shows the neuroplasticity (brain changes) *comes from your thoughts drifting and then bringing them back to your practise.* This means **the benefit comes from that mind wandering, noticing that you've wandered and gently bringing your practise back to your breath.**

It isn't about being 'good' at meditation by having a blank mind – that's not it at all! You will benefit from the gentle wandering of your mind and your gentle return to your focal point. Over time, you can slowly build up your practise (note, the word 'practise'– not perfect) to longer periods with different types of focus areas.

10 Steps to Success with Meditation

1. Decide on a **goal** that you would like to achieve for your meditation practice.
2. Choose a simple action '**anchor**' that you can associate with using your app or the practise you can do on a daily basis. For example, if you eat breakfast every day, set a goal to meditate directly after breakfast.
3. **Plan** when and where you will do your meditation. Be consistent: choose a time and place that you encounter every day of the week.
4. **Design your space** – how can you make it somewhere that promotes you having a few peaceful minutes? A nice cushion, chair, or cosy spot in bed/on the sofa.
5. **Start small** – if you are new to it, start with one minute. That's totally fine. Then work up to two mins and then five etc. Better to just start.
6. **Be flexible and creative** – what space works for you? Perhaps you've just dropped off your kids or been to the gym and can take five mins breathing in the car. Make it work for you in whatever suits.
7. **If you miss a day** – it's no problem, just start again the next day.
8. Try your best to have a **growth mindset** – think of this rewiring challenge as a learning experience and focus on your progress. Changing behaviours is hard, but with a bit of effort and dedication, you can improve your outcomes.
9. Try out **'run streaks'** – if you have a bit of a competitive spirit, these are great ways to keep you going. Many apps have them now, where they track how many days you've done it in a row. Aim for seven days, then fourteen days, then perhaps thirty days in a row.
10. **Socially commit** – tell people you are doing it. That will help.

Remember: it will get easier with time. According to habit-formation research, within ten weeks you should find you are doing it automatically without even having to think about it.

3. THE POWER OF PERSPECTIVE

You're at the theme park with those little people in your life, begging you to take them on the roller coaster ride. "Pleeeaaase" they cry, jumping and dragging you with their little hand. You agree, and immediately start to sweat.

You walk around the long queue, listening to the screams of people whooshing up-down-sideways-inverted and the suspense builds. Your heart starts beating faster, your body tenses and your brain is going into panic mode because of the impending DOOM. But what about the small person next to you? They are bouncing up and down with excitement. They sweat and you see their body tensing up with anticipation at the FUN they are about to experience. Same ride. Similar bodily experiences. Different perspective.

In her research at Harvard[8], Alison Wood Brooks challenged the common belief that calming oneself down is the best way to handle pre-performance anxiety. Through a series of experiments, including scenarios like singing "Don't Stop Believin'" by Journey in front of an audience, she discovered that **simply reframing anxiety as excitement can dramatically shift how we feel and perform.**

The reason? Both anxiety and excitement are high-energy emotions, and they are what's called 'arousal congruent'. Instead of trying to suppress those racing thoughts and that pounding heart, Brooks found that *embracing* the feeling and telling yourself "I am excited" made it easier to channel that energy positively. This is because *the same parts of the brain associated with anxiety are also associated with excitement.* The sweaty palms, heart beating faster, body tensing etc, they are very similar responses, whether you are feeling that sense of fear or excited about what's going to happen next. So, having her research participants reframe their anxiety as excitement by saying "I am excited" before they went on stage, led them to adopt an 'opportunity mindset' rather than a 'threat mindset'. People who practiced this reframing didn't just feel better – they actually did better, taking on tasks with a sense of opportunity rather than fear.

This is a very useful tool for improving confidence, particularly given that so many people feel that sense of deep fear around public speaking or similar

situations. Rather than going into full panic mode, shift your perspective on the situation and reframe that anxiety as excitement:

- I am terrified > I am excited.
- I won't know what I'm talking about > I'm excited about how I can learn.
- I'm going to muck it up > I'm excited about how I can serve and share what I know.

You're moving the energy of anxiety to be used for performance edge. Now that's powerful.

I love the video of Karen Lawson[9] giving an inspiring talk speech to her Duke's Basketball team. She talks about waiting in life for things to get easier, to get simpler, then it will be OK:

> *"It will never get easier. What happens is that you handle hard better. You become someone who handles hard stuff better."*

What an incredible perspective to have. Don't wait for life to get easier. Instead, trust in yourself, trust you will be able to figure it out; trust in that growth mindset and you will be able to handle it better.

Fixed and Growth Mindset

What you may be thinking of here is fixed and growth mindset. It's another important lens of perspective through which we can look over life's twists and turns with confidence. If you are unfamiliar with this, it is a concept discovered by psychologist and Stanford researcher, Carol Dweck[10], which has a significant impact on how we perceive failure.

Fixed Mindset: The belief that a person's capacities and talents are fixed and cannot be changed.

Growth Mindset: The belief that a person's capacities and talents can be improved over time.

People with a growth mindset understand that *effort* leads to improvement and so are *more likely to persist in the face of challenges.* They want to learn more from others; they see effort being part of the puzzle. So naturally, people with a growth mindset will be more successful, as they don't give up too early.

People with a fixed mindset don't persist, they give up (why bother?). They may even avoid the challenge altogether and ignore any negative feedback they get. They may even feel threatened by the success of those around them.

Now, let's be clear, everyone possesses a mixture of fixed and growth mindsets, which evolves with experience. You may be very fixed about one area but have a growth mindset on another. Your perspective on a situation is crucial: can I grow in this? Will I persist? Or will I give up as there isn't any point?

Let's look at an example:

Fixed Mindset: This was my frame of mind about my finance knowledge. I thought 'I don't know what I'm talking about' and 'I don't want to know and I'm not going to learn.' Guess what happened? I found learning about the finance industry really hard work, and I forgot a lot of it as soon as I could!

Growth Mindset: What I could have said to myself was: "I bet I can learn about this and be really good over time. I just need to put in the effort." And in fact, I found I had times where I did learn more deeply, but the reality was that I didn't really care. My mindset was fixed deep down that I couldn't learn or become an expert.

Remember one of our definitions of confidence: 'Confidence is belief in my ability to figure things out.' **Confidence is about having a growth mindset on life. Who knows what will come? But you'll be fine – you'll figure it out and keep moving forward.**

4. SET UP FOR SUCCESS

We've focused on a number of different ways you can manage stress, but how can you actually set yourself up to be confident in the moment? How can you prevent the stress in the first place? One of our goals for success is to elongate the time between stimulus and response. How can you provide your brains with the armour it needs to *not react*, instead responding like a calm swan on the water as the waves bob you up and down?

Stress Inoculation

You're living in the caveman days and you're packing up your meagre possessions to migrate for the season. You feel bit sniffly before you leave, but as you get going, you feel the adrenaline kick in; suddenly you feel stronger and ready to take on the journey. However, your caveman mate, Hairy Henry, isn't doing so well. His cold didn't shift. In fact, it got worse, turning into full blown flu and he can't make the journey. You know what's going to happen to him when the tribe leaves, as cavemen on their own are prime meat for hungry sabre-toothed tigers… Poor Hairy Henry.

Stress is very clever, as is demonstrated by our caveman story. Our ancestors who survived were the ones who had adapted their systems to deal with stress effectively. The adrenaline triggered by migration was crucial for firing up the immune system, beating your cold and enabling you to make that journey.

We all know how this shows up today. We work our butts off for that deadline before we have our well-earned holiday. We pull the long days, the packed diary, just so we can escape for those two weeks of bliss. We arrive at our beachside resort, and we get ill. Why does this happen? Because the adrenaline in our system has been keeping our immune system fired up. You're having your own mini-migration, and your body knows you have to perform during that period. Once you arrive, though, you relax and it's all over; our body finally gives in to the virus.

The good news is that we can use this clever mechanism to inoculate ourselves to stress. It's like having a vaccine of stress which exposes our body to it ahead of time, so we are better at coping with it when it does arrive. Essentially, we can teach our mind and body to be more comfortable with high stress situations, a bit like if you were trying to deal with a phobia.

Here's the process:

1. Identify your sources of stress and what triggers them.
2. Plan how you can manage those stressors and practice relaxation techniques.
3. Gradually increase the exposure of stressors to yourself, while using your relaxation techniques to build resilience against them.

Here's an example. I hate spiders. Properly hate them. I used to scream at even a picture of a spider (and yes, they still give me the heebie-jeebies). Now, English spiders can be a bit spiky and sometimes big, but nothing like Australian spiders. My goodness, those bastards are ENORMOUS. You genuinely feel like they might be looking at you, and some are hairy and as big as your hand (yikes). So, when I moved to Australia, I had more experiences than I would like to remember of these nasty critters (over there the fear is more valid though, as they have spiders that can kill you). But, over time and many experiences of being confronted with yet another hairy eight-legged monster, I did get a bit better at dealing with them. English spiders are now nothing in comparison. I've gone from being terrified of *all of them*, to mildly irritated at the smaller variety and hence screaming a lot less than I used to.

We can do the same thing with stress, and there is something very clever happening in our bodies which explains why stress inoculation works. Essentially, adrenaline can be produced in either or both the brain and the kidneys, however it cannot pass through the 'Blood/Brain Barrier'. This is what it says on the tin: a semi-permeable barrier that regulates molecule and ion movement between your brain and body. It's a clever way to protect your brain from pathogens and molecules which aren't compatible with your brain's make up (water soluble or big molecules).

What this means is that you have the ability to separate the production, and hence impact, of adrenaline in your body and mind. This means your body can feel 'stress' whilst you can stay calm in your mind.

This is why the zeitgeist fad of cold-water immersion works. Having a cold shower or ice bath whilst breathing calmly means that your body is saying

STRESS INOCULATION

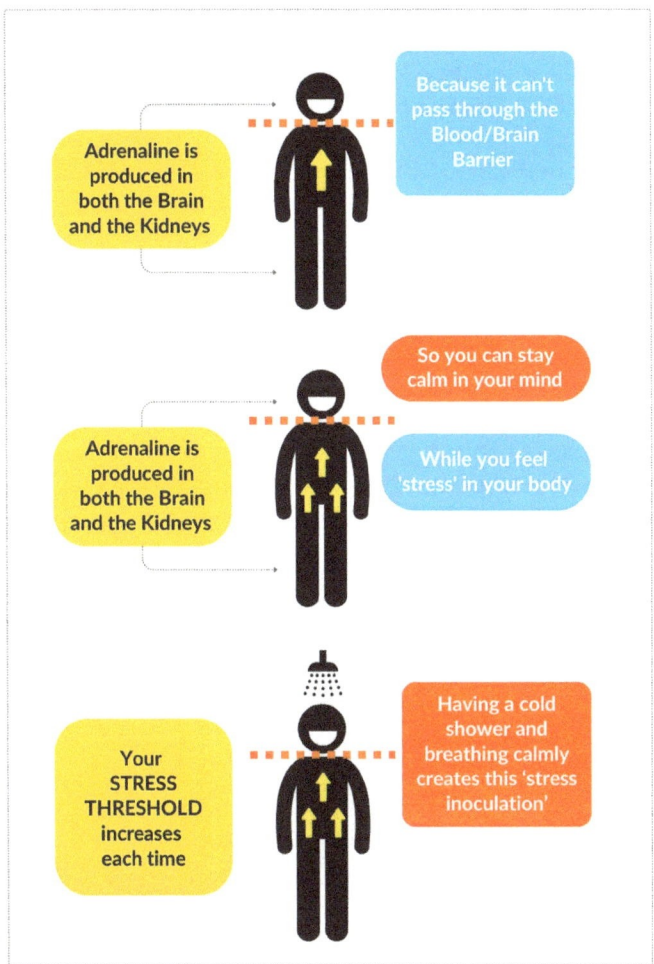

'WTF' and your mind is saying 'I am calm. This is good for me. I'm going to keep breathing.' This becomes your stress inoculation, because each time you do it, your stress threshold increases. The 'stress threshold' is essentially the point at which your body succumbs to stress. So, the higher we raise this through these 'safe' environments, the better we are able to deal with other stresses in our lives. (Note, there are dangers with cold water immersion, so please always do it in a safe environment with someone with you and limit your time in the water).

There's also the benefit of a big dopamine spike and endorphin release after a chilly dip, reducing inflammation and improving circulation. It's a great way to feel that spark of WOW, whilst reducing stress and increasing your resilience levels.

A great example of this was proven in collaboration with Wim Hof, a crazy Dutch athlete and motivational speaker, who has become famous for his methodology of breathing, particularly with cold water. A study by researchers from Radboud University Medical Centre[13] in the Netherlands investigated the physiological effects of Wim Hof's techniques, including breathing exercises, meditation and cold exposure. A group of participants were trained in his techniques for ten days. After that period, they and a control group were injected with endotoxin, a component of a bacterial cell, to induce an immune response.

The participants who had done the training had a markedly reduced immune response versus the control group. *Through this training, participants were able to regulate their sympathetic nervous system response. They increased the cortisol and adrenaline release so their system was primed to defend itself against bacteria.*

This doesn't have to be complicated; you can simply do a cold blast in your shower at the end for thirty seconds to one minute. The key is that it has to feel *uncomfortable* – that's when the magic actually happens.

Final Word

Stress can be a sneaky confidence thief, but learning to 'dance' with it builds resilience. By understanding how stress impacts your brain and taking proactive steps to manage it, you'll not only protect your mental health, but also unlock a deeper, more resilient confidence that can weather any storm. Think of unwinding your brain spring, so you're able to deal with the pressures that come up more easily. Now that you've built resilience, it's time to defend it with 'Empowered Boundaries' (E), ensuring you stay grounded and confident.

KEY CONFIDENCE INSIGHTS

1. **Burnout is a Signal, Not a Weakness:** When our brains say, 'no more', it's a sign that we've pushed ourselves too far without pausing to recover. Burnout is the brain's way of shutting down before it reaches the point of no return. It's not a sign that we're failing; it's a survival response. Recognising this early on allows us to address the causes, overcommitment, blurred boundaries, and constant pressure, before burnout takes hold.

2. **Confidence Thrives When We Control What We Can:** Confidence is deeply connected to our sense of control. When the world spins faster, it's natural to feel unsteady. But by homing in on what's within our power, our responses, routines, and attitudes, we can regain that stability and build confidence from within, rather than allowing external chaos to dictate our state of mind.

3. **Mindfulness Can Rewire Our Response to Stress:** Mindfulness isn't about eliminating stress but about learning to navigate it. By practising even short moments of mindfulness, we can retrain our brains to pause, breathe, and choose how to respond rather than react. This strengthens our ability to face pressure calmly, ultimately creating a more resilient, confident mental state.

4. **Perspective is Our Best Tool in High-Stress Moments:** How we view stress shapes our experience of it. If we see a situation as a threat, our body responds with panic. However, if we frame it as a challenge, we shift into a state of readiness and focus. Reframing anxiety as excitement, for example, can help us channel stress energy into productive action.

5. **Resilience is Built, Not Inherited:** Resilience is a skill we develop by regularly stepping into controlled stress situations and learning how to stay calm. Each time we navigate these moments, our brain rewires to handle future stress more effectively. This process, known as 'stress inoculation', trains us to stay composed and confident when life throws bigger challenges our way.

TIME FOR ACTION

1. **Set Boundaries Proactively:** Let's start by identifying areas where our personal or professional boundaries have blurred. What tasks or commitments drain us the most? How can we gently but firmly start saying 'no' to what no longer serves us? It's about protecting our energy for what matters most and building our confidence to assert those boundaries.

2. **Create a Daily Mindfulness Practice:** Commit to just a few minutes a day of mindfulness, whether it's a quick breathing exercise, a quiet moment of gratitude, or simply observing our thoughts. Practising mindfulness consistently will help us create a mental buffer against stress, giving us the space to respond more calmly in heated situations.

3. **Reframe Stressful Situations in the Moment:** Next time we feel the anxiety rise, try to experiment with reframing: instead of "I'm terrified", say, "I'm excited and ready". Shifting our perspective from 'threat' to 'challenge' can turn nervous energy into focus and drive. Practice this mindset shift in low-stress settings, so it becomes second nature when the stakes are high.

4. **Focus on Our Circle of Control:** In any situation, we can list out the aspects of our current environment that we have direct control over. This might include our daily routines, how we communicate, or even our mindset around challenges. We can channel our energy effectively here, where there's real impact, rather than getting caught up in what's outside our influence.

5. **Introduce Stress Inoculation Exercises:** Remember to start small. Maybe it's taking a quick cold shower in the morning or speaking up in a meeting when we'd usually stay quiet. These 'mini-challenges' will gradually train our brains to handle stress without triggering a panic response. Each step helps us build a more robust, resilient mindset.

CONFIDENCE MASTERCLASS
NICOLINA ANDELL – REJECTIONS TO RESILIENCE

"Seize opportunities. Believe in your ability to figure things out, and don't be afraid to ask for help when you need it."

Nicolina Andall is a Corporate Commercial Solicitor with over 20 years of experience and a Portfolio Non-Executive Director. She is also a Judicial Appointments Commissioner, serving on several boards, government panels and advising on key public appointments. Nicolina founded Inspiring Diverse Leaders in 2022, a growing group supporting ethnic minorities in leadership roles. She is a renowned public speaker, recognised for her advocacy, and was listed in the Cranfield 100 Women to Watch in 2020.

In our conversation I was struck by Nicolina's incredible journey, which is anchored in a deep sense of self-worth and resilience. These traits, she explains, were nurtured by her parents, Windrush immigrants from Jamaica. "They came over with one bag each, thinking the streets were paved with gold," she said with a smile. Her parents' determination to succeed, despite the odds, shaped her mindset to aim high from a young age. Her mother's decision to move her out of a school with limited expectations was a pivotal moment. "The headmaster at my first school thought that if I worked hard, I might get a job at Woolworths. My mother was horrified. She didn't come all this way for me to be told that was all I could achieve."

Reflecting on her journey, Nicolina emphasised that confidence is something that develops over time. "Confidence, for me, is about a steely belief in your ability to achieve. If you don't believe in yourself, no one else will." But it's not just belief in her skills; it's also a belief in her self-worth.

> ***"You have to have the strength to stand up for yourself, especially in environments where gaslighting, backbiting, and negativity are the norm. It's important to be able to say, 'No, it's not me. It's them'."***

Nicolina was candid about self-doubt: "There have been plenty of times when I've struggled with confidence. Early in my career, I faced hundreds of rejections, 139, to be exact, before I finally got my legal training contract. It only takes one yes, but getting there is brutal. It tested my resilience, but it also built it." Now that is resilience!

One of her key strategies in dealing with difficult situations is to seek support from a strong network. "I'm blessed with amazing people around me. When I face criticism or personal attacks at work, I talk to my friends. I ask them, 'Is there some truth in this? Or is it just a toxic environment I need to get out of?' It's important to self-reflect, but also to recognise when it's not you, it's the environment." But even in adversity, Nicolina finds ways to give back. "I'm the culmination of hundreds of pieces of advice from so many people along the way. That's why I set up the Inspiring Diverse Leaders group. People kept saying they wanted to see more diversity in leadership but didn't know how to get there, so we started a little group. Now, we're over 250 strong, sharing our successes and supporting each other."

Despite her many achievements, she remains grounded. "Humility is important. You have to recognise that you don't know everything and that there's always room to grow. But you also have to give yourself credit for how far you've come." Reflecting on her journey, she says, "I didn't start out as a confident person, but over the years, I've built that muscle."

One moment that stands out is a simple but transformative encounter she had: "I was feeling a bit lost when I started my own business. Then one day, I walked into a café and a complete stranger started talking to me. For an hour, he gave me advice on how to set up my practice. It was one of those moments where the kindness of strangers made all the difference. That experience taught me the value of always being open to learning and help."

One of her favourite mottos, a piece of advice her late father gave her, captures her approach to life: "Life is a stage. You have to get up and be on it." Nicolina embodies that belief, showing up every day, not just being on the stage but owning it.

Nicolina's Top Tips for Confidence

1. **Believe in Yourself** – Confidence starts with an unwavering belief in your ability to achieve. If you don't believe in yourself, no one else will.
2. **Embrace Resilience** – Confidence is a muscle that grows through challenges. Learn from rejection and setbacks, and then use them to strengthen your resolve.
3. **Surround Yourself with a Strong Network** – Build a supportive circle of friends, mentors, and colleagues who believe in you and provide honest feedback.
4. **Reflect on Your Achievements** – Take time to acknowledge how far you've come, giving yourself credit for your successes.
5. **Be Brave and Take Action** – Don't be afraid to seize opportunities, even if you're unsure. Confidence grows through action and learning along the way.

CHAPTER SEVEN

> " The difference between successful people and really successful people is that really successful people say no to almost everything. "
>
> Warren Buffett

THE DREAM OF WORK/LIFE BALANCE

I was working in Singapore, running two big regional teams, both with tough stakeholders and high consequences if things went wrong. Every day, as I got in the lift, I would play banging music (Rage Against the Machine, if you're interested). It was to help fill me with strength so I could walk on the trading floor, shoulders back, and take on another day. But the reality was that I was drowning. I was on the edge of tears, if I gave myself two minutes to acknowledge it…. Please, don't let anyone ask if I'm OK; I knew I would just fall apart.

How many times have you felt like this? Maybe you're at your desk, or on your sofa, swamped in so many different tasks, requests and meetings that you feel like an elephant is standing on your chest. You try to take a deep breath, but the weight is too much. I see you. It's really bloody tough. 'Work/Life Balance' feels more like 'Work = Life.'

There are many ways we can get to this point. Sometimes people take advantage of us, piling the work onto someone who is very capable. Caroline gets shit done so give it to her. Mum will do it – she's unstoppable!

Load him up because he's great under pressure. Damn right I'll deliver, but when does it stop? And at what cost?

When I look back, I know now there was more I could have done, had I had more confidence. I struggled with boundaries, which partly fuelled by insecurity; yes, yes, yes, was the answer to all the requests. What would they think if I said no? Would they think I was rude? Unhelpful? Not able to cope? Weak? I shudder at the thought…

When we lack confidence and doubt ourselves, we say 'yes' too much and find ourselves overloaded with both work and personal commitments. We fear that saying 'no' will upset people, or be seen as selfish or rude, so we get caught in a cycle of stress and exhaustion. At an extreme level, this culminates in burnout, which has become an epidemic in itself; over 49% of employees globally in a recent study said that they felt some level of burnout[1].

Within the workplace, it means that we take on too much and then feel like we could be penalised by promotion panels for 'not being able to manage their workload'. In fact, often it is because we are frightened to say no, or simply *don't know how to,* that we end up being the recipient of all the work or action points.

The truth is this:

- It takes confidence to step up and say no.
- It takes courage to speak up when someone compromises your values.
- It is hard feeling like you are being selfish by putting yourself first or declining something you don't want to do.
- It's tough to express your feelings responsibly and talk about your experiences honestly.

So, here are a few important reference points for you so you can achieve more balance in your life:

- You are allowed to say no without being rude.
- You are allowed to say no without people thinking you 'can't cope'.
- You are not the only one who can do it (yes, really).
- People respect people who say no (politely).

- If you want to be seen as a senior leader, it's important that you can say no. Saying no is actually a demonstration of courage, discernment and smart resource management.
- Saying no actually empowers others as it gives them a chance to step up.

BOUNDARIES – YOUR NEW BEST FRIEND

"Personal boundaries are designed to clarify what are acceptable and unacceptable behaviours from others. Just as a fence protects and preserves our real property, so should personal boundaries protect our personal selves."

Positive Psychology

We can break boundaries down into eight different types. Which of these do you need to develop so that you can start being firmer on it?

1. **Mental** – This includes freedom of thought, values, opinions. That is the freedom to say, "I respect your opinion but don't agree."

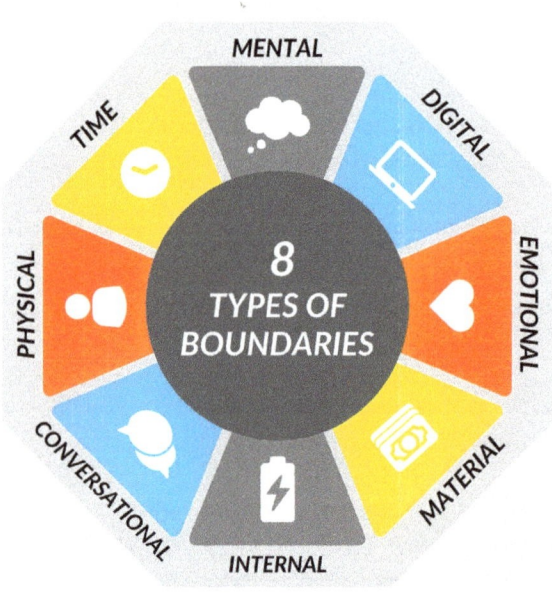

2. **Emotional** – This refers to how emotionally available you are. Sometimes you're all capped out and need to say, "I don't have the emotional capacity."
3. **Material** – This is linked to money, giving it or lending it to people. "I'm just not able to help you right now."
4. **Internal** – Your self-regulation and energy spent on others, which includes knowing your limits with socialising or being in groups: "I'm going to have some me time tonight."
5. **Conversational** – This includes which topics you're comfortable discussing. For example, talking about my dad is hard for me right now and saying that is OK.
6. **Physical** – This area includes privacy, personal space, your body, whether in a relationship or referring to people at work. "I'd like you to stop that please."
7. **Time** – This refers to what you give/spend (other people vs. yourself). "I just need 30 mins for myself."
8. **Digital** – This includes social media and how it can invade your privacy, time and relationships, through trolling and expectations of what you should (or shouldn't) be doing or looking at digitally. Like those dreaded blue ticks on WhatsApp that make people feel they 'should' be responded to because you've read the message (mine are switched off).

Which one of these do you struggle with most? What's the sacrifice you make in your life because of your lack of boundaries? It's so critical we build confidence in our boundaries because it filters through to our whole lives. When we have good boundaries, we see so many benefits:

1. Mental and emotional health
2. Avoid Burnout
3. Clear identity
4. Healthy relationships
5. Recharge to give more

When we don't have boundaries:

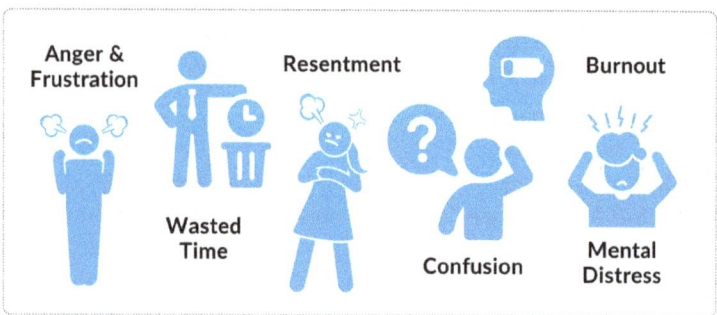

1. Anger and frustration
2. Wasted time
3. Resentment
4. Confusion
5. Mental distress
6. Burnout

"Choose discomfort over resentment."

Brené Brown

HOW TO SAY 'NO'

Part of creating confident boundaries comes from saying no. But how on earth do we start saying no when we've always been a yes person? It can feel like a big mountain to climb, but there are some practical ways you can start.

Always be direct and honest and don't overcomplicate it – keep it simple and to the point. Then try it on something small to start off with and see how it feels (it will feel great, I assure you!). Can you come to ours for dinner on Saturday? We can't I'm afraid, but thanks for the invite. Simple. Honestly, you think it's going to be so much worse than it really is! Remember your negativity bias – people will accept and move on. Some might question at first (especially if you've always been a yes person), but once you start being clearer on those boundaries, you'll be amazed how those requests will reduce. Of course, though, always be respectful. I know you know this, but no-one likes an 'f-you' response. You can be courteous in a way that people will accept what you say, rather than feel rejected.

A great way of doing that is by offering alternatives. This is so important, particularly if you've been pleasing for so long. You'll still itch that 'being helpful' piece, but you're redirecting to better options. Please note, you also don't always have to offer a reason! 'No thank you' is perfectly acceptable too.

There are four key techniques you can use to say No[2]:

1. The Broken Record Technique – repeating what you said and staying firm whilst not getting drawn into more discussion by remaining brief: "no thanks, I'm not interested."

2. Empathetic Technique – acknowledging them and their need, but still saying no: "That sounds like it's really important to you, but I'm afraid I can't help."

3. Sandwich Technique – using the positive, negative, positive response: "I would have loved to if I had time, but sorry I'm at capacity. Perhaps X would be a better option?"

4. Delay Technique – delaying it for now and it may well just go away! "I'm sorry I can't now. Perhaps we can revisit in a few months?"

Here are some other phrases you can use to say no:

Personal

- "Thanks so much for the invitation. I'm sorry we can't make it."
- "That's kind of you to think of me but I'm flat out at the moment so can't take on any more."
- "I appreciate the offer, but I'm focusing on X for the next X period."
- "I can't but do have a wonderful time."
- "I'm not going to do that for you, but I know you have the capability to do it yourself."

Work

- "My workload is full at the moment, but perhaps X team could take a look at it."
- "The current priorities I'm working on are XYZ. How does this request fit in with them, as we will need to amend our delivery dates?"
- "I can take this on, but it means X will be delayed. Is that okay with you?"
- "That isn't my role, so you may need to go and check for the right person to do it."
- "My current workload isn't going to allow for this to give it the attention it deserves."
- "No, I'm afraid this isn't possible for us. Perhaps you could consider X instead?"

CONFIDENT

4 TECHNIQUES TO SAY NO[2]

The Broken Record Technique
Repeating what you said, staying firm and don't get drawn into more discussion by remaining brief.

> No thanks, I'm not interested.

Empathetic Technique
Acknowledging them and their need, but still saying no.

> That sounds like it's really important to you, but I'm afraid I can't help.

Sandwich Technique
Use the positive, negative, positive response.

> I would have loved to if I had time, but sorry I'm at capacity - perhaps X would be a better option?

Delay Technique
Delay for now and it may well just go away!

> I'm sorry I can't now. Perhaps we can revisit in a few months?

PHRASES TO SAY NO

WORK

My workload is maxed at the moment, but perhaps X team could take a look at it.

The current priorities I'm working on are XYZ, how does this fit in with those as we will need to amend our delivery dates.

I can take this on, but it means X will be delayed - is that Ok with you?

That isn't my role so you may need to go and check for the right person to do it.

My current workload isn't going to allow for this to give it the attention it deserves

No, I'm afraid this isn't possible for us. Perhaps you could consider X instead?

PERSONAL

Thanks so much for the invitation, I'm sorry we can't make it.

That's kind of you to think of me but I'm flat out at the moment so can't take on any more.

I appreciate the offer, but I'm focusing on X for the next X period.

I can't, but have a wonderful time.

I'm not going to do that for you, but I know you have the capability to do it yourself.

If they do keep asking, stay firm. You can always acknowledge what they say, "I hear what you're saying, but I'm afraid the answer is still no."

Remember, you own your space. The more you exercise the confident 'no' muscle, the more people will respect you and start to learn about what your boundaries are. You'll be happier and more confident as you won't feel walked all over, and most likely you will have more time – for you and those who you love the most. Win-win!

ENERGY AUDIT

Part of your success is influenced by your mental and physical energy levels. Research indicates that sleep-deprived individuals tend to interpret information more negatively. There was a really interesting study done by the sleep researcher Matthew Walker, where they found that the emotional centres of the brain (the amygdala) of people who had been sleep deprived were *60% more sensitive* than those who had a normal night's sleep[3]. They were also much more impulsive – that feeling of 'being really snappy' when you're tired. What was happening? **We know that the amygdala, your brain's smoke alarm, is more sensitive when you're tired – and this makes your negativity bias more extreme.** So those who were yawning away with limited kip found that their perception was much more sensitive.

We all say 'oh, she's just tired' or 'he needs a good nap' as kids start getting grumpy in the afternoon. Same goes for us adults too. Energy levels matter in how we see the world, how we are showing up and are able to take on challenges with confidence. *If you're exhausted, you will see bigger hills to climb, less support, more difficult people and you're less likely to take on a big new challenge.*

So, first up on your confidence energy audit is check in on your sleep. It's a priority so please make sure you do! Next up, check in on your drains and radiators.

We all have those areas of our lives that make our soul sing (radiators) or fill us with dread (drains). Identifying our energy sources and starting to create boundaries around them is crucial because it allows you to *start respecting yourself*. That new-found respect will bring you confidence, but from a place of authenticity, grounded in who you really are. Setting these boundaries can also lead to stress reduction, better mental health, and improved communication, resulting in reduced anxiety and frustration. You'll be ready to take on the world with a calmer confidence, whatever it brings.

CONFIDENCE GYM: ENERGY AUDIT

Take five minutes to identify the people or activities in your life that either energise you (radiators) or drain your energy (drains). It might help to reflect on how certain people or situations in your life may compromise your core values (often aligned with the drains).

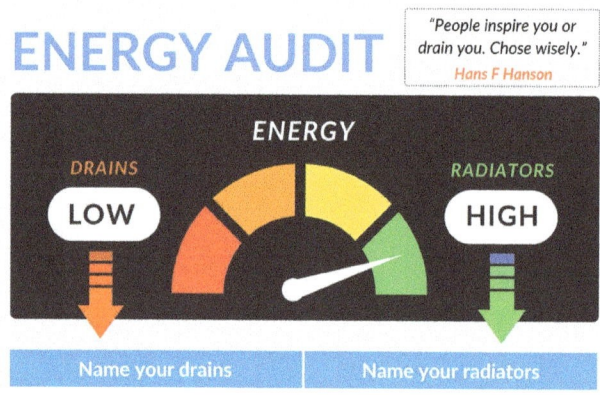

"People inspire you or drain you. Chose wisely."
Hans F Hanson

| Name your drains | Name your radiators |

| What do you need to say no to? | What do you need to say yes to? |

Did you find it easier to identify the drains or radiators? Were there any surprises in your list? What impact do these drains have on your life, or conversely, what positive impact do the radiators provide? What changes do you feel are necessary for you to manage these drains or enhance the presence of radiators in your life?

"Stop asking why they keep doing it and start asking why you keep allowing it."

Chase Hill

CONFIDENCE TOOLKIT: 10 TIPS FOR CONFIDENT BOUNDARIES

1. **Assess your personal boundaries** – these are your values and life priorities. They are crucial to understand at the start.
2. **Communicate effectively up front** – you need to tell people what your values are, what is actually a real emergency to you (not 'I couldn't find the jam'). With your teams, give them clear expectations of what you want and empower them to find the answers. Provide clarity, be respectful and be clear on what you would want/not want/don't like.
3. **Set Limits** – This refers to the times you work, check emails, and your hours. How you prioritise your workload is significant, so make sure you understand what's most important with your boss, so you are both aligned.
4. **Learn to Say, 'No'** – (see Boundary Builders earlier)
5. **Practise Confrontation** – How might they object and what can you do to prepare for that?
6. **Re-energise** – Take time off; no one is going to die if you take 15 minutes for yourself (but you might go mad if you don't).
7. **Create clear structures** – Use techniques like 'time blocking' and creating clear roles and responsibilities so everyone knows who does what.
8. **Delegate when appropriate** – Always ask 'who can I delegate this to?' first, rather than doing it yourself.
9. **Remember to focus on your champagne moments** – 80% of the time 'fine' is good enough.

10. **Use technology to help you** – Make media rules (how and when to use social media), do a digital detox, encourage face-to-face or walking meetings; limit your notifications, manage usage time on your phone, mute and block groups if you need to, use Do Not Disturb on your phone.

Pick one of these now and implement it today. It will be a great start in building confident boundaries for you in your life.

"A boundary is not the point at which something stops, but the point from which something begins."

Martin Heidegger

Final Word

Setting boundaries isn't selfish; it's smart. You've now got the tools to protect your energy and time like the precious resources they are. Next, in our C.O.N.F.I.D.E.N.T. framework, we'll explore how to navigate the tricky world of feedback and failure (N) without losing your cool.

CONFIDENT

CHEATSHEET

KEY CONFIDENCE INSIGHTS

1. **Boundaries are not Barriers**. They are essential frameworks that help you to define acceptable and unacceptable behaviours in your life. When established, they create space for you to thrive, prevent burnout, and help you build healthier relationships and a stronger sense of self. Learning to set boundaries confidently is a profound act of self-care and empowerment. Remember, saying 'no' is not a sign of weakness but a demonstration of courage, discernment, and smart resource management.

2. **Identify Your Boundary Gaps.** Reflect on the eight types of boundaries (Mental, Emotional, Material, Internal, Conversational, Physical, Time, and Digital). Determine where you feel most compromised or where your boundaries are being tested. This awareness is your first step towards asserting yourself more confidently.

3. **Practise Saying No with Confidence.** Start small, be direct, and keep it simple. Use techniques like the Broken Record Technique, Empathetic Technique, Sandwich Technique, or Delay Technique. Remember, 'No' is a complete sentence. Offering alternatives or reasons is optional!

4. **Conduct an Energy Audit.** Evaluate what drains you versus what energises you (radiators and drains). Identify people, tasks, or situations that sap your energy and consider ways to reduce or manage their impact. Focus on increasing the presence of energising activities and people in your life. Use the tools and strategies to reinforce boundaries and regularly reassess them and adjust as necessary to maintain your wellbeing.

5. **Adopt a Mindset of Courage and Self-Respect.** Setting boundaries takes courage. Be prepared to confront resistance, but trust that as you consistently maintain your boundaries, others will learn to respect them, and you will gain confidence in your ability to protect your own well-being.

TIME FOR ACTION

10 Tips to Create Confident Boundaries:

1. Assess your personal boundaries and align them with your values.

2. Communicate expectations clearly and effectively.

3. Set limits on your time and workload.

4. Learn to say no.

5. Practice confrontation to prepare for objections.

6. Re-energise regularly with breaks and self-care.

7. Create clear structures and responsibilities.

8. Delegate tasks when appropriate.

9. Focus on high-impact activities and avoid perfectionism.

10. Use technology wisely to manage your time and mental space.

CONFIDENCE MASTERCLASS
OLI SPENSLEY-CORFIELD – NAVIGATING THROUGH CHALLENGES

"It's not how good your good sailing is; it's how good your bad sailing is."

Oli Spensley-Corfield is a former elite sailor turned sports psychologist and performance coach. A specialist in mental resilience, he draws on his experience in competitive sailing to help athletes and business leaders build confidence and focus. Through his consultancy, Think to Win, Oli provides strategies to enhance performance and achieve peak results.

Oli's path was marked by several pivotal turning points that shaped his career and his perspective on confidence. Early on, he was drawn to both medicine and competitive sailing, but he eventually faced a choice. "I had to make a bit of a choice," he explained to me, recalling advice from a teacher who reminded him, he could always return to education, while the opportunity to represent his country in sailing was rare. This advice led him to sports and exercise science, where he merged his passion for sailing with a newfound interest in sports psychology, deepened by his own Olympic campaigns and coaching journeys.

Oli emphasised that high performance in any field relies heavily on mental resilience and the ability to "control what you can and let go of the rest." He explained, "You can't control whether you win or lose… but you can control your process." This focus on the controllable is central to his confidence philosophy, and he has applied it to both his athletic and business coaching roles. He found that "a high-performing person in the business world is so similar to the high-performing person in sport."

According to Oli, confidence rests on five key areas: **performance, context, experience, super skills, and reflection**. Confidence, he explained, isn't a blanket feeling but "your belief in your ability to achieve that certain skill or task." He broke down these five pillars to illustrate how confidence can be developed in a practical, focused way:

Performance: Consistent, steady performance – even on difficult days – is crucial. Oli's father had advised him, "It's not how good your good sailing is; it's how good your bad sailing is." This focus on steady performance underpins lasting confidence, proving that even on challenging days, you can achieve a reliable outcome.

Context: He underscored that confidence is often situational and depends on preparedness and awareness of the environment. He explained how an athlete might feel highly confident on the field but less so in a new setting. Recognising and preparing for different contexts helps tailor confidence to specific demands.

Experience: Reflecting on past successes is vital. "Use the negative experiences to learn from, but reflect on the positive," Oli said. Building a foundation of positive experiences over time can reinforce confidence, even in high-pressure situations.

Super Skills: Oli encourages identifying and leaning into "super skills" – those areas of natural strength or passion. For him, excelling in Q&A sessions is a super skill that anchors his confidence. Recognising these strengths provides a dependable confidence boost when needed.

Reflection: Finally, Oli highlighted the value of regular reflection and self-assessment. He suggested tracking progress through tools like 'performance profiling': scoring oneself on specific skills each month. "Seeing progress is something that really allows you to develop your confidence," he said, adding that tangible self-improvement offers a clear path for growth.

To maintain mental stamina, especially in extended competitions, Oli also emphasised the importance of "zoning in and out." In sailing, for example, athletes must keep their minds ready for action even amid long waiting periods. This adaptable readiness is crucial to staying mentally resilient.

Oli's perspective on confidence applies to both introverts and extroverts, with a focus on self-awareness and adaptability. Introverts, he noted, often bring depth and thoughtfulness, while extroverts may thrive in social engagement. "We're not fixed," he said. "We can move to different spaces" to meet situational demands - and that's something important for us to embrace.

Setting boundaries is also vital, as Oli explained. He noted that it's essential to understand personal needs without guilt, reminding us that "people want you to do well...but they don't care about you that much." This perspective is a practical reminder to prioritise self-care and recognise that our lives are our own to shape.

Oli's journey reflects a clear-headed approach to high performance and personal growth. Confidence, he reminds us, isn't a fixed state but can be nurtured intentionally through these five pillars, providing a roadmap for anyone seeking to build lasting self-belief in both personal and professional pursuits.

Oli's Top Tips for Confidence

1. **Control What You Can:** Focus on aspects you can control or influence rather than fixating on outcomes.
2. **Track Your Growth:** Regular self-assessment lets you see progress and builds a solid foundation.
3. **Lean into Your Strengths:** Identify your "super skills" and use them as anchors for confidence.
4. **Stay Present:** Ground yourself in the moment to counteract anxiety and stay focused.
5. **Reflect on Wins and Lessons:** Learn from setbacks and remember past successes to reinforce self-belief.

Want more? Oli offers world class psychology, mental coaching, event preparation and mentoring. You can find out more on his website: www.think2win.co.uk

CHAPTER EIGHT

> " Failure is success in progress. "
>
> Einstein

TRIBES AND TRIBULATIONS

Most people remember that terrible feeling when the teacher says, "OK. Let's pick teams" and the brutal selection process begins. The dread ensues as one by one people are picked before you, smiling to their gaggle of teammates... 'Oh goodness, no. Please don't let me be last!'

The fear of exclusion does not disappear as we grow up. I even had it at a wedding aged thirty-five when the bride and bridegroom decided to pick teams for a treasure hunt. The same thing happened as people were called up before me. Clearly the happy couple had never been picked last. Even at that age the process was horrific!

This brings us to our next important Evolutionary Fact:

EVOLUTIONARY FACT #4

Our brain wants to be part of a *TRIBE*

Evolutionary Fact 4: Our brain wants to be part of a tribe

Fear of exclusion can be hugely triggering and has even been shown to be actually *physically* painful[1]. **Whether caused by social rejection or physical pain, brain scans showed the same areas associated with distress were activated**. So, when you feel the threat of being excluded, whether it be from a sports team, work team or through a performance review, it can actually be a painful experience for your brain.

Conversely, social support, which is known to reduce social pain, can also reduce physical pain. Research shows that pain killers normally used to reduce physical pain can also reduce social pain[2] (yes, really. It's not that we are condoning it. It's just really interesting how the brain works, isn't it…?)

Why is this?

We are built and motivated chemically for connection. Oxytocin is a neurotransmitter released in the brain that is generated during social bonding, reproduction, childbirth and ongoing child rearing. This is what wires us for connection, whether with a parent, as a parent, partner, loved one or even colleague. Oxytocin gained the nickname as the 'trust', 'cuddle' or 'love' hormone. American Neuroscientist Paul J. Zak showed that high levels of oxytocin cause people to actually work harder to help their team achieve its goals[3].

Why is this so important? Because social connection is a crucial part of existence and the ability to stay safe. Human offspring are not born able to fend for themselves, like reptiles, who just lay an egg which the offspring emerges from, ready to go. We need care and support for many years before we are able to cope in the world. Likewise, when homo sapiens first roamed the Earth, we needed our tribe to protect us from the perils of the times, whether it be the woolly mammoth, sabre-toothed tiger or hazardous environment. So, **acceptance into a group is crucial for our brains to feel safe. Being part of a tribe is, to our brain, a matter of life and death.**

The Confidence Connection

So, we are wired for social interaction – how does this relate to confidence?

When we have a strong network of support, this paves the way for us to act with confidence and take risks. If there is a perceived threat of exclusion from our tribe, our confidence can be shattered, and our stress levels go sky-high. Existence of core human values (integrity, honesty, kindness) builds a social safety net that leads to better sleep, less stress and better health[4]. In fact, research from Waldinger et al[5] shows that the level of social connection you have is the best predictor of well-being and longevity. Yes, the social connections you have are a key determinant of how long you will live.

Lonely people die sooner, which is a kick up the butt for anyone to connect more with their elderly neighbour! But, and this is important, it's not the *number* of connections, it's the *quality* of connections. Popular people don't live longer, just the people who have really deep social networks.

There's also most likely a connection between the oxytocin we gain from these social interactions, the level optimism we feel about our lives and hence our confidence levels. Remember the confidence definition from Brendon Burchard – belief in my ability to figure things out? Optimistic people are more likely to have this belief and so will 'have a go'. They will assume a good outcome is possible, as their level of self-efficacy (the belief in their ability to succeed) is greater. Although there is no research directly connecting the two, research in Frontiers in Psychology (2017)[6] highlighted that oxytocin is associated with increased emotional resilience, which is closely tied to optimism and confidence.

It makes sense that if we are able to create an environment where we nurture and increase our oxytocin levels, it could well be a key contributor towards how confident we feel overall. All the positive habits and practises that you have been learning in this book can also be levers for this, so there's even more reasons to keep them up!

So, let's look at this from two perspectives – getting feedback and giving feedback.

GETTING FEEDBACK

What happens when you are headed towards your annual performance review? Your manager talks at length about the many areas where you've exceeded expectations. They highlight how you've grown and challenged, dealing with tough clients and stakeholders. You feel good, but are listening with trepidation, waiting for the dreaded 'development area'.

Then here it comes. It's just one small thing: 'try and speak up more in meetings' or, that mistake you made 6 months ago, which was explained well at the time.

As they go through the example, the red mist ensues, as you feel yourself getting angry, upset and maybe holding back hot tears. You can't think straight as they rush through the point, themselves stumbling over their words as they see your reaction. What do you then think about for the next two weeks? There's little reference to the fifty-five minutes of praise. Instead, you are only turning the development area (bah!) around like a Rubik's cube in your mind. How could they? Why me? It's so unfair! I'm rubbish at my job. I should resign now before they sack me. I wish I had thought to say X when they had brought it up!

Let's look at this situation through the lens of all the Evolutionary Facts we have learned:

Evolutionary Fact 1: Our brain prioritises energy for a survival response.

Evolutionary Fact 2: Our brain is wired to notice danger (negativity) more than positivity.

Evolutionary Fact 3: Our brain sees lack of control as danger.

Evolutionary Fact 4: Our brain wants to be part of a tribe.

Which of these four facts do you think is triggered if you are the person called into the performance review, *getting* the feedback?

The answer is ALL OF THEM. No wonder we find it difficult!

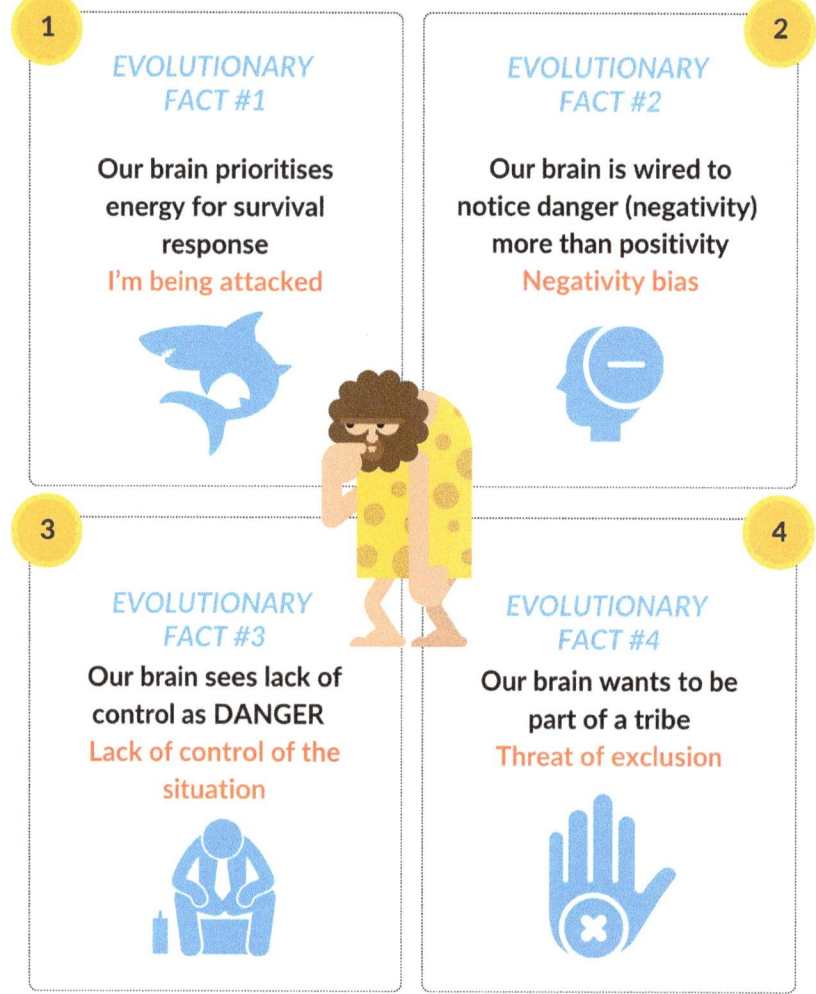

GIVING FEEDBACK

Anyone who has been a manager will have had one of those trickier employees. The ones that get really defensive, aggressive even, when you raise an issue. It makes you really *dread* the discussion, thinking about how they are going to respond. As you walk in, you have a knot in your stomach; your hands get a bit clammy and your heart's racing. Then you start talking quickly and a bit squeaky, as you approach the thorny part of the chat. There's that mutual knowing that this isn't going to be pleasant. This is key to understand in this situation:

Even if the feedback or criticism is about only one person in the interaction, the threat response can be triggered in both parties.

Let's look at which of our Evolutionary Facts would be triggered in the person *giving* the feedback. Most likely it's 1,2 and 3, but in a different order and perhaps even circular!

- Evolutionary Fact 2: Your brain is anticipating danger (negativity) more than positivity (negativity bias). You know this isn't going to be pleasant, so you're prepping for that. That may then lead to more of…
- Evolutionary Fact 1: You have a survival response in anticipation of their reaction. If they are actually being very defensive, this gets worse as you feel like you're being attacked. The energy in your brain moves to the survival mechanism, not executive functioning in your pre-frontal cortex. You then can't think clearly, get your point across, nor have good clarity in your responses. You then feel like…
- Evolutionary Fact 3: you have lost control of what's happening, and the brain sees a lack of control as DANGER.

What's the outcome of all this activity? ***Most people shy away from any possible confrontation, including giving feedback.***

We don't like that feeling of discomfort; knowing or even just *imagining* that the threat response may occur.

There is a real danger that this can impact your performance overall, as happened to Sarah. She was a top performer, and she always had been throughout her career. She had always worked really hard to make things successful, at the cost of much of her personal life, but there was no doubt she had a great reputation. She was used to running her team across the region, no problem at all, remaining independent, decisive and a great leader. Then a new manager arrived; a lady who had been in the company for a long time, so she knew her way around. They had a weekly team meeting and Sarah set up a one-to-one with her manager every two weeks, which was ample communication for her to be able to run the team.

They had their ups and downs; it was a tough business and volumes had gone through the roof, so the team had struggled. But Sarah navigated her way through it with a positive attitude and regular deep breaths.

Then it came to her year-end review.

She could sense something was wrong by the pitch of her manager's voice. She was trying to be light and breezy, however Sarah knew something was coming.

"So, if we talk about the development areas, there was something in particular that I wanted to raise with you," said her boss. "I feel like your communication could've really been improved."

"What do you mean?" Sarah asked.

"Well, we could have had meetings every week rather than every other week. That would've been much better, connecting us up more effectively."

It turned out this was the only example she could give of really where things hadn't gone to plan communication-wise. And guess what? She was marked as an 'average' having been 'exceptional' her whole career.

The key lesson here is that Sarah's manager did not like conflict. What she should've done, is given Sarah this feedback right at the start, but instead she was steaming away all year, not bringing it up until she was *forced* to give year-end feedback.

What's the lesson? **It is very important that you take control of these situations and compensate for others where they lack confidence in conflict.** This really can impact you, your career, your personal life and your overall happiness.

With so much fear in the system now around bullying, sexual harassment, inequality and more, this danger of not getting the feedback you need is heightened. Whether its gender, ethnicity, LGBTIQA+, neurodiversity, religion, age or disability, if the manager feels nervous about saying the 'wrong thing', it's likely they will avoid it.

In contrast, if a manager feels it's easier to communicate with someone (probably people who are like them), it is *those* people who will get the feedback they need and be able to course-correct. They will hear the messages, get the advice, so the inequality that exists will perpetuate.

Knowledge is power

If knowledge is power, **it's time to take control,** so you get the knowledge you need to improve. You need to identify your blind spots (yes, we all have them, even you) and learn what we need to work on to improve personally/professionally. From there our competence and confidence can grow.

Some statements I hear a lot:

- **"I shouldn't have to say anything, my manager will see what I deliver. Hard work gets rewarded."** Sorry, but you need to assume the opposite. Your manager isn't going to do this for you. They are managing multiple people, teams, stakeholders and a whole lot you don't even know.
- **"I don't get feedback from my manager."** Well then, ask for it! Take control, set your expectations and ask for the feedback you deserve (more to follow on how).
- **"I'm really bad at asking about promotions, pay rises and performance."** Yes, many people are, but confidence in this is a muscle. You just need the right language and then you will nail these discussions going forward.

So, here are three tips for how you can gain the confidence you need to ask for feedback:

1. Invite It

Feedback and criticism are better received when they are invited. By asking for feedback, you take control of the situation, rather than it being imposed on you. You don't need to be needy, just logical and practical.

There is also **less of a stress response** on both sides when you ask for it; the invitation means it's not a surprise. How should you ask for it? State early with your manager that "I'm really open to feedback as it helps me learn." You'll create safety around the subject, which means it will be more likely to be shared, allowing you to course-correct as needed.

Regularity also breads familiarity, so try to make it a habit – you will both feel comfortable that it can happen without a negative outcome (we tend to fear the worst). "What went well in that meeting and what can I improve?"

If you are a leader, make this part of all the interactions you have, so your staff get super comfortable with the feedback. They will appreciate the fact that you're trying to help them, rather than dropping a bomb on them in an annual review.

2. Don't React, Respond

Reactions (getting aggressive, angry or upset) is partly a function of your stress levels, how much sleep you have had and so how sensitive your amygdala is at the time. If, on the whole, you tend to react strongly to feedback, give yourself some space or time to breathe before responding. You have a couple of options. When you are given feedback, ask questions – don't interrogate the other person, but be curious about the feedback. Your pre-frontal cortex will be re-engaged and you're more likely to calm down. Responding thoughtfully like that can diffuse tension and lead to a more productive conversation.

You could also ask for a quick 'time out' (rather than losing your mind, telling your boss they are an idiot and storming out). This could be just a simple bathroom trip or a 24-hour break so you can gather your thoughts meaningfully.

3. Don't Ruminate

Ruminating over criticism or feedback doesn't solve anything – your negativity bias and critic are likely to spin out of control! Instead, focus on taking constructive action to address any concerns or areas for improvement. Perhaps chat with a friend, partner or colleague to diffuse the fire. What is the gift in the feedback you have been given?

CRITICISM AND FEEDBACK 🔥 HOT TIPS!

Knowledge is Power   **Elimination of Blind Spots**

REMEMBER
- ✓ Invite it
- ✓ Don't react, respond
- ✓ Don't ruminate

Invite it — Feedback is much better both **given** and **received** when you have **asked** for it (a 50% lower stress response!). You don't need to be needy, just logical and practical.

Why? — There is less of a stress response on both sides: we have asked for it so you're in **control**.
Regularity also breads familiarity - you will both feel safe it can happen without the negative outcome we expect.

How? — State early "**I'm really open to feedback** as it helps me learn". You'll create **safety** around the subject, which means it will be more likely to come up, allowing you to course-correct as needed.

Practice — These discussions are tough for most people. Don't be afraid to **practise** with a friend or trusted colleague - it will get much easier the more you do it!

Separate — It helps talking about **the 'role'** rather than MY role. For example, "a role of this type in the market demands XYZ salary". By separating the role from your **identity**, you aren't judging yourself and defining yourself by the job - that makes it much less emotional!

 *PepTalkHer is a great organisation who help women negotiate pay rises - look them up if you want more help from the experts!*

 ## CONFIDENCE GYM: FEEDBACK REVIEW

Take a couple of minutes to note down:
- An area of your work where you should ask for feedback.
- An action you can take based on this feedback.

CONFIDENCE TOOLKIT: CRITICAL QUESTIONS

IMPORTANT

CAREER QUESTIONS

Want to take control of your career?

These are questions you need to be discussing with your manager. Use these questions as a guide to build your confidence in having the best possible, targeted, quality discussions. They are especially important with a new manager so you can figure out how they work and how you will best work together.

PERFORMANCE

What can I do more/less off?

What's working? What needs to be improved?

How are the communications working for you? Do you need more/less /different channels (email / verbal)

What are the 3 things that you see as the most important from this team/me?

These are really important if you have a new manager

- *You never know how they like to communicate and if what you are doing is working for them!*
- *Are you aligned on priorities?*

Make them happy by checking :)

CONFIDENT

Please let me know if there's anything I can shift to improve

If you were in my position what would you change?

This is a great one if they struggle to give feedback! Everyone finds it easier to talk about themselves rather than have perceived conflict

I'd appreciate having 10 mins each month on what went well / could go better

What can I do to support you more?

What specifically worked / didn't work?

If they say you need to improve, get specifics, then you can take real action to change it (and measure when you have improved). Ask for an example if needs be.

I'd love to hear your thoughts on how things are going? How can I develop?

Where do you see me in 1/2/5 years?

I'm keen to discuss my career direction and promotion. Where do you see me now and what are any gaps I need to fill to reach the next level.

If you struggle with talking about Promotion, this is a wonderful way to approach it. Nice and neutral, acknowledging you may have some gaps. Try and get a timeline from them - 1 year, 2 years? Get alignment on that and don't let them skulk out of it!

What was your pathway to promotion? How did you get to where you are now and what would you do differently?

What does success look like in my role?

Everyone loves talking about themselves! With these two, you're connecting with them and respecting their journey to where they are. Write some notes as there will be gems in here!

What advice do you have for me?

PAY RISES

Getting a pay rise isn't easy. It's important you know the process in your organisation and how you can be proactive to manage it. You have to earn a pay rise with great performance, then just make sure you do your homework of the facts around your market value. Here's some langauge you could use to frame the discussion:

Please can we look at my roles & responsibilities and performance, with a view to potentially reviewing my salary?

Have a view of your $$ number
Wish > Dream Number
Want > You'll be happy with
Walk > I'm out the door!

Make sure you can articulate all the great things you have done - keep track of them and the impact they have made - use metrics wherever you can.

With my achievements over the past 12 months and given the value I've brought to the organisation recently, I'd appreciate it if you would consider a review of my current salary.

I've also reviewed my current compensation levels for roles similar to mine in comparable companies and believe I have a clear view of the industry standard salary.

Do your homework - it's very important you understand your value in the market. Ask recruitment agents, look at The Glass Door or other benchmarking sites.

For pay rise discussions, we love the advice of PepTalkHer[7] – a great organisation and community helping close the pay gap and supporting professionals to negotiate pay rises. Look them up if you want more help from the experts! This is their advice:

- Research your worth (online & talk directly to folks)
- Wish = Dream Compensation Number
- Want = A figure you think is fair & reasonable
- Walk = NOPE. I'm worth more. I'm out the door!

Plus:

- Make sure you can articulate all the great things you have done. Keep track of them and the impact they have made. Use metrics wherever you can (and check out the free PepTalkHer app on the app stores that helps automate this).
- Do your homework. It's very important you understand your value in the market.
- Ask recruitment agents, talk to people (men and women) and check out job ads in jurisdictions where listed compensation is mandatory.
- It helps talking about 'THE role' rather than MY role. For example, 'a role of this type in the market demands XYZ pay.' By separating the role from your identity, you aren't judging yourself and defining yourself by the job. That makes it much less emotional!

CEO Meggie Palmer says:

"You should be asking for a pay increase every year. Sadly, the squeaky wheel gets the oil. Learning to self-advocate in a way that feels authentic to you and your personality is the best investment you can make in yourself, and your bank balance! Our community of 60,000 women has had HUGE success following the PepTalkHer framework. From $5k to $50k pay increases in one negotiation, it's unreal what is possible for folks who thought there was zero salary wriggle room. But these results don't happen by simply saying, 'Please may I have a pay raise.' There's strategy and serious preparation behind it. You can't expect your boss to know and remember every excellent achievement you've had in a year. It's your responsibility to consistently document your success and reflect that back so leadership is aware of your value. If you don't do your own PR, who will?'

REMEMBER when you are feeling nervous about asking for feedback:

- Confidence comes from stepping out of your comfort zone and doing hard things.
- Evolutionary Fact 2: Your natural negativity bias. It's probably going to be MUCH easier than you thought it would be.
- These discussions are tough for most people. Don't be afraid to **practise** with a friend or trusted colleague. It will get much easier the more you do it.

FAIL FORWARD: BUILDING CONFIDENCE THROUGH SETBACKS

Fear of failure can hinder our progress significantly, but it's essential to remember our negativity bias. It is often much less likely to happen than we believe. This bias can lead us to overestimate the likelihood and consequences of failure. So many of the clients I work with try a micro confidence challenge and then say, "It wasn't nearly as bad as I thought it would be!" It's important that we acknowledge this natural tendency and remind ourselves to focus on the facts rather than fear. Remember that when you are feeling nervous about taking a step forward.

Perception of your failures is driven by how much we believe we can grow, hence so is your confidence. Having a 'growth mindset' is crucial when we consider our perception of our abilities – whether they are fixed or can grow and develop. We can choose to redefine how we perceive it:

- No or just not yet.
- Not getting the job or celebrating we had the courage to try.
- Not getting that date and feeling rejected, or being proud of ourselves for stepping outside our comfort zone.

What is crazy is that we forget failure is part of the process. As Einstein said, "Failure is success in progress." Making mistakes is entirely natural and actually means we will come up with a better tested solution. It's even beneficial as our brain *learns more effectively when it makes mistakes first.* **Neuroplasticity, the brain's ability to reorganise itself by forming new neural connections, occurs when you encounter challenges and learn from them.**

It's funny how as adults we try so desperately to avoid failure, and yet as children we are doing it all the time. Think of a child learning to walk. How many hundreds of times do they fall over? But we don't say, "Don't bother" or "Give up". We say, "Keep going. Nearly there!" Why don't we give ourselves the same grace when we try new things?

If we go back to your life/career timeline, reflect on how much you learned from the failures you have had through the years. How much you have grown, personally and professionally. How much resilience have you gained? Part of the problem is we aren't integrating and celebrating the struggles. If you can make that part of your process, you will always be building on that strong foundation.

So, it's important to analyse failure objectively. When something goes wrong, we need to ask ourselves why it happened. Was it within our control? What could have produced a better outcome? After gathering the facts, step back and reflect on what you learned from the experience. How can you apply this newfound insight going forward? Consider keeping a 'Failure Journal' to track what you've learned and how you're applying those lessons in the future.

Remember, failure is not a setback but an opportunity for growth and improvement.

Every successful person has faced failure at some point. It's not the failure itself that defines them, but how they rose again after falling. Let failure fuel your determination and confidence and drive you to achieve your potential.

CONFIDENCE TOOLKIT: BRAIN RESET

When facing failure, tough feedback or criticism, here's how to manage yourself and reset your thoughts:

BRAIN RESET TOOL

Whether you haven't achieved something you hoped, or have been given some tough feedback or criticism, it's important to have the mechanism to reset. Once you have taken a breath and acknowledged your emotional response, work through these steps:

Breathe and Acknowledge to move you from from survival mode to using your prefrontal cortex

> "Let others know you are thinking out loud and in a "first draft" when you are unclear about a concept and trying to work through it. Don't wait to engage until you have it "all figured out." If you do that, you will never jump in".
>
> *Schiff*

1. It's not personal — There's a difference between what you have **done** and your **identity**. Focus on the former and manage your inner critic - is the feedback triggering a value?

2. Don't Ruminate — **Rumination won't change things**, so use the STOP sign to shift your thought pattern. Write it down so it's out of your mind, and then move on

3. Consider different perspectives & context — **Perception is everything** for you and those around you. What's their **context**? Have they had a terrible day? Do they understand your context too?

4. Be curious: What can you learn? — Ask Questions. Analyse the facts. What went wrong what can you change? What have you learned and how can you adapt?

5. Adapt and Action — **Try a few options, take calculated risks**, see which one works and course correct if you need to. Be a **speedboat**, nimble and responsive!

6. Ditch the Approval — Don't give too much power to others' opinions! If their intention isn't to help, then just move on.

Final Word

There are plenty of successful individuals who faced rejection before achieving success:

- Oprah Winfrey was fired from her job as a television reporter because she was 'unfit for TV'.
- Twelve publishers rejected J.K. Rowling's manuscript for *Harry Potter and the Philosopher's Stone.*
- Walt Disney was fired from a newspaper job early in his career because his editor felt he 'lacked imagination and had no good ideas'.
- Michael Jordan, often considered the greatest basketball player of all time, was cut from his high school varsity basketball team as a sophomore.

The fact is that feedback and failure can be tough, but you've now learned how to turn them into stepping stones rather than stumbling blocks. Now that you've got that mastered, let's face the biggest challenge of all: change. We're heading to **T** to learn how to 'Triumph Through Change'.

CHEATSHEET

KEY CONFIDENCE INSIGHTS

1. **Evolutionary Fact 4: Our brain wants to be part of a tribe:** The fear of exclusion is real: that dread you feel about being left out is not just in your head – your brain is hardwired to see social rejection as a threat to survival. It's no wonder feedback or criticism can feel so intense.

2. **Social Bonds are Everything:** Your social connections aren't just a nice-to-have; they're a must-have for reducing stress and living longer. But remember, it's the depth of those connections that counts, not the number.

3. **Psychological Safety Equals Confidence:** When you feel safe to be your true self within a group, your confidence soars. This is why creating and maintaining these safe spaces is critical both for individuals and teams.

4. **Feedback is Tough, but Essential:** Receiving feedback triggers all our evolutionary survival mechanisms, which is why it can feel so challenging. But feedback is the key to growth.

5. **Knowledge is Power:** Understanding what you need to improve and preparing how to approach tough discussions gives you back control. It's how you reduce stress, build confidence, and drive your success forward.

TIME FOR ACTION

1. **Proactively Invite Feedback:** Don't wait for feedback to come to you – ask for it. By doing this, you create a safe space for constructive criticism, and it becomes a tool for growth rather than a threat.

2. **Respond, Don't React:** When feedback lands, take a breath. Instead of reacting emotionally, get curious: ask questions, seek clarity, and use the feedback to your advantage.

3. **Don't Get Stuck in Negativity:** It's easy to let negative feedback spin out of control in your mind. Instead, focus on what you can learn and how you can act on it. Talk it through with someone you trust to gain perspective.

4. **Nurture Quality Connections:** Invest in deep, meaningful relationships, both at work and in life. These connections are your safety net, reducing stress and enhancing your overall well-being.

5. **Prepare for the Tough Conversations:** Use the tools and questions provided to guide discussions around things like performance, promotions, and pay raises. The more you practice, the more natural (and powerful) these conversations will become.

Remember, your brain is powerful, and by understanding its wiring, you can harness that power to boost your confidence, handle feedback like a pro, and strengthen the connections that matter most. It's all about stepping into the unknown, shining a light on areas for improvement, and growing stronger every time you do.

CONFIDENCE MASTERCLASS
ROB CAINE – THE FIGHTER PILOT

"If you don't know something, admit it. That's real confidence."

I had the privilege of interviewing Air Commodore Rob Caine, the Head of UK Military Flying Training – a profession where confidence couldn't be more important! Rob is responsible for overseeing the training across the Army Air Corps, Royal Navy, and Royal Air Force, a role that involves preparing pilots for fast jets, rotary-wing aircraft, multi-engine aircraft, and air traffic controllers. As he put it, "Confidence is at the heart of everything I do."

Rob's passion for becoming a fighter pilot began early. "I knew I wanted to be a fighter pilot when I was just eleven," he shared. That dream drove him to work hard, seize every opportunity, and eventually join the Royal Air Force. With over 30 years as a fast jet aviator, Rob has been tested countless times, often under intense scrutiny. Through these experiences, he's come to understand that:

"Confidence is not about being fearless or flawless; it's about the ability to keep making decisions without ending up in paralysis."

Rob emphasised that his confidence has been shaped by both successes and failures. He recounted his initial attempt at the Qualified Weapons Instructor Course (akin to the Top Gun program in the U.S.), where he didn't pass on the first try. "I failed," he admitted, "but instead of letting that defeat define me, I used it as a learning experience." He returned better prepared, passed the course, and eventually became one of the instructors.

> ***"You can learn through success and failure as long as you have an open mind. That failure taught me that growth often comes through failure as much as through success."***

Building confidence, according to Rob, is a gradual, step-by-step process. "We train our pilots to fly fast, powerful jets almost instinctively," he explained. "By the time they reach the front line, they've gone through rigorous training, so the technical aspects are ingrained, and the focus shifts to decision-making." This is where confidence is crucial.

> ***"It's about making the right call, even without all the information, in high-pressure, fast-moving situations."***

He also shared his belief in trusting one's instincts. "In combat, there is often no time for overthinking; you must rely on that gut feeling, that intuition built from thousands of hours of experience," Rob explained. He called it 'seeing the shot' – the ability to recognise an opportunity before your conscious mind catches up. "That kind of decision-making has saved my life more than once," he said. "It's a skill we teach our pilots because it's crucial for their survival and effectiveness."

Psychological safety is another cornerstone of Rob's approach to leadership. "It's essential to create an environment where people feel safe to admit mistakes, learn from them, and grow," he emphasised. He rejects the notion of 'fake it till you make it,' especially in critical fields like aviation. "There is no room for faking it in our field; that could cost lives," he stated. "If you don't know, say you don't know." This kind of transparency builds trust and, ultimately, true confidence.

How about what he sees from working in a predominantly male environment? "I treat everyone as an individual. Confidence isn't about gender; it's about creating a culture where everyone feels valued and safe to express their strengths and weaknesses." He added:

> *"I've seen bravado in some men to hide insecurity and self-doubt in some women, but I've also seen the opposite. Confidence comes from competence, trust, and fostering an environment where people feel safe to be themselves."*

Rob's Top Tips for Confidence

1. **Prepare thoroughly**, then trust in that preparation.
2. **Be kind to yourself**; understand that confidence ebbs and flows. Use breathing techniques if you need to calm yourself.
3. **Surround yourself with a strong team** and **seek mentors**.
4. **Remain open to learning from every experience**, whether it's a success or a failure.
5. **Focus on the present**, because that's where you have control.

> *"Authenticity and honesty are crucial; if you don't know something, admit it. That's real confidence."*

Three Mottos he loves: **'Look at the whole board.'** It serves as a reminder to take a broader view and not get lost in the details. Another is from Eisenhower: **"When you're successful, it's the team that's successful; when there's a failure, you as the leader take responsibility."** And finally, he mentioned, **'The obstacle is the way,'** which he uses to remind himself to view challenges as opportunities for growth and new paths.

Speaking with Rob reinforced for me how central confidence is to all aspects of life and leadership. As he put it, "Confidence isn't about being perfect or never feeling fear; it's about preparation, resilience, and having the courage to keep moving forward, one decision at a time, in the face of uncertainty." Rob believes confidence is built on "trusting yourself, your instincts, and your team" and knowing that together, you can achieve extraordinary things.

CHAPTER NINE

TRIUMPH THROUGH CHANGE

> *Character cannot be developed in ease and quiet. Only through experience of trial and suffering can the soul be strengthened, ambition inspired, and success achieved.*
>
> Helen Keller

Life happens, and it is full of joy and happiness, as well as sorrow and really tough times. There are many things that completely knock us for six, like grief from losing a loved one, to divorce, redundancy and the pleasure/pain of parenthood.

Through my research and working with many clients, the four big life changes which we have seen fundamentally impacting confidence are **Motherhood, Redundancy, Menopause and Divorce**. This doesn't mean other big life events don't have a huge impact on your life, but these are the ones we are going to focus on, as they can have such a sizable impact on that confidence scale.

Now, if you're a man, you might be tempted to skip ahead. You might be thinking, "What about being a dad?" or "Does this really apply to me?" And I hear you. While the physical experiences of motherhood and menopause are specific to women, the emotional terrain they open up—loss of identity, changing roles, fatigue, guilt, and the pressure to do it all—is something many people can relate to.

So don't skip this chapter. If you're a father, partner, son, or friend—what's shared here might give you a deeper understanding of someone you love.

Or even reflect something in your own story you hadn't quite put words to yet. The truth is that parenthood is hard. Taking time out for caregiving or just trying to survive a season of change is hard. And the hit to confidence that often follows? That doesn't discriminate.

From our research[1], 48% of people have had a career break (for whatever reason) and subsequently really struggle with their confidence. When we dig into those numbers of people who have had the career break, we found:

- 74% of them don't always speak up in meetings because they doubt themselves.
- 67% of them have feelings of being a failure.
- 82% of them are stressed from taking on too much.
- 90% of them get anxious about dealing with senior leaders.
- 93% of them worry about making mistakes.
- 84% of them compare themselves to others and think they may be more intelligent or capable than themselves.

So, whatever the reason for the break, the fact is this: confidence really suffers. Let's dig into each of these four huge life changes, exploring the what, why and how of managing them so you can rebuild that confidence.

1. MOTHERHOOD

"I don't know what happened. Before I was a mum, I was all over it, kicking goals and at the top of my game. Now I feel like I've lost it all: I don't know who I am, what the hell is going on and my confidence is shattered."

Familiar? It's something I hear A LOT. Let's look at what you have just done, CREATED A HUMAN (no less), and you should be giving yourself massive high-fives, walking tall and proud for completing the most complex task known to humanity.

Full disclosure: I don't have kids (and I honestly don't know how you parents all do it!). But I've seen and heard a huge amount from my friends, family, clients and colleagues, as well as from research and experts, all of which has built this chapter. So, please read this hearing their voices and experience, as this is a culmination of their work for you!

What happens in your brain? Neuroscientist, Dr Sarah McKay explained that pregnancy fundamentally rewires a woman's brain. She explains that pregnancy is a time of profound brain plasticity, where the brain adapts to care for a new-born. "Pregnancy prepares your mind for motherhood," she notes. "It doesn't mean you instantly know how to be a mother, but your brain becomes a willing learner." Structural changes occur, particularly in regions involved with social cognition and understanding the thoughts and emotions of others. This adaptation helps mothers become more attuned to their babies. While the term 'baby brain' is often used to describe the fogginess some women feel during pregnancy, Sarah clarifies, "We're not picking up cognitive decline – same as at menopause." Instead, she believes it is more about the brain *prioritising the baby's needs over minor everyday tasks,* rather than any true cognitive decline.

WHY THE DROP IN CONFIDENCE?

Firstly, your body has probably changed beyond what you could imagine; whether it's stretch marks, breast shape, unwanted weight or all the complications that can come up having given birth. No wonder you aren't leaping to pop on a bikini and or get your profile photos updated.

MOTHERHOOD: WHY THE DROP IN CONFIDENCE?

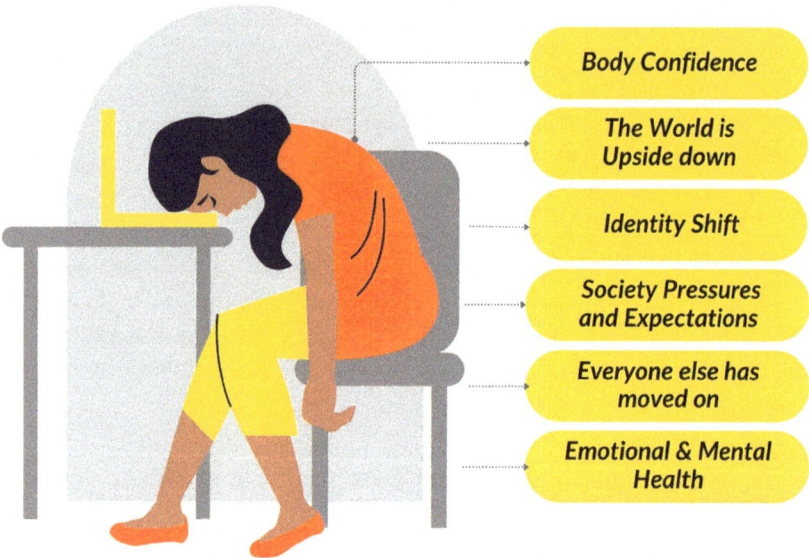

- Body Confidence
- The World is Upside down
- Identity Shift
- Society Pressures and Expectations
- Everyone else has moved on
- Emotional & Mental Health

Your life has also turned upside down and may be hardly recognisable! Keeping a small human alive with raging hormones, lack of sleep, postpartum depression and your life flipped on its head is enough to make anyone question themselves.

You're also having a huge identity shift, which is so rarely talked about with motherhood. Before your identity was clear: Corporate Queen, Party Princess, Dynamic Deliverer. You owned your world and how you interacted with it. Now, how do you balance old you with the new 'Mum' you? Perhaps you've taken to it like a duck to water, or perhaps you're struggling not to drown. There's a constant pull in multiple directions, never feeling like you're doing well *in any of them*. Independence? What's that? Amy Taylor Kabaz is CEO and founder of Mama Rising and the Global Matrescence Foundation. She thought that when she went back to work, she would remember who she was – she would feel like herself again. "I just couldn't find the place where I felt like me anymore," she said (see more from Amy in our Confidence Masterclass section at the end of this chapter).

Aside from the identity shift, there's the huge society pressures and expectations of what your identity should be: the curse of 'you can have it all!' (complete with a smile, a ribbon in your kids' hair and perfect nails/outfit/hair, all by 9am). The reality? *Please stop me from being so tired that I put my top on inside out again and leave one of the kids at the door.* I mean, it was hard enough performing at work before, let alone adding entire new humans to the equation (and band practice, ballet, football, touch rugby… the list goes on). Include lack of support; a judgemental mother-in-law or school mum with their standards and expectations and the edge may seem rather close.

You may well find too that the organisation you once knew has moved on. The systems have changed. You've forgotten it all (or so you think) and you just don't feel like you're 'current' anymore. The people seem younger and more ambitious. Or maybe you just care a little bit less, as your perspective has changed on what's really important in life. In Amy's words: "You don't have room for that crap anymore. I don't care what you think about my Instagram post now. I'm just trying to get my two kids through gastro and get back to work." The fact is that you can feel like everyone else is on a motorway and you're jogging alongside, trying to hitch a ride.

There can also be a physical impact on your emotional and mental health. Postpartum depression and anxiety can hugely impact your confidence and overall mental wellbeing. The worry of your child's wellbeing, shift in your identity and being a good parent can be overwhelming. With comparison everywhere, it's hard to ever feel like what you're doing is enough.

So, what can you do about it? Let's go back to the Confidence Gym for a good workout!

1. Repeat after me: "I'm doing the best I can."

And again. And again. I know you are, because you're *you* and you expect the best of yourself. So, you strive to thrive in your life (but maybe just survive). Wherever you are, be kind to you. Know that love, kindness, laughter and safety is what your child needs. Give them that and they will flourish (even if your hair isn't brushed and your Lululemon has stains down the front).

Hannah Porteous-Butler is a maternity coach at her company The People Practice. She knows it's easy to dwell on mistakes or what didn't go perfectly, but Hannah encourages mothers to celebrate small wins, such as getting the kids to school or simply keeping them happy and healthy. Practicing gratitude can shift your mindset to a more positive and affirming one.

She reminds us:

> *"Emotions are like weather—they can change all the time. And as parents, we need to understand our emotions better and recognize that if we're struggling, it's just a moment in time. That moment will change."*

2. You are not alone

Whether they admit it or not, everyone struggles with the change to parenthood and the lifetime role that involves. No one had done it before they first did it – they just figured it out, just like you. Hopefully you have supportive people around you who tell you that and you can share your concerns with. If you don't, find them with a friend or a mother's group (in person or online).

3. You are better now than you ever were before

Yes, really! Let's look at what skills you have learnt! Unbelievable prioritisation, organisation, anticipation, communication, perspective, multitasking, decision making, resilience, resource allocation, planning, teamwork, leadership, networking, conflict resolution, patience, creativity, adaptability, emotional intelligence and more. Procrastination? Bullshit? Bah – no time for that! Your efficiency will make you a better leader and valuable contributor to your job. Write down all you have gained from this experience and congratulate yourself for it; you should be so proud!!

In her book *Baby Brain*, neuroscientist Dr Sarah McKay notes that although there is reduction in grey-matter volume in the brain during pregnancy (same as in adolescence), it actually reflects reorganisation, refinement and streamlining, not degeneration[2]. Even your brain has got more efficient!

Danielle, single mum and corporate legend, is all about accepting this next stage for what it is:

> *"A baby may very well change your priorities of what's important, and this may have a huge impact on your career choice, level of satisfaction, keenness to climb the corporate ladder further. That's okay. You have permission to re-assess. Take your time, there's no race. Be wise. Be measured. Meditate. Let your mind explore ideas."*

4. Work on the rebuild

You have the skills, you have the capabilities, you just need to remind yourself of that (I promise they weren't wiped out when that child popped out). So, gently work on that muscle and step into things you've not done for a while – you'll be amazed how it all comes back. If it's something new, don't chastise yourself for not knowing, just think, 'Great, I'm learning!' and enjoy the process of your brain and capabilities growing.

5. Social Media Comparison

Forget it. Everyone's life will look more perfect and organised than your own; no one is posting the really hard stuff. The parenting accounts you see probably are full-time social media mothers, which is fine but please don't compare.

6. Release the control

There is no doubt there are some things men can't do. These are primarily having a baby and breast feeding (although Robert De Niro in *Meet the Fockers* might argue with that). Men can take part in almost all other aspects of childcare, including feeding (through bottle-feeding), changing nappies, soothing, bathing, playing, discipline, schoolwork, drop off etc.

However, primarily society, often alongside practicality, means that the woman takes the primary load.

Please, you don't have to. Let go of some of that control. Let them figure it out too, go through the hard bits and gain the rewards of bonding with their kids. I know it's tough, but *you don't have to do it all*. As they grow up, let them wash their clothes, put things in the dishwasher and learn to cook. Your future daughter or son-in-law will be so grateful! How to release control? Be clear about what you need and want. Your other half doesn't have a crystal ball, so be clear on what you require and how they can help you. Cassie, mother and career queen said, *"It's about taking control of what you need and how your partner can be part of the team!"*

You also need to set up clear boundaries about how the picture is going to look parenting as a team. Try to avoid the 52-point list of 'how to' when you are sharing that responsibility! They will figure it out, just like you did, and would you believe, maybe even have a few improvements...

WHAT CAN YOU CONTROL?

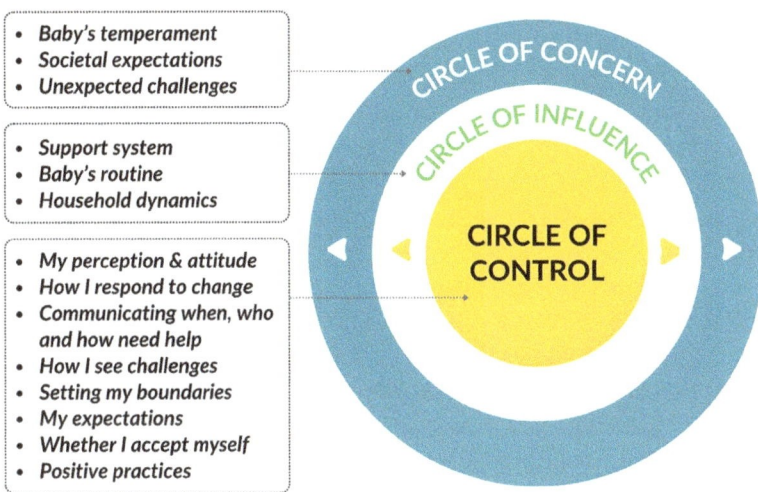

Adapted from Covey, S. (1989). The 7 Habits of Highly Effective People

Consider this permission to also outsource as much as you can. There is no shame in outsourcing work or chores, so that you can be less stressed and more present with your family.

RETURN TO WORK WITH CONFIDENCE

So, you're having time off for the wonderful celebration and nurturing of your new child. However, the joy may be slightly marred by the dread of going back to work. There are a few things you can do to minimise this dread and make sure you go back to work with confidence.

1. **Get on the front foot for your diary** – agree with your manager on what you can/can't do, including calls between specific times of the day, early meetings and weekends.
2. **What support do you need from your manager?** Speak proactively with your manager on what you need from them to be successful. How can they help you with this transition? Do you need more support or feedback for the first period? Or perhaps a morning of full download of the corporate changes when you first get back? I was a caring

manager, but needed to be educated on what the returning mums needed from me.

3. **Block Guilt-Free Me Time.** You will be a better mother, partner, colleague and friend if you have some time for yourself. Block it in your calendar and communicate it if appropriate. You'll feel more confident about work if you feel better about yourself, so make it a priority. Maternity coach, Hannah Porteous-Butler 'clocks off' from parenting at a set time each evening, signalling to her children that she also needs personal time. This teaches children about independence and the importance of self-care – mum is done for the day!

4. **KIT (Keep In Touch) Days.** Some companies offer these as part of their standard maternity policy. It's basically a day you can come into work, attend meetings or whatever you want it to look like for you to 'keep in touch'. You may well feel like you don't want to 'power up the work mindset' whilst you're on maternity, but these are a great thing to attend/implement if you feel up to it.

5. **Dress for Success**. Stretch marks, changing shapes and weight fluctuations are all part of the experience. But here's the thing: your body tells a story of strength and transformation, so start to see it that way. Then, when the time comes to get back into the workforce, consider a personal styling session at one of the big department stores (they don't have to be expensive). Your body and styles may have changed (and we all feel more confident when we are dressed for the part).

6. **Networking.** Spare time = zero, so using precious time to network will feel like time wasted. However, this time can be extremely important in how you get support, confidence and manage your career. Just give yourself permission for at least one connection coffee a week – just one. You might have to race off whilst others are able to have the drinks after work – that's OK, but build in the networking in a way that works for you. It is not time wasted, it is a very important brick in the wall of your identity, self-esteem and longer-term career.

7. **Embrace the Hacks.** If you're a full-time working mum/dad the first thing to remind yourself about is the fact that *you're not the first.* Everyone has had to create their own hacks, whether that be the two-minute meal, the no-iron work clothes, after school care etc. Developing your own short cuts and systems (and they can be little ones like lunch boxes at night or a huge Sunday weekly meal prep) will help you feel more in control.

8. **Set up your support structure.** Mother's groups at work may have made you squirm in the past, but these can be powerhouses of support at this time when you most need it. Seek them out, whether within work, personally or online. Health warning: some people are more neurotic than others, so make sure you follow what's authentic to you and don't get caught up in unnecessary panic.

PROSECCO TIME

We've discussed 'Champagne moments' – those times where you are over-performing and killing it at work. When you've *just brought a human into the world* and are trying to figure out your balance, identity and career, know that it's OK to drink Prosecco for a while. Embrace the young child season for what it is, a time of new skills and expansion in so many ways. You don't have to go at 1,000mph, judging yourself versus your old standards and chastising yourself for not being where you were or progressing at that rate. Life is long (hopefully), and your career will be too.

Leadership expert and best-selling author, Robin Sharma, talks about this in his book, *The Wealth Money Can't Buy*. He talks about embracing those different seasons of work, rest and recovery; elite performers always have this time for exceptional performance and then recovery. It's time to plan out what will be possible for *you*, how you will make it work and feel confident that that's the right thing for you, in your personal circumstances, for this season in your life. It may not seem like it now, but you're building extraordinary skills that will be needed further on down the track. And please note, having a baby or young child is perhaps not an ideal time to do an MBA (even with built-in childcare).

A DIFFERENT LENS

University of Colombia research[3] shows that men often receive a pay increase when they become fathers, a phenomenon known as the 'fatherhood wage premium'. This isn't associated with harder work or better performance, but the perception of men being the bread winners with more responsibilities. With the world shifting so much to where responsibilities are so much more shared, why shouldn't you ask for a pay rise too? You have nothing to lose (see how in the section from PepTalkHer CEO Meggie Palmer in the Navigating Feedback chapter).

Final Word

Remember your parents saying, "I just want you to be happy"? It may have felt like a throwaway comment when there were so many other things in our lives as a child that seemed so important. But the truth is this, as said again by wonderful mum Danielle:

> *"Motherhood serves you up a mirror, with a reflection of the past and a view of the future: why don't we deserve the same confidence and happiness that we want so deeply for our kids?"*

Remember, you are stronger and more capable than ever. This is a time of growth, not just for your child, but for you. You've got this! Like many, you'll feel for a while that you are failing at every aspect. This is not true. There are days when, if everyone is fed, alive and even remotely happy, that it has taken the effort that delivering a huge project would have required before. And on those days, it is enough.

CONFIDENCE MASTERCLASS
AMY TAYLOR-KABBAZ – MAMMA RISING

*"In the process of female empowerment,
we ignored motherhood."*

Amy is a single mama of three children, best-selling author, journalist and podcast host. She is founder and director of Mama Rising, a coaching certification training that specialises in Matrescence (the process of becoming a mother) and supporting mothers differently[A].

From a very early age, Amy set her sights on becoming a journalist, and in particular, telling stories of women around the world. After graduating from university, she began working at the ABC (Australian Broadcasting Corporation) and continued to work towards her ultimate goal for the next fifteen years, including during the birth of her three children. But motherhood brought unexpected challenges, including a thyroid disease and post-natal burn out, and she struggled to reconcile her professional identity with the realities of motherhood and the sense of isolation she felt.

> **"As I was walking through the doors, I'd thought I'd be myself again. But you're a new self. That identity shift is gripping onto something which is in the past, which just doesn't exist anymore. You're an entirely different person."**

In her years of working with women, she finds the biggest pain point is that they *don't know who they are anymore*. But this is something that needs to be acknowledged: "You've changed and that's okay; you'll be stronger on the other side."

The big lightbulb for Amy was learning about matrescence (think of it as a life stage like adolescence). Just as teenagers navigate identity shifts, mothers experience a massive transformation that impacts their confidence, identity, and relationships. This transformation is underappreciated and rarely discussed, leading many women to internalise feelings of inadequacy. Society and workplaces often expect women to remain unchanged, ignoring the profound internal shifts that motherhood brings.

Why does confidence drop? Not because of a personal failing, but due to lack of preparation and understanding of the changes they will undergo.

"Before being a mum, whatever I faced I could beat it. If I just got up earlier, if I just did another list, if I just did this, then I would do it. Motherhood doesn't work like that, and it is crumbling if you're not prepared for that."

Amy advocates for educating future parents about the identity shift (how you'll feel different about work, how your goals will change) to help you to better navigate the transition. The knowledge that you will have 'competing devotions' and feel pulled between worlds is an important check-in, which needs to be aligned with your values (again, this reflects why it's important to be aware of your values and how these will change over time!).

"The biggest fear in all the women that I have seen over the last decade is that they're not enough."

Amy is adamant we need to accept that *it's not our fault that we couldn't do it all*. It's just not real, not possible (no matter what time you wake up!). From that place is a huge feeling of relief as then you can start to think about what you really want. She uses her mantra **'I'm getting ready to be ready'** to remind herself that, even when the gap between where she is and where she wants to be feels too big, she is preparing herself for that next step.

What is her view on confidence? She believes that true confidence comes with grace, forgiveness and space:

> *"Because you know who you are, you don't need to buy into the drama. You don't need to buy into any of that. You're all good."*

Amy's Top Tips for Confidence

1. If you can, **prepare yourself** for the change to come – expect things will change and realign your expectations of what 'enough' looks like.
2. **Acknowledge you are a *completely different person*** and take the time to think who you want to be.
3. **Be kind and learn to forgive yourself** – you cannot do it all.
4. **Rebuild your foundations** – check in with your values and make sure you prioritise what is most important to you *now*. This might change but stay true to this for this moment in time.

Want more? You can find more about Mamma Rising and Amy's work at https://amytaylorkabbaz.com or follow her on social media: @amytaylorkabbaz

2. REDUNDANCY

Jobs for life are no more. The twenty-year commitment is now unusual, from both employers and employees. In fact, the latest research from the world economic forum states that the average person has twelve jobs in their working lifetime[5]. Whether that terrifies or excites you, there is a reality ('R') you may find yourself facing at some points: redundancy.

It used to be whispered with an awkward face 'she's been made redundant' (insert judgment and shame). Now, it happens to many people, regardless of quality of performance! Absolutely, there are times when performance is considered for redundancy (and if it keeps happening, it's time for a good self-audit) but this is no longer the only reason.

The truth of it is, that sometimes:

- You outgrow the organisation.
- You don't have the right skills for a new role that has emerged.
- The organisation takes a different direction to what you offer.
- You don't fit company culture.
- You put yourself on a list as you can't see a future for yourself there.

There are plenty of fantastic books out there which can guide you how to navigate redundancy effectively, so I'm not going into the nitty gritty of this. However, your confidence absolutely can take a hit from this life event, so it's important that we address it.

THE NEUROSCIENCE OF REDUNDANCY

When faced with redundancy, it's natural for our brains to perceive this as a threat. As we know, the brain, particularly the amygdala, is wired to detect threats and activate a 'fight, flight, or freeze' response. This is because redundancy, like any form of change, triggers uncertainty, which our brains interpret as a potential danger (our third Evolutionary Fact). In this state, our bodies produce stress hormones, like cortisol and adrenaline, which can cause anxiety, fear, and a lack of clarity.

However, knowing this is just our brain's way of trying to protect us, we can start to shift our response. Understanding how the brain works under stress, allows us to create space for calm and conscious decision-making.

We can begin to engage our prefrontal cortex, the part of our brain responsible for rational thinking, planning, and emotional regulation, to guide us through this challenging period with confidence.

MANAGING REDUNDANCY WITH CONFIDENCE

How can we deal with finding out we are being 'put at risk' of redundancy? We can break this down with a number of mindset strategies (please also see our Confidence Masterclass with some fantastic practical tips and the six-step Career Navigation Cycle, from our Redundancy expert Steve Preston).

First, we need to acknowledge the impact on our brain and body: Start by recognising the physical and emotional sensations that arise with redundancy. Increased heart rate, sweaty palms, or a feeling of dread are completely normal. Instead of resisting these sensations, acknowledge them. Labelling your emotions can help activate the prefrontal cortex, reducing the amygdala's grip and calming your nervous system, which is so fired up. Use a journal and write down, 'I'm frightened, I'm scared, I'm anxious.' Whichever emotions are there for you, just hear them. It's OK.

Second, you can reframe redundancy as a growth opportunity: Your brain loves stories – it's how we make sense of the world. By consciously reframing redundancy as an opportunity rather than a threat, you begin to rewrite the narrative your brain is telling you. This activates the brain's reward system, releasing dopamine, which enhances motivation and creativity. Practice saying this affirmation, *'This is the best thing that could have happened for me,'* and notice how this shift changes your energy and outlook. Consider the redundancy being the universe giving you a big kick up the butt to make the change you've needed to for a while. You're allowed a short 'wallow in tracksuit bottoms' period (48 hours) then it's time to put on the big pants, change your mindset and start taking action.

Third, get yourself moving and engage your body to regulate your brain: Movement is medicine for both the brain and body. Physical exercise, even a brisk walk, releases endorphins – our body's natural mood enhancers – and can help reset our stress response. Mind-body practices like yoga, deep breathing, or mindfulness meditation can also help quiet the stress response, fostering a sense of calm and increasing resilience.

Another crucial strategy with redundancy is to focus on the controllables: Remember, our third Evolutionary Fact: our brain sees lack of control as danger. By focusing on what you can control, such as ensuring you are getting a good package, acquiring new skills, building your network, or exploring new industries, you create a sense of agency. Spend some time thinking: What do you love? What are you good at? What are you trained in? What are the gaps you need to fill? There's an intersection of these which can be really helpful. Set small, achievable goals that can help you to regain control over your career path. This not only activates the prefrontal cortex but also boosts serotonin levels, promoting a sense of well-being and satisfaction.

A growth mindset can change your experience of redundancy too. Neuroscience shows that our brains are incredibly plastic; they can change and adapt throughout our lives. By cultivating a growth mindset, you prime your brain for resilience. Embrace curiosity, experiment with new ideas, and be open to learning from failures. What are the benefits? Write down all the personal and professional benefits of this redundancy. More time with your kids? Finally take that trip away with your mates? Get out of the industry you've always hated? Get more aligned with your true authentic values? Whatever those benefits may be, get them down and focus on the gratitude for this enormous nudge from the world.

Final Word

Trust and patience: I know it's hard. I've been there too. You feel like your world is upside down, but I promise that you'll be looking back on this with such relief and gratitude before you know it. I honestly don't know a single person that hasn't benefited from being made redundant. Repeat these words:

- 'I trust that everything is unfolding just as it should be.'
- 'I am excited about what the chapter holds.'

"Disaster is opportunity."
Winston Churchill

CONFIDENCE MASTERCLASS
STEVE PRESTON – REDUNDANCY IS OPPORTUNITY

"Redundancy is not the end of the world; it's an opportunity to rethink and take stock."

Steve Preston is a renowned career coach, author, and speaker, specialising in helping individuals navigate career transitions, particularly through redundancy. With many years of experience in corporate, coaching and mentoring, Steve developed his six-step Career Navigation Cycle, guiding people through life and career changes with a focus on mindset, resilience, and personal growth.

Just like many people, Steve's path was filled with unexpected turns, key moments, and a mindset shift that ultimately reshaped his professional life. His major turning point came when the company he worked for was acquired, and he was asked to relocate. His response? "Thanks, but no thanks." This marked the moment when he first chose to prioritise his personal values over career ambition. It was a defining decision, as he explained: "It was wrong for the family, but I hadn't a clue what I wanted to do next."

When he joined a government training programme for out-of-work executives, he noticed: "Mindset is everything." Some participants were stuck in negativity, while others, like himself, were more open to embracing change. "Before I knew it, I was actually coaching and mentoring other people… and that's how it all started." What had started as a career setback eventually became the foundation for his new career: supporting others through redundancy, career change, and life transitions. He encourages us to view redundancy not as the end, but as an opportunity for personal growth, re-evaluation, and even reinvention. As Steve puts it, "You're never too old, or too young, to change."

However, he acknowledges, redundancy can also be an emotional rollercoaster, with unexpected highs and lows. "It's like a bereavement," he said. It's vital to recognise and manage the ups and downs that come with major life changes. His advice is to remain open to support, whether through professional coaching or personal networks, as going through such transitions alone can be isolating and more challenging.

> *"You spend more waking hours at work than in any other activity. Life is too short, so why be unhappy? Take the leap of faith and do what you love."*

Steve has distilled his experience into a six-step Career Navigation Cycle, which he says applies to not just career transitions, but life changes too:

1. **Let Go and Look Forward:** Release negative experiences from the past and shift your focus to the future. Holding onto baggage from previous roles or setbacks can hinder progress. It's crucial to mentally prepare for new opportunities by embracing change and letting go of the past.
2. **Re-evaluate:** Assess what's truly important to you in both your career and personal life. This includes identifying your core values and ensuring they align with your goals. Understanding these values helps to guide better decision-making as you face the next steps in your career.
3. **Establish Your True Marketability:** Go beyond skills and consider your full range of abilities, including attributes, passions, mindset, interests, strengths and knowledge. Recognise the unique value you bring to the table, which can enhance your confidence and open up new possibilities.
4. **Explore Opportunities:** Conduct research, network, and be open to new roles or industries that align with your skills and values. This step is about considering different paths and finding the right fit based on your re-evaluated priorities.
5. **Decide What to Do:** After exploring options, make a clear, informed decision about your next career move. This is about

Adapted from Preston, S. (2002). Winning Through Career Change. Kogan Page.

narrowing down the choices and committing to a direction that aligns with your values and marketability.

6. **Take Positive Action:** Once a decision is made, follow through with concrete steps to make it happen. Whether it's job applications, networking, or starting a business, creating an action plan and then taking positive action is crucial to achieving success and transitioning smoothly into your next chapter.

If networking makes you cringe, Steve believes it is crucial for this time (and before it too). Networking, he believes, is about developing relationships and finding people who can open doors, not simply asking for a job. He recounted a story about a client who didn't tell anyone he'd been made redundant, not even his best man, as he was too ashamed. After floundering for a year, he eventually opened up to his friend who then quickly helped him land a new role through a personal connection. This is why it's so important to build a strong support network and to be open and honest about your situation!

Is there a difference in how men and women handle redundancy and career transitions? From his experience, Steve has found that women tend to be much more open about their emotions and more willing to seek help, whereas men often put up a front, waiting until a crisis point before asking for assistance, as in the example mentioned above. Please don't wait; there's no shame in redundancy at all. Stay positive and believe that the majority of people are happy to help, as they would like to think you would do the same for them if roles were reversed.

Steve's Top Tips for Confidence

1. **Focus on Personal Development to achieve a Positive Mindset:** Stay open to change and approach challenges with a growth mindset, letting go of the past as it won't serve you!
2. **Re-evaluate Your Values:** Align your career and life goals with what truly matters to you.
3. **Recognise Your Marketability:** Understand and value your full potential beyond just your skills to showcase to a potential employer or maybe to run your own business.
4. **Build a Support Network:** Surround yourself with positive people who can provide emotional and practical support whilst also boosting you up.
5. **See Opportunities in Challenges and Take Action:** Use setbacks as an opportunity to reassess and grow, then take that action to move forward, even in the face of fear.
6. **Celebrate 'small wins':** Small wins are a key part of your transition journey and should be celebrated, or at least recognised, as they show you are moving you forward (e.g., making new connections, letting go and banishing negative thinking, getting invited to interviews etc).

Want more? You can find Steve and details about his books at: https://www.linkedin.com/in/steveprestonsmpsolutions/

3. MENOPAUSE

This chapter is for *everyone*, whatever your gender. True, men don't go through menopause, not directly. However, you'll have women in your life who will, so understanding this phase will help your ability to relate, support and champion those women. It can be challenging, but it's not a disaster and nor should we treat it as such! The fact is, the impact of the changes that are happening in a woman's body when she goes through the menopause can really impact her confidence.

MENOPAUSE LOW-DOWN

Let's start with a brief overview from neuroscientist Dr Sarah McKay. She gave me the low down on menopause itself. Essentially, it's when our ovaries run out of eggs. Our normal cycle consists of what Dr McKay says is "a lovely conversation between the ovaries and the brain" and that regulates your menstrual cycle. But then, things start to change, because the oestrogen production becomes erratic and irregular, so the conversation "starts to splutter and stall." Instead of it being a smooth discussion, it becomes very rollercoaster-like. Dr McKay says:

> *"It's almost as if the brain is saying to the ovaries, 'I can't hear you,' and the ovaries going, 'Okay, sorry, we'll be louder.' And then the brain going, 'Not quite that loud!' And it all becomes chaotic."*

This is where we see the knock-on effects on the brain and body, like hot flashes, which are caused by a change within the mechanisms that manages our temperature (the hypothalamus). However, because we have oestrogen receptors all over the body and throughout our brain, the impact of these changes can be much more wide ranging.

Why would Mother Nature do it? Why would we have to go through all of this? The first key fact was what I realised when I was complaining to my husband. "I mean, honestly, we have to deal with periods our whole lives, and then menopause! It doesn't make any sense!"

Well, it turns out it does make sense - total sense: we were meant to be dead.

Now that might sound dramatic, but it's true. Just one hundred years ago, the menopause was rare *as we just weren't living as long*. In the late nineteenth and twentieth century, the average age of death for women in the United States was forty-nine[6]. Mother Nature probably thought she had provided plenty of wiggle room giving us eggs and hence oestrogen for that period of time. However, as life expectancy has gone up, this clearly unexpected situation where we would run out has emerged and our bodies are trying to cope with the consequences. We now understand the extraordinary impact a lack of oestrogen has on our bodies (yes, every cell) and so why this is such a crucial area to address.

We spoke to Executive Menopause Coach, Claire Hattrick[7] to get the low-down on what it can look like. Claire emphasised that menopause is a lifelong phase affecting many women and can significantly impact both their personal and professional lives. Symptoms can range from physical (e.g., joint pain, hot flushes) to psychological (e.g., anxiety, depression). Menopause affects a wide range of women with diverse symptoms and can be over a long period of time (some women start having symptoms of perimenopause in their thirties).

Let's start with the truth: perimenopause and menopause can be hard. It's not just the hot flashes or the sleepless nights; it's the profound physical, emotional, and mental changes that can feel like they're turning your world upside down. You may feel like you're not yourself, like your brain and body are at odds with each other, and it's okay to admit that.

However, it's not all doom and gloom. Dr McKay noted that the longitudinal studies show that around a quarter of women have symptoms that interfere with their daily lives and need some kind of help. About 50% of women notice some symptoms, but they're fine and another 25% don't even notice anything. "We need to be careful not to lump everyone in together and say all women experience all of these symptoms," she says. The danger is that there's the unintended consequence of discrimination against women, because it's perceived that they are all going to fall apart at this stage of their lives! It's just not true – it can be an opportunity to thrive.

Whatever your experience of this, even when it feels overwhelming, you have the power to navigate this phase with resilience, self-compassion, and real, practical strategies. Let's explore how you can better understand what's happening in your brain and body, and how to support yourself through it.

MANAGING MENOPAUSE WITH CONFIDENCE

1. Understand Your Brain–Body Connection: It's Not All in Your Head. Your body is in transition, and so is your brain. During perimenopause and menopause, the decline in oestrogen impacts neurotransmitters like serotonin and dopamine, which are crucial for mood, sleep, and cognitive function. This is why you might feel more anxious, emotional, or experience 'brain fog'. It's not just you – it's your brain chemistry shifting in response to hormonal changes. So, when you find yourself forgetting where you left your keys or feeling inexplicably anxious, remind yourself: 'My brain is adjusting to these changes. I'm not losing it; I'm adapting.'

2. Give Your Mind What It Needs: Calm the Storm. Your brain is more sensitive to stress during this time because of these hormonal shifts. When you're feeling on edge or overwhelmed, it's your body's way of signalling that it needs a reset. Practicing the psychological sigh, mindfulness or deep breathing can help calm your brain's stress response and bring you back to centre.

Take a few minutes each day to practice a simple mindfulness exercise. Sit quietly, close your eyes, and focus on your breath. Inhale for four counts, hold for four, exhale for four. Repeat. This isn't about clearing your mind – it's about giving your brain a break from the constant noise of this crazy world.

3. Sleep Smarter, Not Harder: Support Your Brain's Natural Rhythm. Insomnia and disrupted sleep are real challenges during menopause. With less oestrogen, your body struggles to regulate temperature and maintain stable sleep patterns, leaving you feeling exhausted and foggy. But sleep is when your brain does its repair work, so it's crucial to find ways to support better rest, however you possibly can.

Create a wind-down routine that signals to your brain that it's time to sleep. This could include reducing screen time before bed, keeping your bedroom cool and dark, having a hot shower before bed or using calming practices like reading or gentle stretching.

4. Move with Intention: Exercise for Your Body and Brain. We know exercise is good for the body, but it's just as important for the brain. Physical activity releases endorphins, which can lift your mood, reduce anxiety, and help counteract the cognitive dips that sometimes come with hormonal changes. Regular movement also helps regulate hormones, improve sleep, and increase overall energy levels.

Find a form of movement that feels good to you, whether it's a brisk walk, yoga, dancing, or strength training. Aim for thirty minutes a few times a week. Remember, it's not about punishment; it's about joy and caring for your body and mind. Celebrate and congratulate yourself when you do it; you'll be much more likely to do it again. And remember: **You never regret exercise.**

5. Nourish Yourself Deeply: Food Is Fuel for Your Brain and Body. Your brain and body need the right fuel to navigate this transition. Hormonal changes can affect everything from mood to metabolism, so a balanced diet becomes even more essential. Think of it as giving your brain and body the best support possible.

Focus on foods that stabilise blood sugar and support brain health. Include plenty of leafy greens, lean proteins, healthy fats like omega-3s, and whole grains. Minimise refined sugars and caffeine, which can spike anxiety and disrupt sleep. Dr Mary Clare Haver, author of *The New Menopause* has some excellent suggestions on recipes that can support your needs at this time[8]. There are also some great supplements out there that women say have really helped them (Dr Vegan's 'Menofriend' is a great example of this and a favourite of many women I know![9]).

6. Acknowledge the Emotional Rollercoaster: It's Not Weakness, It's Biology. Your brain is recalibrating to a new hormonal environment, and that can trigger mood swings, irritability, or even feelings of sadness. This isn't a sign of weakness or failing; it's a natural, biological response to change.

Give yourself grace. When you feel emotional, pause and recognise what's happening: 'My brain is adjusting; it's okay to feel this way.' Allow yourself to feel what you feel without judgment. It's okay not to be okay all the time. It's worth having a way of **communicating to the people in your life** when you know you are gripped by the claws of irrational hormones. They can give you grace then too. I just put up a flag: **'I'm feeling quite hormonal today**.' It makes everyone a bit more understanding of what might come out of my mouth!

7. Stay Connected: Your Brain Thrives on Community. Isolation can make everything feel harder. Your brain actually craves connection; social interaction helps release oxytocin, the 'bonding/trust hormone', which can counteract the stress response and help to stabilise your mood.

Reach out to your support network, whether that's a friend, a partner, or a group. Be honest about what you're going through. You don't have to do this alone. Sometimes, just knowing someone else understands can be incredibly healing.

8. Speak Up for Your Needs: You Deserve to Be Heard. This is your body, your experience, and your health. Don't shy away from advocating for what you need, whether that's at the doctor's office, at work, or at home. Your needs are valid, and your voice matters. Practice clear, direct communication. Use 'I' statements: "I'm experiencing... and I need..." Whether it's asking for a quieter workspace or exploring different treatment options, your needs deserve attention and respect.

9. Control What You Can: Small Steps to Take Charge. While you can't control the fact that menopause is happening, there are small, actionable steps you can take to feel more in control of your life. Your brain will feel much happier if you can focus on what is in its control, rather than the uncontrollables. This might mean speaking to your healthcare professional about menopausal hormone therapy (MHT, which was previously referred to as 'HRT', or hormone replacement therapy), adjusting your diet, incorporating more movement into your day, or finding new ways to manage stress.

Write down what you can really control in this situation and take action today. Set a realistic goal for yourself each week, whether it's going for a walk, booking an appointment, trying a new recipe, or practicing mindfulness. Focus on progress, not perfection, and celebrate each small step.

Final Word

There's no denying that perimenopause and menopause bring real challenges, but it isn't a foregone conclusion that you are only facing despair and doom! Understanding what's happening in your brain and body can help you to navigate this phase with more confidence and grace. It's not about pretending it's easy. It's about knowing that, even when it's hard, you have the tools and strategies you need to support yourself. You're stronger than you think, and you have what it takes to face this phase with resilience, self-compassion, and empowerment. Trust in yourself, be kind to yourself, and remember that you're not alone on this journey.

If you're someone supporting a woman through menopause, then patience, understanding and asking how you can support them can make all the difference. The fact that you have read this chapter means you are up for learning (good on you), but following through on that education is key.

CONFIDENCE MASTERCLASS
CLAIRE HATTRICK – EXECUTIVE MENOPAUSE COACH

"I experienced ten years of menopausal joint hell."

Claire Hattrick's experience of menopause is the reason she's now an Executive Menopause Coach[7]. She experienced such severe pain that it often left her crawling on her hands and knees. After consulting numerous doctors and specialists, she still had no clear answers until a male physiotherapist suggested that her hormones needed to be looked at. This was her 'light bulb moment', which led her to educate herself and eventually launch her website, The Executive Menopause Coach, in 2020, with the support of her twin daughters.

Claire emphasises that menopause is a crucial part of life for many women, especially now that we're living longer. "We are going to be post-menopause for maybe 40 years," she noted, pointing out the urgent need for greater awareness and education around the topic.

She is passionate about her mission to ensure that everyone, especially men, became informed about menopause. She wants "to make the world a kinder place" by increasing awareness and understanding, stressing that menopause isn't just about "hot flushes and old women". It could manifest itself in a wide range of symptoms, from anxiety and panic attacks to joint pain and sleep disturbances. "Menopause will impact 51% of the population," she says, affecting not only women, but also everyone around them.

> *"There is still a taboo surrounding menopause and we need to break the silence. We need to educate everybody so it becomes the norm."*

Claire points out the importance of using correct terminology and openly discussing the challenges women face. Changing workplace cultures to better support menopausal women is an important part of that. After all, retaining talented women is crucial. She shared that some male employers, after learning from her workshops, have told her, "You saved my marriage," having come to understand their partners' experiences better.

How can menopause affect a woman's confidence? Claire herself had gone from being a confident, outgoing person to someone who couldn't leave her house for four years due to anxiety and pain. She understood the literally 'crippling' impact menopause could have, but also demonstrated how, through education and sharing her story, she had managed to rebuild her confidence. "I feel quite confident and happy in my own skin," she told me, underscoring the power of resilience and how confidence can come back.

She stressed the importance of empathy and understanding, particularly from men. She encouraged both men and women to approach these conversations with care and sensitivity, emphasising that empathy and kindness were crucial.

Claire's Top Tips for Confidence

1. **Being informed** about menopause is vital: 'Forewarned is forearmed.'
2. **Each menopause journey is unique.** Symptoms, treatments, and the impact vary widely, and understanding this diversity is crucial for providing the right support and solutions.
3. **Break the silence** around menopause – women need to share their stories, support each other, and seek help because 'a problem shared is a problem halved.'

4. While menopause can significantly impact a woman's confidence, **education, community support, and openness** could help in reclaiming it.
5. **You are more resilient than you know,** and your confidence can return!

Want more? See Claire's website: https://www.theexecutivemenopausecoach.com or follow her on social media: @theExecutiveMenopauseCoach

4. THE DIVORCE/BREAK UP

"I can't do this anymore!" It came out of the blue from the man I thought I was going to marry. It was the beginning of the most painful period in my life, where the tears didn't stop for over a year.

Now, we hadn't actually got *married*, we were everything but, having bought a home and spent five years of our lives together. I'm hugely grateful that we didn't have the complexity of kids to add to the equation. On my part, I felt like someone had died; the grief was crippling and my confidence was shattered.

Whether it's actually a divorce or a similar break up, the impact on our personal and professional life can be enormous – totally suffocating. We can't sleep, eat, focus or maybe even get out of bed. The foetal position starts to feel like an excellent strategy to deal with the world. So, what's the neuroscience? Let's guess which of the different Evolutionary Facts are being triggered in this scenario…

Evolutionary Fact 1: Our brain prioritises energy for a survival response.

Evolutionary Fact 2: Our brain is wired to notice danger (negativity) more than positivity.

Evolutionary Fact 3: Our brain sees lack of control as danger.

Evolutionary Fact 4: Our brain wants to be part of a tribe.

Yep, the lot. Add in the impact of the grief and loss our brain is experiencing, and it's no wonder this tips us on our heads.

When we think about this kind of massive change in our lives, there is a really useful model called The Kübler-Ross Change Curve (derived from the 'grief curve'[10]). This is a useful tool to understand how massive changes can have an impact on people and the different ways we respond, whatever the change is.

THE STAGES OF CHANGE

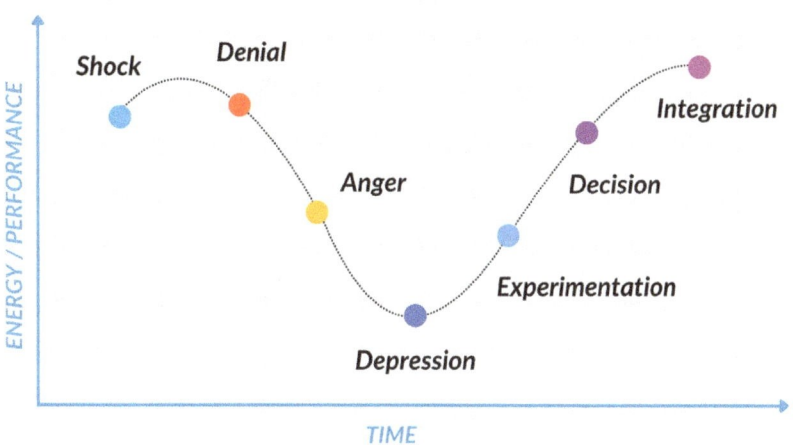

Adapted from Kübler-Ross, E., & Kessler, D. (2005)

Let's look at it through the lens of a break-up:

- **Shock** – Oh my goodness, this break-up has come out of NO WHERE!
- **Denial** – It can't be true. We will get back together once we have talked it through.
- **Frustration/Anger** – How could they do this? Why is it happening? I can't believe they are being such an idiot!
- **Depression** (otherwise known as the 'tracksuit bottom' phase) – No-one loves me. I'm going to be alone forever.
- **Experiment** – Hmm. OK. Perhaps there could be some benefits. There were some parts of them that were quite annoying.
- **Decision** – Right, that's it. I'm moving on. We weren't meant to be together and that's okay.
- **Integration** – How do I download Tinder again?

When people understand this and the emotions they may well feel during a breakup, that in itself can allow them to 'be' and let the parasympathetic system calm the sympathetic nervous system response.

Understanding that these are *entirely natural responses,* based on our brain's constant desire for safety, can provide real comfort and confidence in uncertainty. What's very important is to know everyone goes through this at different paces, and with different interpretations. Some people may skip a phase. In fact, some might whip all the way through to making a decision. However, we need to be patient with people (and ourselves). The key is not to linger too long in any one part – that's when we get stuck and can't make progress.

Breakups and divorces can be some of the most challenging experiences we will face, shaking our confidence to the core. Whether it's the end of a marriage or a long-term relationship, it's not just about parting ways with someone we cared about; it can feel like we're losing a part of ourselves, too. Navigating this change is tough, but it's also a time when we can rediscover our incredible strength and get back in touch with what really matters to us.

HOW BREAKUPS AND DIVORCES IMPACT CONFIDENCE

When we've been in a long-term relationship, our brain literally rewires itself to form a bond with our partner. We create habits, routines, and shared memories that shape our daily lives and our sense of self. After a breakup or divorce, our brain needs to adjust to a new reality, which can feel confusing and disorienting; it's going through loss physically. This is partly because our brain is working to undo those neural pathways that were tied to our relationship, leading to feelings of being lost or unsure of who we are.

We can, in fact, use this time as an opportunity to consciously rewire our brain. We can engage in new activities that help to heal us, revisit old hobbies, or try something we've always wanted to do. These new experiences help create fresh neural pathways, which can gradually help us to rebuild our sense of self outside of the relationship. When I broke up from my partner I dug deep on yoga, meditation and acupuncture. I felt a real need to heal myself and avoid the destruction of alcohol and partying.

When you go through a breakup or divorce, your brain is dealing with a flood of neurochemicals. The emotional pain we feel isn't just 'in your head', as mentioned before, it's a real, physical response. Those studies show that the same areas of the brain that register physical pain light up when we experience social rejection or *loss*. This is why we might feel like we're in a fog, distracted, or even physically unwell. The drop in dopamine and oxytocin, the 'feel-good' chemicals that were plentiful in a happy relationship, can lead to feelings of sadness and a lack of motivation. During my break-up period, I would wake up every day feeling like I was in a daze; I couldn't focus, think straight or eat.

Knowing that these feelings are linked to real changes in our brains can help us to be kinder to ourselves. Practising self-care activities that help boost these neurochemicals, including exercise, connecting with friends or doing activities we enjoy, can help elevate our mood and counteract the emotional lows.

Dealing with Others' Opinions

During a breakup or divorce, our brain's threat detection centre, the amygdala, can become more sensitive. This heightened sensitivity makes us more reactive to perceived criticism or judgment from others. We might feel overly defensive, anxious, or worried about what people think of us. This is a natural survival response; our brain is trying to protect us from what it perceives as social exclusion from our tribe, our fourth Evolutionary Fact, which historically could have been a matter of life or death.

It's important that we recognise that our brain is wired to care about social connection, but it's also adaptable. Other people's opinions are just that – opinions, not facts. We can use mindfulness techniques, like deep breathing, meditation or simply more sleep, to calm our amygdala and reduce anxiety about the judgement of others.

Financial Uncertainty

Financial stress can be high when we are going through a breakup or divorce, as so many people rely on their partners for financial security. This fear can activate our brain's stress response system, releasing cortisol, the body's primary stress hormone. High levels of cortisol can impact everything from sleep and digestion to concentration and decision-making, making us feel overwhelmed and out of control. This can diminish our confidence in even the simple ability of handling day-to-day life.

You can manage things by breaking down your financial concerns into manageable steps. The act of taking control brings our brain calmness (remember, your brain doesn't like a lack of control). Create a budget, speak to a financial advisor, or plan for the future – these steps all can reduce cortisol levels by giving your brain a sense of order and predictability. This, in turn, can help you to feel more empowered and less anxious about the future.

Molly Benjamin, author and CEO of the brilliant Ladies Finance Club[11] says:

"If your relationship is ending, gain confidence by understanding your financial status. Key steps include seeing a lawyer, dividing assets, and reviewing spouse maintenance, property settlement, and child support. Build a trusted support team – lawyers, financial advisors, or counsellors – and seek legal advice early to protect your interests.

Gather important documents, like property deeds, bank statements, superannuation records, and photograph documents, early in case your partner tries to hide them. Secure liquid assets by notifying your bank and consider two-to-sign access for joint accounts. If assets are in your partner's name, consult a lawyer.

Document your separation date clearly, even with a text, to avoid confusion. Change passwords, log out of shared devices, and secure your accounts to protect your privacy. Separation can be tough, but with the right steps, clarity and control are within reach – and there's always light at the end of the tunnel."

Parenting Adjustments

If you have children, your brain might be on high alert for their well-being during a breakup or divorce. You may feel a surge of worry or guilt, which can be tied to an increase in oxytocin, the bonding hormone that makes you feel protective and connected to your children. While this can cause anxiety, it also shows your brain is wired to care deeply about your role as a parent. Use this heightened awareness to your advantage. Stay focused on your parenting goals and remind yourself that these feelings of anxiety and guilt are rooted in love and concern. This can help you to approach parenting with intention, building a new sense of confidence in your ability to navigate this new chapter.

MANAGING DIVORCE WITH CONFIDENCE

1. **Be Honest with Yourself:** Acknowledge that this process is triggering both your emotional and physiological systems. Your brain is working overtime to make sense of the change. Allow yourself to feel everything without judgement, knowing that each emotion is a natural response to what your brain perceives as a significant loss. Accepting your feelings helps to calm the brain's alarm systems and makes space for healing.
2. **Redefine Your Identity:** As you move forward, use the brain's plasticity to your advantage. Your brain is capable of creating new pathways and adapting to new circumstances. Think about who you are outside of the relationship and what you want to cultivate in your life now. That can be a really exciting prospect! Whether it's a new skill, a hobby, or a goal, engaging in these activities helps your brain to create a new narrative about who you are and a brighter future ahead.
3. **Build Your Support Network:** That 'trust hormone' I've mentioned, oxytocin, is released when we connect. This can help soothe our nervous system and rebuild a sense of safety and trust. Reach out to those who uplift you, make you laugh and understand what you're going through. Surrounding yourself with a supportive network can help your brain feel less isolated and more connected, which is crucial for rebuilding confidence.
4. **Enlist the Professionals:** The support network that you build may also include a professional, such as a coach or therapist. I highly recommend you do this if you can! I'm not sure how I would have got through my breakup without my coach, Sian. She helped me find confidence in myself when I thought I was empty; it meant I managed to get to work and function. There's a huge amount that you need to process when you have a breakup, and that may take time, energy and space with a professional. It's worth it, though, as it's part of your healing and how you learn from the experience. From that place, you'll be ready to be confident in the relationship you have in the future, and you deserve that!

5. **Take Charge of Your Finances:** Facing financial fears head-on can activate the brain's reward centres. As you make progress, however small, you'll release dopamine, the neurotransmitter associated with reward and pleasure, which reinforces positive behaviour and boosts confidence. Break down your financial goals into small, manageable steps, and celebrate each achievement to keep those dopamine levels up.
6. **Focus on Small Wins:** Your brain loves a win, even a small one – each time your confidence grows. Completing simple tasks, or setting small, achievable goals, triggers the release of dopamine, which reinforces positive feelings and builds momentum. Take a micro confidence challenge and celebrate these moments as signs of progress and resilience. Over time, you'll find your confidence returning as that muscle starts to grow.
7. **Practice Self-Compassion:** Self-compassion isn't just a nice idea; it's a way to rewire your brain for resilience. Being kind to yourself activates the brain's self-soothing system and reduces the production of cortisol, helping you to feel calmer and more in control. Remember, growth isn't linear, and setbacks are part of the process.

Final Word

The end of a relationship, whether through breakup or divorce, is a significant life event that affects both your brain and body. But it's not the end of your story. Your brain is adaptable, your body is resilient, and you have the power to create a new chapter for yourself. By understanding what's happening inside your mind and body, you can make choices that help you to heal, rebuild, and find your confidence again.

CONFIDENCE MASTERCLASS
SARA DAVISON – DIVORCE COACH

*"It's not what happens to you in life that defines you;
it's what you do about it that makes you who you are."*

Sara Davison is a leading divorce coach, author, and speaker known as 'The Divorce Coach'[1][2]. Drawing from her personal experience of a difficult divorce, Sara develops practical strategies to help others rebuild confidence and navigate the challenges of separation. She has trained hundreds of breakup coaches globally and is recognised for empowering individuals to transform their pain into growth. Sara is a sought-after expert in media and continues to guide people through the process of moving forward after a relationship ends.

In our discussion, Sara emphasised that many people, around 50% globally, go through divorce, and it profoundly affects their confidence. "When someone unexpectedly ends a relationship," she explained, "it can leave you doubting yourself, wondering why you didn't see it coming. You find yourself on what I call the hamster wheel of questions: What's wrong with me? Why don't they love me anymore? What could I have done differently? These questions just take you around in circles and often made you wary of future relationships, fearing the same thing might happen again."

*"Divorce, even when you're not legally married,
can shatter your confidence."*

Sara had been married for less than three years when she discovered that her husband was in love with someone else – a woman twelve years younger and stunningly beautiful. "That wasn't great for my confidence," she admitted. "We had a son who was almost one, and we were running a business together with over two hundred staff. The humiliation was public and painful. Everyone knew before I did, and she was even made a director of our firm. It was a daily struggle to show up to work."

Sara realised she needed to regain control, and as a coach with fifteen years of experience, she tried to find resources to help her through. But there was nothing specific to her situation. So, she began to create her own toolkit, combining coaching skills with strategies to handle the divorce process. "I tested these techniques from the bathroom floor up. Will this help me get dressed today? Will this help me make a call or eat something?" This toolkit eventually became a foundation for helping people worldwide, giving her pain a purpose.

Sara believes confidence is multi-faceted. "I was confident in my professional life, managing a team of two hundred people, but that wasn't the same as confidence in my personal life. Going through such a public and painful breakup made me feel ashamed and doubt myself. But I realised that true confidence wasn't about how you appeared in public; it was about what I did behind closed doors when no one was watching. Did I get up and go to the gym, or did I just take that one selfie a month to show the world?" She vowed not to let her circumstances break her.

> *"My motto, 'Screw you, watch this!' was born there.*
> *I decided to turn my pain into power, my trauma into triumph.*
> *Confidence comes from taking steps forward,*
> *even when it's hard."*

Building confidence, she realised, also involves leaning into uncertainty, reducing it where possible, and focusing on what you could control. "You can't control other people's actions, but you can control how you respond," she explained. "Find people who can help you reduce uncertainties, create a support system, and always ask better questions. Instead of focusing on what was wrong, ask yourself, 'What can I do to move forward?'"

For anyone facing the aftermath of a breakup, Sara encourages them to find a community, lean into the fear, and take control of what they can. "Confidence isn't the absence of fear. It's doing it anyway, despite the fear," she said.

Her final thought was a reminder: "It's not what happens to you in life that defines you; it's what you do about it that makes you who you are. You might feel like giving up, but remember, it's your choice to grow stronger and find a way to thrive. You can do this!"

Sara's Top Tips for Confidence

1. **Turn your pain into power.** Remember her motto: "Screw you, watch this!"
2. **Reduce the uncertainties** by controlling what you can.
3. **Ask questions** that move you forward.
4. **Lean into the fear** as it's going to make you stronger.
5. **Find a community** of people who can support you.

Want more? Sara offers one-to-one and group coaching. You can find out more on her website www.saradavison.com or follow her on social media: @Saradavisondivorcecoach

Final Word

Change may feel daunting, but you've weathered it before and come out stronger. With your new resilience, you can embrace life's shifts with confidence. And as we wrap up this framework, know that every letter in 'CONFIDENT' has led you to this point. It has led you to being unapologetically, confidently *you*.

KEY CONFIDENCE INSIGHTS

1. **Confidence Takes a Hit with Major Life Changes:** Life is going to send you curveballs – fact. These life events often trigger stress responses in the brain, leading to anxiety, self-doubt, and reduced self-esteem. You aren't alone; many others in the history of time have gone through this, survived and come out stronger.

2. **Understanding the Brain-Body Connection is Crucial:** Recognising how your brain and body respond to these changes can empower you to manage your reactions more effectively. Knowledge about how hormonal shifts, stress responses, and brain chemistry affect your emotions and thoughts is essential to rebuilding confidence.

3. **Reframe Challenges as Opportunities:** Shifting your mindset to view these events not as setbacks but as opportunities for growth and self-discovery can change your brain's narrative, activating the reward system whilst boosting motivation and resilience. Trust that the future holds better opportunities; whatever is happening, know that there is a gift in that lesson and you'll be stronger as a result (I promise).

4. **Build New Skills and Strengths Through Change:** Each of these life changes presents an opportunity to develop new skills and strengths, whether it's the multitasking abilities gained from motherhood, the resilience developed through redundancy, or the new self-awareness and health focus prompted by menopause or a breakup.

5. **Support Systems and Self-Compassion are Vital:** Navigating these changes successfully involves reaching out to supportive networks, communicating your needs, practicing self-care, and fostering self-compassion. These strategies help regulate the brain's stress response, reduce anxiety, and build confidence.

TIME FOR ACTION

1. **Acknowledge and Normalise Your Feelings:** Recognise the emotions you're experiencing as normal responses to change. Labelling your emotions helps to activate the rational part of your brain and reduces anxiety, allowing you to regain control and clarity.

2. **Practice Mindfulness and Stress Management Techniques:** Engage in daily practices (like deep breathing, mindfulness meditation, or physical exercise) to calm your brain's stress response and promote that calmer sense of balance and well-being.

3. **Reframe Your Mindset to Focus on Growth:** Use affirmations and positive self-talk to shift your perspective. Remind yourself that this challenge is an opportunity to learn, grow, and build a stronger, more confident version of yourself. There is a reason this relationship has ended and, with time, that will become clear. Focus on the controllables and let the uncontrollables go; you always, always, have the power to ask 'what can I control?' and focus on that.

4. **Take Small, Empowering Steps Toward Change:** Once you know what you can control, set small, achievable goals. Whether it's learning a new skill, finding a support group, or creating a new daily routine that brings you joy and purpose, you really can move forward each day.

5. **Build and Lean on Your Support Network:** Actively seek out and connect with supportive individuals who understand your experience. Get in the experts when you need them. From doctor to therapist, there is no shame whatsoever in asking for help. It is perfectly normal (and actually very smart) to get it sorted out. Don't delay, just take a deep breath and take action.

PART 2

CHAPTER TEN

BEYOND THE FRAMEWORK: UNDERSTANDING GENDERED CONFIDENCE

> "Brains reflect the lives they have lived, not just the sex of their owners."
>
> Gina Rippon, Neuroscientist

"I was literally just so upset and he didn't even notice." How many times have you heard a female friend say that (or thought it yourself)? It's then only when the tears come that the man leaps panicked into action, trying to do anything to stop the floodgates. (I generalise, but with a lot of data points on this!). In fact, if men and women understood each other's brains a little bit better, perhaps we could give each other a bit more grace and the world could be a calmer place.

Let's go back to the womb – a great place to start the journey of understanding.

WHERE IT ALL STARTS

Initially, in utero, we all start as females (yes, all you men, you're welcome). Then when the Y (male) chromosome kicks in, there is a surge of testosterone which starts the process of making the male the male. But there is a consequence of this process. This surge actually shrinks the male brain's centres for communication, observation and processing of emotions[1]. So, **the male foetus actually has a physical change to their brain which means they are less able to see the nuances of a sly look, shift in emotion, or notice that uneasiness that a women would**.

I had a great example of this recently. I'd been at my fitness class in Sydney and we were sitting round afterwards having coffee, four guys and me. I noticed the owner looking a bit anxious; something definitely wasn't right.

"You OK, Dan?" I asked.

He took a deep breath. "Yeah. All good."

I asked again, because he clearly wasn't alright.

The guys around me didn't even blink. "Of course, he's fine!" they said, and carried on with their jokes and jibes.

Turns out Dan wasn't fine.

Two weeks later he confided in me that the business nearly went bankrupt. That day had seen him come very close to folding the whole thing.

A similar thing happens with my husband. If I'm upset, he often carries on with what he's doing, whilst in my mind, I'm waiting for acknowledgement for the fury/upset/sadness I'm feeling. Unfortunately, though, his crystal ball is broken, so it's only when I burst into tears that he will rush, concerned and full of hugs. I've learned not to hold it against him and actually be better at confidently communicating what I need.

One evening, I noticed something similar with one of our friends. Something was off and I prompted my husband to check in on him, properly. "He's fine. I didn't even notice anything." I insisted and when they had a proper chat, it turned out he had cancer.

In fact, the science indicates that girls are more wired for connection and being successful in a social group. Even as babies, little girls typically quickly engage, looking for visual cues of reassurance and connection, which is all part of our inbuilt survival mechanisms as we need to be aware of danger. Little boys can happily stare into space, thinking of who-knows-what (if anything) whilst their female counterparts are busy interacting with the world around them. In her wonderful book, *The Female Brain*, Louann Brizendine, MD, explains why this may be useful[2]:

> *"If you can read faces and voices, you can tell what an infant needs. You can predict what a bigger, more aggressive male is going to do. And since you're smaller, you probably need to bond with other females to fend off attacks from a ticked off caveman… or cavemen."*

Essentially, we female cavewomen need to have our wits about us as we are (physically) the weaker sex. We need to notice that thunderous look or shift in pace from a thousand yards, clear off the screaming children and make ourselves scarce. We also need to be super sharp to look after our young, keeping an eye out for snakes, tigers or other predators that may elicit catastrophe. Our brain was built that way, and it still operates like that today.

Consider a mother in a modern-day setting. She's at a busy playground, constantly scanning the environment for potential dangers: an approaching stranger, a child climbing too high, or an unattended bag left nearby. Her ability to pick up on subtle environmental cues might seem like 'over-caution' to some, but it's rooted in evolutionary survival instincts honed over millennia.

As girls grow older, the language they use is collaborative: they make decisions together and avoid stress, conflict and displays of status. "Let's play together." It's about partnering in their interactions and building relationships. It's less about winning, more about the interaction in the game. This may be because females in a bonded social group are more likely to help each other in a time of threat – they are stronger together. Boys, on the other hand, focus on the competition; they want to beat the other, with less focus on or care about what they think of them[2].

First-hand experience has shown me time and time again that this plays through into adults and organisations. I would often see the men compete and argue, with the women able to broker a win-win solution. The men were about empire building, the women just wanted to get the job done.

The point here is that there is a wonderful gift of having a balance of male and female brains creating the greatest outcomes, particularly in teams. This is also very important for a balanced approach to risk, people-matters, clients and the rest of the critical decisions an organisation faces.

So, let's answer the question that keeps on getting asked.

Are men actually more confident than women?

It's now quite an accepted norm that the messages we get when we are younger shape how we see the world. The message for girls tends to be that you are 'good' if you are quiet, polite, don't cause trouble and aren't demanding. For boys, they are expected to be more noisy, boisterous, competitive and loud: 'boys will be boys.' Unfortunately, the outcome we see is a perceived lack of confidence amongst girls.

In our research of over 17,000 people, approximately 21.2% identified themselves as 'male' or 63.3% as 'female' (0.4% identified as LGBTIQ+ and 15.1% preferred not to say). When we look at specifically comparing male and female results, we saw:

33% of women always feel like a failure, vs 28% of men.

41% of women don't speak up in meetings because they doubt themselves, vs 34% of men.

53% of women always compare themselves to others and think they may be more capable or intelligent than them, vs 45% of men.

So, there is a difference in these figures, with women showing less confidence than men, although perhaps not as much as you may have thought. That was certainly what struck me. It's clear from the data that men struggle with confidence too, a lot of the time. So, what could be some of the reasons for a difference in confidence, or rather, the *behaviours* that we see that *demonstrate confidence*? Perhaps the key here is that men (in the words of the book) 'feel the fear and do it anyway'. The science may give us some insights to this confidence conundrum (and if you would like to see more information on our research, please go to the book resources area at www.brainpoweredcoaching.com/book)

THE BRAIN-BODY CONFIDENCE CONNECTION

Testosterone, the hormone most associated with male behaviour, is known to drive risk-taking, aggression, and a greater focus on competition. For example, studies have shown that men with higher testosterone levels are more likely to engage in competitive sports[3], assert dominance in social situations, or take on high-stakes challenges at work, like pitching a bold, new idea to senior management or taking a more aggressive approach[4], even when they don't have all the facts.

In contrast, oestrogen and oxytocin, more prevalent in females, play critical roles in nurturing, bonding, and collaborative behaviour. Oestrogen can enhance emotional processing and the ability to empathise, allowing a woman to understand the emotional states of others and respond with appropriate care. Meanwhile, oxytocin drives the need to connect and collaborate with others.

Think of a project meeting where a male leader, influenced by higher testosterone, may quickly push for a decisive outcome, emphasising speed and competition. In contrast, a female leader might take more time, ensuring everyone's input is considered and aiming for a more inclusive decision that aligns with the group's overall goals. Both approaches have value, but they stem from different hormonal and psychological influences.

Structural Differences in the Brain

Male and female brains don't just differ in hormonal influences, they work differently, too. Research at the University of Pennsylvania[5] used functional Magnetic Resonance Imaging (fMRI) to reveal some incredible evidence. Nearly one thousand brain scans of boys, girls, men, and women, aged eight to twenty-four, showed female brains having much greater activity *between* the two hemispheres (left and right), while male brains primarily functioned front to back, within one hemisphere or the other.

Illustration of fMRI Images of Brain Networks

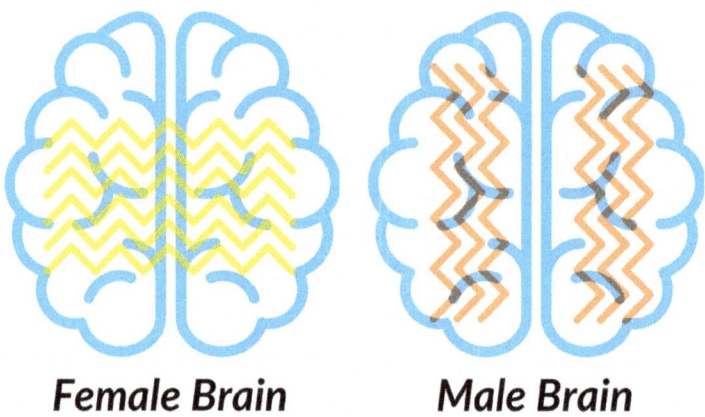

Female Brain **Male Brain**

This seems to imply and back up the experience of men making decisions quickly, looking at a problem from a more binary perspective 'this or that' (often interpreted as being more confident). In contrast, it would suggest the idea that women would look at things from a broader perspective 'both/and', so apparently being slower (and perhaps seen as less confident). In fact, the research implies that the female brain processes across more data points to come to decisions. Both modes of operating have their merits, but a team knowingly taking advantage of a combination of the two will likely be much more powerful than another depending on one alone.

This might play out in a crisis situation: a male firefighter might focus narrowly on the immediate danger, putting out the fire quickly and efficiently. Meanwhile, a female firefighter, processing more data points across both hemispheres, might simultaneously consider multiple factors, the safety of all team members, alternative escape routes, and the potential impact on nearby structures. Neither approach is inherently better; both are crucial for effective problem-solving under pressure.

Beyond the Brain:
Neuroplasticity and Evolving Confidence

It's crucial to understand that these brain differences aren't set in stone. Enter neuroplasticity, the brain's incredible ability to change and adapt throughout life. Both men and women can develop new neural pathways through experience and learning, which can influence their initial predispositions.

Consider a woman who, early in her career, felt hesitant to speak up in meetings dominated by male colleagues. Over time, through conscious practice, feedback, and encouragement (and reading this book!), she develops the confidence to assert her ideas and becomes a leader known for her strong, balanced perspective. Her brain literally rewires itself to support these new behaviours, demonstrating that confidence can be nurtured and enhanced, regardless of your starting point. Everyone has the potential to grow their confidence.

Early Socialisation and Its Lasting Impact

From an early age, the messages we receive shape how we see the world. As we have mentioned, they often say that 'being good' for a young girl looks very different to that for boys. These early social norms often culminate in perceived confidence differences, as girls learn to minimise themselves, while boys are encouraged to take up space and assert themselves.

Picture a classroom scenario where a teacher praises a boy for speaking up loudly and confidently, even if he interrupts, while a girl who waits patiently to be called on may be overlooked. This reinforces the notion that being assertive and dominant is positive for boys, while girls are subtly encouraged to be more reserved.

CULTURAL NORMS AND COGNITIVE BIASES

It's also important to consider the role of cultural norms and stereotypes. Different cultures have varied expectations for gender roles, which in turn shape how confidence is expressed and perceived.

In many Western cultures, confidence is often equated with extroversion and assertiveness – traits which are traditionally associated with masculinity. In contrast, in some Eastern cultures, confidence might be more closely linked to humility, patience, and harmony, which align more with traditionally feminine traits. This can affect how men and women are perceived in leadership roles across different cultural contexts. Confidence across cultures is a whole different book! However, what I do believe is that, no matter where you are from, you still deep down want to be your authentic self.

Cognitive biases, such as stereotype threat (the fear of confirming negative stereotypes) can significantly impact performance and confidence, especially for women in male-dominated fields. Understanding these biases is key to fostering an environment where everyone feels empowered to contribute.

When we look up towards the top of organisations, many of the traits that are valued and rewarded are those of the traditional, hierarchical, white middle-aged male. Sadly, often, the women who are sitting at the table with them have got there because they have had to shape themselves in a similar fashion: 'they may not look like us, but they *act* like us so they can join our club.' This misses out on the fundamental value of neurodiversity (both within gender and beyond it) and hence the opportunity that would exist if you invited different, authentically confident brains around the table.

BRIDGING THE CONFIDENCE GAP IN ORGANISATIONS

"Twelve promotions. One woman. *Twelve*. So, you are telling me that we had eleven men better than all the other women up for Managing Director?" I was on the warpath. My manager was looking uncomfortable as I drew a pie chart of the result, just to ensure the message was getting across.

"They just weren't ready, Caroline. *They weren't good enough.*"

"But *what does good look like?*" I replied. "It looks like white middle-aged male!"

This conversation has echoed in my mind for years and I believe it is a big part of the foundation for the ongoing struggles for gender equality at a senior level.

I saw this several years ago when I decided I wanted to help women within the finance industry with professional coaching. I sat down with each manager and applicant to get feedback on their key development areas: things that were holding them back from being promoted to that next level.

What was interesting was that the feedback came in different wrappers:

- She's not good at presenting.
- She doesn't speak up in meetings.
- She isn't 'seen' at that level.
- She lacks 'gravitas'.
- She's not ready.
- She's not ambitious or hungry.
- She lacks leadership qualities.
- She's not really focused on progression.

The lens through which decisions are being made are often where 'success' looks like the characters and behaviours of the past. Sadly, this is even true for women too. They do not see that they match up to those standards and hence they *believe* the message that they are also not ready. Many of those who are perceived to be modelling confidence, and perhaps demonstrating control, charm and decisiveness, often also show some elements of arrogance, bullying, brashness and perhaps even aggression. Unless this perception of 'what good looks like' changes, the environment is unlikely to change enough to support the incredible power of the *combination* of male and female brains.

While it's clear that confidence levels can differ, it's equally clear that organisations benefit from both male and female strengths. The data is compelling: Studies from three hundred and fifty FTSE companies found that executive committees with at least thirty-three percent female representation had ten times the profit margin of those with fewer women[6]. McKinsey's research[7] found that diverse executive teams were twenty-five percent more likely to financially outperform their peers.

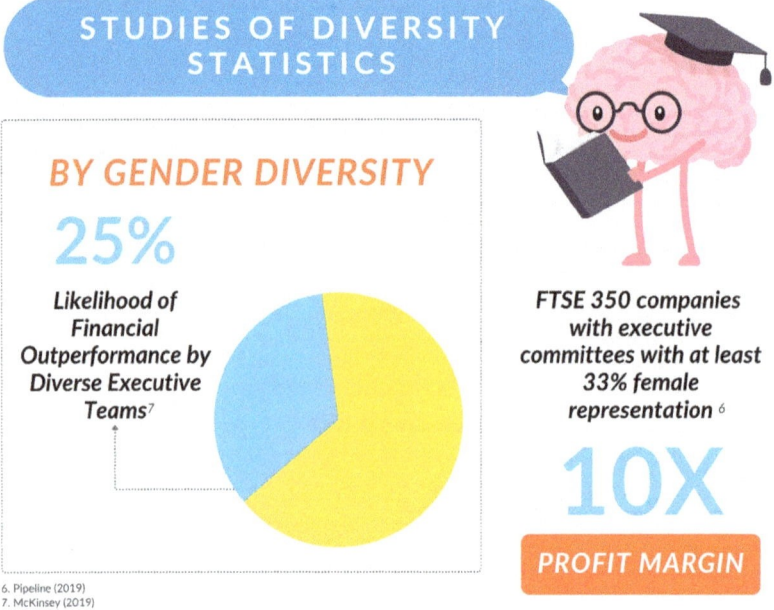

A big 'bang for your buck' also exists in investing in upcoming female leaders. This is the talent not yet at board level, but among the emerging mid-level leaders. It may be those who are weighing up their priorities in regard to family and work: they want to progress but, if they do not feel that the compromise is really worth it, then why bother?

If they can truly grow into their potential and see that it is *worth the effort* (because they see an environment where they are not minimised, taken for granted or their skills undervalued) then they will continue to invest their precious time and talent towards the more senior roles. They will have the confidence to apply for new opportunities and stretch roles, areas that they would have otherwise seen as beyond their capabilities. This is the talent pipeline to feed the precious upper echelons of leadership and inspire those below.

To be clear, this is not about 'fixing the women'. That is a misconception masking the problem at hand. This is not addressing a weakness. It is instead doubling down on and releasing their strengths. Enabling confidence here is about bringing out the deepest level of potential from the female brains in the organisation. It is about lifting the lid on your company's performance. It is about giving the women permission to be themselves and to flourish in that form, not squashed and moulded into an alternative that limits their contribution.

However, achieving true balance goes beyond numbers. It requires a shift in mindset. Confidence needs to be seen as not the person who speaks the loudest or takes the biggest risks. It's also about who brings the most thoughtful insights, who asks the tough questions, stays true to company values and who fosters a culture where everyone feels safe to contribute.

Emotional intelligence (EQ) is the ability to recognise, understand, and manage our emotions and those of others. Research suggests that women, on average, score higher in empathy and interpersonal skills, which are critical components of EQ. A large-scale study done by the University of Cambridge[8], involving nearly three hundred and six thousand people across fifty-seven countries, found that women scored significantly higher in cognitive empathy (the ability to understand others' mental states) compared to men. For example, in a team setting, a female manager might notice a team member is unusually quiet during a meeting and, sensing discomfort, they might later check in privately to ensure everything is okay.

This empathetic approach can build trust and strengthen team cohesion, traits that can sometimes be mistakenly viewed as a lack of confidence but are, in fact, critical to effective leadership. In contrast, men may excel in areas like self-confidence and risk-taking, which are often seen as more visible markers of confidence in traditional leadership roles. This is where bringing together the blend is so important.

Imagine a world where men and women from all backgrounds, with all their brain-based strengths and differences, come together to create the best outcomes-whether in boardrooms, classrooms, or living rooms. To harness the incredible power of both male and female brains, we need to redefine what 'good' looks like.

A successful product development team might include both men who are eager to push the boundaries and take bold risks and women who excel at anticipating customer needs and fostering collaboration. Together, they bring a blend of confidence styles that can drive innovation and create products that truly resonate with the market.

We need environments that encourage everyone, regardless of gender, to bring their full selves to the table. Confidence isn't just a male or female issue – it's a human issue. We all have strengths, and we all have areas where we could use a boost. The challenge, then, is to create spaces where both men and women feel confident to step up, speak out, and share their unique perspectives.

Practical Steps Forward

To get there, we need to invest in immersive and engaging development programs that increase adaptability and foster psychological safety. As McKinsey's research[9] points out, this is crucial for the brains of an organisation to operate at their maximum potential. Psychological safety, defined as 'a shared belief held by members of a team that the team is safe for interpersonal risk-taking'[10] is key.

We can focus on building environments where confidence can grow, where the diverse strengths of male and female brains are seen, valued, and utilised to their fullest potential. Because when we give both women, and men, the permission to be themselves, we unlock a deep ocean of talent that can truly transform organisations and societies alike.

A simple starting point is reframing some of the negative language we use to describe confident women:

Ditch...	Reframe as...	Ditch...	Reframe as...
Arrogant	Confident	Timid	Thoughtful
Bossy	Assertive	Flaky	Flexible
Emotional	Passionate	Overbearing	Detail-oriented
Aggressive	Driven	Gossiping	Communicative
Difficult	Strong-willed	Weak	Persevering
Too sensitive	Empathetic	Lucky	Successful
Overly ambitious	Goal-oriented	Unapproachable	Focused
Overreacting	Responsive	Too independent	Resourceful
Selfish	Self-assured	Cold	Composed

If you're worried about coming across as arrogant, there are some really simple ways you can mitigate that, with our SHARE Model:

SHARE Model
CONFIDENCE... NOT ARROGANCE

S — STAY HUMBLE
Emphasise humility over humiliation. Acknowledge your growth and others' strengths without diminishing yourself.

H — HIGHLIGHT EXPERIENCE, NOT SUPERIORITY
Share the ups and downs and what you've learned from your journey, making your insights relatable and valuable.

A — ASK AND LISTEN
Engage others by asking questions and actively listening, showing genuine interest and confidence in others' contributions.

R — RADIATE OPENESS
Use open body language and an approachable demeanor to convey warmth and invite connection.

E — EMBRACE VULNERABILITY
Be willing to admit mistakes and share your imperfections. This shows real confidence, rooted in self-awareness and a willingness to learn.

Final Word

The next time you face a decision or challenge, if you are a women ask yourself, 'What would a man do?' You might then just access a different, useful perspective. If you're a man, then ask, 'What would a woman do?' The most powerful answer may lie somewhere in between.

KEY CONFIDENCE INSIGHTS

1. **Biological Differences Affect Emotional Perception:** Men and women have different neurological wiring and hormonal influences from birth. Men's brains are less sensitive to emotional cues, while women are more attuned to subtle emotional changes and nonverbal signals due to developmental and hormonal factors.

2. **Early Socialisation Shapes Confidence:** Societal expectations for boys and girls from an early age impact their confidence levels. Boys are encouraged to be bold, competitive, and assertive, while girls are taught to be polite, cooperative, and restrained, leading to perceived confidence gaps.

3. **Hormonal Influences on Behaviour and Decision-Making:** Testosterone in men drives risk-taking and competitiveness, whereas hormones like oestrogen and oxytocin in women enhance emotional processing, empathy, and collaborative behaviour. These differences can manifest in various decision-making and leadership styles. This is why combinations of teams are the key!

4. **Cognitive and Neurological Diversity Benefits Teams:** Teams that balance male and female perspectives, taking advantage of both 'either/or' and 'both/and' brain processing styles, tend to make more informed and holistic decisions, optimising outcomes in organisations and other group settings.

5. **Promoting True Confidence Requires a Cultural Shift:** Encouraging confidence in both men and women involves moving beyond traditional stereotypes, creating environments where diverse strengths are recognised and nurtured. Neuroplasticity shows us that confidence can be developed in both genders over time.

TIME FOR ACTION

1. **Increase Awareness of Biological and Social Differences:** Educate yourself and others about the fundamental differences in male and female brain wiring and how these impact behaviour, communication, and decision-making. Awareness can lead to better empathy and collaboration.

2. **Foster Inclusive Environments**: Promote psychological safety and encourage both men and women to share their unique perspectives and ideas. Support development programs that focus on building confidence, adaptability, and diverse thinking.

3. **Challenge Traditional Gender Norms**: Encourage behaviours in boys and girls that transcend stereotypical expectations, supporting assertiveness in girls and empathy in boys. In professional settings, value a variety of leadership styles beyond the typical male-dominated traits.

4. **Promote Balanced Team Dynamics:** Create teams that leverage both male and female strengths, balancing risk-taking and empathy, competition and collaboration. Recognise the value in diverse decision-making approaches to achieve better outcomes.

5. **Encourage Self-Reflection Across Genders:** Ask yourself how you might approach situations differently by considering the opposite gender's perspective. Women could ask, 'What would a man do?' and men, 'What would a woman do?' to explore new ways of thinking and acting.

CONFIDENCE MASTERCLASS
DR SARAH MCKAY, THE NEUROSCIENTIST'S VIEW

"Confidence is more about how the brain assesses risk and reward."

Dr. Sarah McKay is a neuroscientist specialising in translating brain research into practical insights. She founded Think Brain and directs The Neuroscience Academy, focusing on applied neuroscience. Author of The Women's Brain Book and Baby Brain, she explores how neurobiology impacts women's health and motherhood. Sarah's wonderful work is regularly featured on TV and in major outlets like The Wall Street Journal and The Guardian.

In the interview with Dr. Sarah McKay, we explored her deep insights into the neuroscience of women's health and also on the broader differences, and surprising similarities, between male and female brains.

While male and female brains develop differently due to hormonal influences, particularly during puberty, Sarah was keen to stress that these differences are far subtler than many people believe. "Everyone likes to talk about male brains versus female brains, but the truth is, there's a huge overlap," she points out. The Y chromosome triggers the formation of testes in the male embryo, which then starts producing testosterone. Interestingly, Sarah explained that testosterone in the male brain is actually converted into oestrogen, which masculinises the brain. "It's wild," she said. "Testosterone is turned into oestrogen in the male brain, and it's oestrogen that masculinises it to respond to testosterone later in life."

Sarah also reflected on how the societal environment can exaggerate or diminish these gender differences. "So much of what shapes boys and girls is their social environment," she explained. As children enter puberty, the brain begins to develop in line with the hormonal changes that come with adolescence. However, the structural changes between male and female brains are not as pronounced as the way these changes influence behaviours, especially around risk-taking.

These can often be influenced by social contexts rather than just brain development. "Both boys and girls need courage during adolescence," she noted, "but boys might show it more through physical bravado, like jumping off cliffs or taking dangerous risks, while girls might take social risks, like speaking up or engaging in challenging relationships." While society tends to view physical risks as more dangerous, Sarah points out that social risks can carry equally significant consequences for girls. "Teenagers can make cool, rational decisions when they're alone, but peer pressure and the need for social approval lead to more risk-taking when they're in groups."

So, is risk-taking connected to confidence? Sarah agreed, but with nuance: "Risk-taking can definitely be seen as an element of confidence, but it's about context. A teenager standing up to give a speech may look confident, but really, it's about having the courage to take that social risk." She emphasised that confidence is more about how the brain assesses risk and reward, rather than a specific brain area being responsible for it.

Sarah is not afraid of failure, viewing it as an opportunity to learn and improve. In fact, she recalls a moment of what she jokingly calls "reverse imposter syndrome" when she was asked to narrate the audiobook version of her second book. After several attempts, the publisher hired a professional voice actor instead, but Sarah turned the experience into a funny story. "If I fail, that's fine. I'll turn it into a story," she says, embodying the resilience and confidence she encourages in others.

Sarah's closing thought captures her positive and reflective mindset: **"Today is the good old days."** It reminds us to cherish every moment and recognise that, even amid challenges, we will look back on these times fondly.

Sarah's Top Tips for Confidence

1. **Practice confidence like a muscle** – Repeatedly putting yourself in challenging situations builds resilience.
2. **Turn failures into stories** – Embrace failure as a learning experience and move forward.
3. **Take social risks to grow** – Build confidence by taking small social risks, like speaking up or stepping out of your comfort zone.
4. **Be present in your body** – Focus on physical presence to avoid overthinking.
5. **The audience wants you to succeed** – Remind yourself that others are supportive and rooting for your success.

CHAPTER ELEVEN

> Everyone shines, given the right lighting.
> For some, it's a Broadway spotlight;
> for others, a lamp-lit desk.
>
> Susan Cain

One of the most common areas I get asked questions is around introversion and confidence:

- What if I'm an introvert? How can I succeed in a world of extroverts?
- Do I need to be extroverted to be confident?
- Does confidence = being loud?
- What happens if I'm shy?

Let's start with the difference between extroverts and introverts, which are often misunderstood:

QUIET VS. BOLD

Introverts are like batteries – they carry a steady charge but need time to plug in and recharge themselves after use. They shine brightest in calm, controlled settings where they can focus and recharge their energy in solitude or with a trusted few. They're not afraid of connection, but they prefer smaller, meaningful interactions rather than spreading themselves thin.

Think of them as slow and steady builders – they take their time, reflect deeply, and craft ideas or relationships with care. Their strength lies in staying grounded and seeing things from a thoughtful, nuanced perspective.

For introverts, confidence builds quietly through preparation, reflection, and a sense of inner alignment. They often feel most confident when they've had the chance to prepare, whether practising a speech, doing research before a meeting, or planning their approach to a social situation.

Although they may not be the loudest voice in the room, introverts' confidence shines in thoughtful contributions and deeply considered actions. For them, confidence comes from knowing they've done the work and staying true to themselves, even in a noisy world.

Extroverts are like solar panels – they draw energy from the world around them. The more stimulation and interaction they receive, the more energised and dynamic they become. They thrive in environments filled with activity, movement, and people, whether it's a bustling office or a lively social event.

They're the first to intervene, make connections, and keep the momentum going. Their gift is their ability to draw on the world's energy and radiate it back out, inspiring action and excitement wherever they go.

Extroverts often feel most confident when they're in the middle of the action – brainstorming ideas with a group, getting positive reactions from an audience, or simply feeding off the energy of a lively environment.

Their confidence is outward-facing, often expressed through boldness, spontaneity, and an eagerness to engage. For extroverts, confidence thrives in connection and movement – it's about the energy they give and receive in the moment.

The key difference? It's all about energy and stimulation. Introverts get their best ideas and energy in quiet, reflective spaces, while extroverts light up in the buzz and chaos of the world around them.

Neither is better – each brings its own kind of power to the table.

Speaking from an extrovert's perspective, it's rare that my brain doesn't have some thought, opinion, question or point to make! It's not always terribly well thought through, but it can sometimes feel like I have to get it out, which may be seen as confidence. The introvert in the room may be listening much more intently to the discussion and, hence, can analyse, assimilate and only then, take well-directed action (whatever that is). Notice the difference: one person blabbering away and another talking clearly and concisely at the right moment.

Introverts: Please know that you have great superpowers, and your confidence will improve if you recognise those strengths.

Here are some of the world's most remarkable introverts:

- Barack Obama: Despite his incredible charisma, Obama identifies as an introvert, preferring reflection and preparation in his leadership style.
- Taylor Swift: Known for her introspective and powerful songwriting, Swift has described herself as naturally introverted, finding energy in creative expression.
- Mahatma Gandhi: A deeply introspective leader, Gandhi drew his strength from quiet reflection and inspired millions with his thoughtful, nonviolent approach.
- Marissa Mayer: The former CEO of Yahoo has spoken about being an introvert and how it helped her focus on solving complex problems.
- J.K. Rowling: The author of Harry Potter famously conceived her magical world during a quiet train ride. She's shared that her introversion helps her to focus and write.
- Bill Gates: The co-founder of Microsoft attributes his success to his ability to focus and think deeply, qualities often linked to introversion.

These people are still extraordinary leaders in their field, without having to be extroverted. Authentic confidence doesn't have to shout to be heard – it's about leaning into who you are and trusting your natural strengths.

In 'Quiet: The Power of Introverts in a World That Can't Stop Talking',[1] Susan Cain says:

> *"There's zero correlation between being the best talker and having the best ideas."*

She reminds us that confidence isn't reserved for the loudest voice in the room. For introverts, it's about recognising that your quiet thoughtfulness, creativity, deep focus, and ability to connect meaningfully are your superpowers. You don't need to fake extroversion or force yourself to fit into someone else's mould to be confident. Learn to trust who you are more through doing the reflection exercises in this book – because the more you know yourself, the more you will trust yourself and your unique capabilities.

If you are an introvert, you can build genuine confidence by preparing, reflecting, leaning into your natural abilities and showing up authentically. It's not about competing with others' energy – it's about trusting that your calm, steady presence is powerful, valuable, and precisely what the world needs. Remember what Kim Winser OBE said at the start of this book: *it should not be about how others perceive you, but how you feel inside.*

THE QUIET MODEL

Here's my QUIET model that you can use to help build that confidence and show the world your brilliance – they deserve to see it!

Final word

Confidence doesn't require a spotlight; it grows quietly and steadily from self-awareness and authenticity. For introverts, the power lies not in becoming louder but in embracing their unique voice – and trusting that it's more than enough.

the CONFIDENT INTROVERT
QUIET Model

Q — QUALITY OVER QUANTITY
Focus on meaningful interactions rather than trying to be everywhere or say everything. When you do speak, aim for substance and depth, which often resonates more powerfully.

U — USE PREPARATION
Preparing ahead of time can help you feel grounded and ready to share valuable insights. Having key points thought out can boost your confidence and show you're thoughtful and prepared.

I — INTENTIONAL LISTENING
This is your superpower! Your insights will be unique because of this ability to listen, analyse and make critical observations or recommendations.

E — EMBRACE AUTHENTICITY
Be genuine in your interactions, speaking at your natural pace and avoiding the pressure to be louder or extroverted. Authenticity is one of the most respected forms of confidence.

T — TRUST YOUR PRESENCE
Even without many words, your presence—calm body language, strong posture, and thoughtful eye contact—conveys confidence. Trust that these subtleties speak volumes about your self-assurance.

CHAPTER TWELVE

> " What lies behind us and what lies before us are tiny matters compared to what lies within us. "

Henry Stanley Haskins

TAKE THAT FIRST STEP FORWARD

As we reach this final chapter in our journey together, take a moment to pause and breathe.

You've made it through the pages of this book, but the real journey is just beginning. This is where theory meets practice and where understanding meets action. The truth is, confidence isn't something we arrive at – it's something we build, step by step, with every choice we make, every risk we take, and every challenge we embrace.

Our brain is an incredible tool, constantly evolving, adapting, and learning. But it's also a creature of habit. For years, it may have been conditioned to avoid risks, stay safe, and protect us from failure. So, now it's time to rewire by taking those steps. Remember, our brain's survival instincts, like the 'amygdala hijack', aren't there to hold us back. They're there to protect us. Now, armed with lots of knowledge and a bucketload of tools, you can recognise those moments when fear tries to take the wheel. You can consciously choose to override that autopilot, to breathe deeply, and to step forward with intention, confidence and purpose.

Your confidence is a muscle. Just like any other muscle, it grows stronger with use. The more you practise confident thinking, the more those neural pathways will strengthen. And here's the beautiful part: every single one of us has the power to shape our brains. You are not at the mercy of your past experiences or your doubts. You are the architect of your future. Every time we go to Confidence Gym and exercise, we get stronger!

EMBRACE THE JOURNEY OF GROWTH

Confidence is not a destination; it's a journey of growth. It's about believing in your ability to figure things out. It's about showing up for yourself again and again, even when the path isn't clear. It's about accepting that mistakes are a part of the process, not the end of the road. Remember, you are *guaranteed failure* if you don't even try!

Each time you push past your comfort zone, you're sending a powerful message to your brain: 'I can do this. I am capable.' Whether it's speaking up in a meeting, pursuing a new job, or simply choosing to be unapologetically yourself, every action builds the muscle of confidence. Take those micro confidence challenges and I promise, you will be so pleasantly surprised.

Think of it like our '5A Confidence Formula' Iceberg. Your physical and mental attributes as well as your abilities: your skills, competencies and talents, are just the tip. This is where most people think confidence starts and ends. But the real magic happens beneath the surface, through awareness of your thoughts, your beliefs, and your values. When you live in a way that honours who you really are and truly accept your authenic self and then move into action; your confidence will flourish.

CONFIDENT

5A CONFIDENCE FORMULA

1. ABILITIES
2. ATTRIBUTES
   ➕
3. AWARENESS
4. ACCEPTANCE
5. ACT & ADAPT

TRUE CONFIDENCE IS...

Remember the tools we've covered: the power of the physiological sigh to calm your nerves, the strength that comes from celebrating your successes, and the transformative practice of gratitude, and so much more. Use them. Lean on them. They are here to support you as you step into your next chapter.

> *"Don't be afraid to fail. Be afraid not to try."*
> *Nelson Mandela*

YOUR NEXT STEPS: MOVING FROM KNOWING TO DOING

Now, it's time to act. If you haven't already, make sure you work through the exercises in this book. They will provide you with the foundation you need for unstoppable confidence.

Reflect on Your Values: What matters most to you? Are you living in a way that aligns with those values? Use this clarity to guide your decisions and actions. When you live in alignment with your values, confidence becomes second nature.

Celebrate Every Win: Big or small, celebrate it. Your brain thrives on recognition. Each celebration builds a stronger belief in your abilities and reinforces the neural pathways of confidence.

Practise Self-Compassion: Be kind to yourself. Confidence doesn't mean never feeling fear or doubt; it means having those feelings and moving forward anyway. Recognise that self-doubt is a natural part of the process. Treat yourself with the same compassion you would offer a friend.

Build Your Resilience: Remember, confidence is about being able to say, "I don't know how this will go, but I trust myself to handle whatever comes." Life will throw curveballs. Your strength lies in your ability to adapt, to learn, and to grow. Doing the life timeline exercise will really help with this, as well as exercises like the energy audit and building some better boundaries. So, I recommend you revisit them now if you skipped over them as you read.

Learn from the Masterclasses: What stories and lessons did you resonate with most? What are the top tips you are going to try out? There is so much wisdom from these people. Absorb and put into practice whatever feels authentic to you.

Taking Bold Action: What is one thing you've been holding back on? What is one step, however small, that you can take today that will move you toward the person you want to be? What would you do if you weren't afraid?

Your **Confidence Action Plan** is your next step on the Confident pathway to achieving your goals and building true, authentic confidence. You've got the tools and learnings from this book, now this is about putting it into action, so you have some clear steps to making progress.

You can download the different formats for the Confidence Action Plan on my website www.brainpoweredcoaching.com/book, but the key points to consider are in the confidence action plan diagram.

Don't wait for the perfect moment, because it doesn't exist. Start now. Begin messy, start scared, but begin.

BELIEVE IN YOUR ABILITY TO FIGURE IT OUT

Life is not about having all the answers. It's about having the courage to start, to try, to fail, and to try again. Your confidence grows each time you step into the unknown with the belief that you have what it takes to figure it out.

So, as you close this book, remember that this is not an end, but a beginning. You are stepping into a future filled with possibility. You have the tools, the knowledge, and most importantly, the power to create a life that truly reflects who you are.

This is your time.

Embrace your uniqueness.

Trust in your journey.

Take bold, courageous steps toward the life you truly want.

You have everything you need within you.

And remember,

Confidence is not about being perfect. It's about being authentically, powerfully, unapologetically YOU.

CONFIDENCE ACTION PLAN

LIST YOUR VALUES

🚩	**GOAL**	What is my big goal? (be specific)
☔	**FEAR**	What am I frightened of that is stopping me from starting the goal? What is the worst thing that could happen?
🔍	**EVIDENCE**	What evidence there to support this fear? How likely is it to happen on a scale of 1-10?
✓	**LIKELIHOOD**	Likelihood that I could produce at least a moderately good outcome from 1-10? Have others done this before & pulled it off?
🏷️	**COST OF INACTION**	What does it cost me if I don't take this step? Financially, emotionally & physically - where will I be in 1, 5, 10 years
🏆	**WIN FROM INACTION**	What do I win by overcoming this? Financially, emotionally & physically - where will I be in 1, 5, 10 years
?	**IF... THEN**	What is my If.... THEN plan? Prepare for obstacles that may come up with an If x happens then I will do Y
⚙️	**PEOPLE & TOOLS**	Who and which tools I can I use to help me? e.g. Circle of Control, 54321, Inner Critic, Hacks

TARGET DELIVERY DATE

DEAR READER

Firstly, thank you. Time is our most precious commodity, so thank you for taking the time to read this book. It is greatly appreciated and I really hope you have found it worthwhile. If you found this useful, I would greatly appreciate a quick **review**. It would mean a lot to me and hopefully will enable others to find this message too. You can find the link for this and all your **additional book resources (workbooks, research and much more)** here:

www.brainpoweredcoaching.com/book

Secondly, I encourage you to spread the word, because confidence has a ripple effect. When others look up and see you taking risks, speaking up and being authentic, you will inspire them to do the same.

This book is the result of years of research, personal reflection, and heartfelt conversations. I've done my best to ensure the information is accurate and thoughtfully presented. That said, I'm human – and so is this book. If anything here feels unclear, incomplete, or doesn't quite land with you, I ask for your kindness and understanding. My intention is to inspire and empower, not to prescribe or assume every idea will resonate perfectly. Your journey is unique, and while I hope this book serves as a valuable guide, it's not a substitute for professional advice or support. Take what feels right, leave the rest, and always trust your own instincts.

Finally, my challenge to you is this: get out there and keep trying those Micro Confidence Challenges, whether it be:

- Speaking up in a meeting
- Standing up for someone
- Going to a networking event
- Asking a question
- Saying No
- Going for a role or project you wouldn't have done before.

Connect with Caroline

www.brainpoweredcoaching.com

@brainpoweredcoaching

www.linkedin.com/in/caroline-brewin

To get regular inspiration, confidence tips and encouragement, sign up for our weekly newsletter at www.brainpoweredcoaching.com

Grab all the good stuff here

ABOUT THE AUTHOR

Caroline Brewin is a former corporate leader turned entrepreneur, with a passion for helping others unlock their inner confidence. For eighteen years, she navigated the high-stakes, predominantly male world of Investment Banking, a challenging environment that shaped her resilience, leadership, and drive. Leading global teams and inspiring them to reach their full potential was her true joy, but it wasn't until a coach pointed out, "Have you considered coaching? You're already doing it," that she realised her true calling.

This sparked a new chapter in Caroline's life, leading her to launch Brain Powered Coaching, where she now helps women, men and leaders transform self-doubt into self-belief. Drawing from her own struggles, successes and raw moments, Caroline created **Confident** as a guide for those who feel alone on their confidence journey. It is a book filled with practical insights, hard-won lessons, and a reminder that no one should have to shrink because of fear.

Her mission? To empower one million people by 2034, especially women, to live boldly, embrace change, and step fully into their confident power.

Thank you for being part of this movement.

ACKNOWLEDGEMENTS

There are many contributions to creating this wonderful picture of where I am now. The first thank you is, undoubtedly, to my amazing parents, Adrienne and Peter. They gave me an incredible foundation of self-belief, core values and positivity, whatever life throws my way. They taught me to work hard, try anything, and smile while doing it all. Their energetic, caring, 'yes' approach to life is incredibly inspiring and appreciated by anyone who meets them. Thank you for everything – I couldn't have done it without you.

Secondly, to my wonderful husband, George. Despite your own remarkable success, the way you support me in this journey, with pride and joy, is appreciated more than you know. I'm so grateful for your patience as I tap away, create whiteboards out of cupboards and make Post-it note shrines around the house. Thank you for giving me the confidence to continue and thrive on this voyage with you by my side.

To the rest of my family: your unwavering support and positivity have made this adventure so much easier. I feel incredibly lucky to have your enthusiasm cheering me on at every step.

None of this would have started without my coach, Sian, who introduced me to the world of coaching and supported me through the toughest times of my life. She challenged me to see my potential and gave me many of the insights I needed to write this book.

My neuroscience passion wouldn't have been ignited without Professor Paul Brown; dearly missed from this world, but still felt from the next. We still feel the ripples today of his extraordinary insights and passion for transforming coaching through applied neuroscience. I sincerely hope he approves of this book, given his influence is woven through its pages.

To the Masterclass interviewees throughout the book; I'm very grateful for your insights and generous time in giving them. I know that people will benefit so much from these vignettes of wisdom from each of your amazing lives, thank you.

To my Brain Powered team, particularly Liane and Trixie, thank you for the work you do and all you've done to make this book possible. Trixie - your magic in the illustrations for this book in particular is hugely appreciated.

Finally, to my wonderful friends - you know who you are – thank you for being an unwavering source of support throughout this journey. From surviving and leaving corporate life, to building a business, to reviewing book covers, sharing recommendations, and giving honest feedback – you've brought so much sparkle and inspiration into my life. I am so lucky to have you.

GLOSSARY

1. **Amygdala** – A small, almond-shaped part of the brain located deep within the temporal lobes. It is responsible for processing emotions such as fear and aggression. The amygdala is part of the limbic system and is crucial for triggering the body's fight-or-flight response (the brain's smoke alarm).

2. **Amygdala Hijack** – A term used to describe the process when the amygdala, the brain's emotional centre, takes over control from the logical prefrontal cortex in response to a perceived threat, resulting in an emotional response that is disproportionate to the situation.

3. **Autonomic Nervous System (ANS)** – A part of the peripheral nervous system that controls involuntary bodily functions, such as heart rate, blood pressure, digestion, and respiratory rate. It operates automatically without conscious effort and is divided into two main branches, the Parasympathetic Nervous System (PNS) and Sympathetic Nervous System (SNS).

4. **Boundaries** – Personal rules or limits that protect your time, energy, and wellbeing. Setting and maintaining boundaries ensures you're prioritising what matters most and avoiding burnout.

5. **Brain Fog** – A common symptom during perimenopause and menopause, characterised by forgetfulness, with a lack of concentration or mental clarity. It is linked to hormonal fluctuations, particularly changes in oestrogen, which affect neurotransmitter levels and brain function.

6. **Change Curve** – A model that illustrates the stages individuals typically go through when facing change or transition. Commonly adapted from the Kübler-Ross Grief Cycle, the stages include Denial, Anger, Bargaining, Depression, and Acceptance. Understanding the Change Curve helps people navigate and manage change more effectively, both personally and professionally.

7. **Cognitive Behavioural Therapy (CBT)** – A form of psychological treatment that focuses on changing negative patterns of thinking and behaviour. CBT helps individuals identify and reframe unhelpful thoughts and beliefs, leading to more adaptive emotional responses and actions.

8. **Cognitive Bias** – Systematic patterns of deviation from norm or rationality in judgment. These biases often influence decision-making and can affect confidence by reinforcing negative thought patterns.

9. **Cognitive Reappraisal** – The process of changing one's interpretation of a situation to alter its emotional impact. This technique is used in cognitive-behavioural therapy to manage stress and anxiety.

10. **Cortisol** – The body's primary stress hormone, released by the adrenal glands. Cortisol helps regulate metabolism, inflammation, and the body's response to stress. However, chronic high levels can impair cognitive function and suppress immune responses.

11. **Diversity, Equity & Inclusion (DEI)** – A framework and organisational practice that promotes a diverse workforce, equitable opportunities, and an inclusive environment where everyone feels valued and respected. DEI aims to address systemic inequalities and create spaces where people from all backgrounds can thrive.

12. **Default Mode Network (DMN)** – A brain network that becomes active when the mind is at rest and not focused on external tasks. The DMN is associated with self-referential thought, daydreaming, and rumination.

13. **Dopamine** – A neurotransmitter involved in motivation, pleasure, and reward.

14. **Emotional Regulation** – The ability to influence and manage one's emotional state. This includes strategies to control the intensity, duration, and type of emotion experienced, contributing to emotional stability and resilience.

15. **Evolutionary Facts:**
    - **Evolutionary Fact 1:** Our brain prioritises energy for a survival response.
    - **Evolutionary Fact 2:** Our brain is wired to notice danger (negativity) more than positivity.
    - **Evolutionary Fact 3:** Our brain sees a lack of control as dangerous.
    - **Evolutionary Fact 4:** Our brain wants to be part of a tribe.

16. **Executive Functioning** – This refers to a set of mental skills that include working memory, flexible thinking, and self-control. These

processes help people manage their behaviour, plan for the future, and regulate emotions.

17. **Extrovert** – Extroversion is a personality trait typically characterized by outgoingness, high energy, and/or talkativeness. In general, the term refers to a state of being where someone "recharges," or draws energy, from being with other people.

18. **Fear Response** – This is a physiological reaction initiated by the amygdala when a threat is perceived. This response can include increased heart rate, rapid breathing, and heightened focus, preparing the body to 'fight, flight, freeze, faint, or fawn.'
    - **Fight:** Confronting the threat.
    - **Flight:** Running away from the threat.
    - **Freeze:** Becoming temporarily paralysed by fear.
    - **Faint:** Passing out as a last resort survival mechanism.
    - **Fawn:** People-pleasing or appeasing behaviour to pacify the threat.

19. **Fixed Mindset** – A belief that abilities and intelligence are static and cannot be changed. People with a fixed mindset tend to avoid challenges and view effort as fruitless, leading to stagnation in personal growth.

20. **fMRI (Functional Magnetic Resonance Imaging)** – This is a neuroimaging technique that measures brain activity by detecting changes in blood flow. fMRI is used to identify which areas of the brain are active during certain tasks, providing insights into cognitive functions and emotional responses.

21. **Growth Mindset** – A belief that abilities and intelligence can be developed through dedication, effort, and learning. This mindset encourages embracing challenges and persistence in the face of setbacks, ultimately leading to improved outcomes.

22. **Hot Flashes** – A sudden feeling of warmth that spreads over the body, often most intense in the head and neck areas. It is one of the most common symptoms of menopause, caused by changes in the body's temperature regulation due to declining oestrogen levels.

23. **Hypothalamus** – A small region of the brain that controls many bodily functions, including temperature regulation. During menopause,

changes in oestrogen levels can affect the hypothalamus, leading to hot flashes and night sweats.

24. **Imposter Syndrome** – A psychological pattern in which individuals doubt their accomplishments and fear being exposed as a fraud, despite evidence of their competence and success. This leads to persistent self-doubt and anxiety.

25. **Inner Critic** – The negative, internal voice that criticises, judges, and undermines one's self-worth and abilities. The inner critic often triggers self-doubt, perfectionism, and feelings of inadequacy. Managing this inner dialogue is crucial for building confidence and self-compassion.

26. **Introvert** – Introversion is a basic personality style characterized by a preference for the inner life of the mind over the outer world of other people. Introverts do not fear or dislike others, and they are neither shy nor plagued by loneliness. They enjoy one-on-one engagement in calm environments, which is more suited to the make-up of their nervous system. Evidence suggests that, unlike with extroverts, the brains of introverts do not react strongly to viewing novel human faces; in such situations they produce less dopamine, a neurotransmitter associated with reward.

27. **Limbic System** – This is a complex system of nerves and networks in the brain, including the amygdala, hippocampus, and hypothalamus. It is involved in emotion, memory, and the regulation of autonomic functions, such as heart rate and blood pressure.

28. **Matrescence** – The process of becoming a mother, akin to adolescence in its psychological, physical, and social changes. This term acknowledges the profound identity shift and the impact on confidence that motherhood brings.

29. **Meditation** – A mental practice that involves focusing attention, often through techniques such as deep breathing, visualisation, or repetitive chanting, to achieve a state of mental clarity, relaxation, and heightened awareness. Meditation is used to reduce stress, promote emotional health, and enhance mindfulness by training the mind to observe thoughts and feelings without judgment. Regular practice has been shown to improve concentration, reduce anxiety, and support overall well-being.

30. **Menopause** – The stage of life when a woman's menstrual cycles permanently cease, defined as having gone 12 consecutive months without a period. It typically occurs between the ages of 45 and 55 and is caused by a natural decline in reproductive hormones.

31. **Menopausal Hormone Therapy (MHT)** – Previously referred to as Hormone Replacement Therapy (HRT), MHT involves the administration of hormones by a medical professional to alleviate menopausal symptoms such as hot flashes, night sweats, and bone density loss.

32. **Mindfulness** – The practice of being fully present in the moment and aware of one's thoughts, feelings, and surroundings without judgment. Mindfulness helps reduce stress, improve emotional regulation, and increase overall mental well-being.

33. **Mirror Neurons** – Specialised neurons that fire both when an individual performs an action and when they observe someone else performing the same action. Mirror neurons are thought to play a role in empathy, learning, and social interactions.

34. **Negativity Bias** – The brain's tendency to pay more attention to and be influenced by negative experiences than positive ones. This bias can lead to placing too much emphasis on setbacks and criticism, impacting confidence and mental well-being.

35. **Neural Pathways** – Networks of neurons connected by synapses, allowing information to be transmitted throughout the brain. Repeated thoughts and behaviours strengthen these pathways, forming habits over time.

36. **Neurodiversity** – The concept that variations in brain function and behaviour, such as autism, ADHD, and dyslexia, are natural differences rather than deficits. Neurodiversity promotes understanding and acceptance of these differences, advocating for inclusive environments that leverage diverse ways of thinking.

37. **Neuroplasticity** – The brain's ability to change, adapt, and reorganise itself by forming new neural connections throughout life. Neuroplasticity is fundamental to learning new skills, overcoming challenges, and recovering from injuries.

38. **Neurotransmitters** – Chemical messengers in the brain that transmit signals between neurons. Examples include:

1. **Adrenaline (Epinephrine):** Both a hormone and neurotransmitter associated with the body's stress response.
2. **Dopamine**: Associated with reward, motivation, and pleasure.
3. **Serotonin**: Involved in mood regulation and emotional stability.

27. **Oestrogen** – A key hormone in the female reproductive system that regulates the menstrual cycle and supports various body functions. During menopause, fluctuating oestrogen levels lead to symptoms such as hot flushes, night sweats, and changes in mood.

28. **Oestrogen Receptors** – Proteins located throughout the body and brain that bind to oestrogen, enabling its effects on various tissues. During menopause, the decline in oestrogen affects these receptors, contributing to a wide range of symptoms.

29. **Oxytocin** – Often called the 'love hormone', oxytocin is associated with social bonding, trust, and emotional connection. It is released during childbirth and positive social interactions, enhancing feelings of trust and security.

30. **Parasympathetic Nervous System (PNS)** – The branch of the autonomic nervous system responsible for 'rest-and-digest' activities. It is the brake. It promotes relaxation, reduces stress, and restores the body to a state of calm after a stressor has passed.

31. **Perimenopause** – The transition period before menopause when a woman's ovaries gradually begin to produce less oestrogen. This stage can start in a woman's 30s or 40s and can be marked by irregular menstrual cycles, mood changes, and other physical and emotional symptoms.

32. **Physiological Sigh** – A natural breathing technique where two short inhales through the nose are followed by a long exhale through the mouth. This method is known to quickly reduce stress levels by rebalancing oxygen and carbon dioxide in the body.

33. **Post-Menopause** – The stage after menopause has occurred. Post-menopause is marked by lower hormone levels and an increased risk for certain health conditions, such as osteoporosis and cardiovascular disease, due to reduced oestrogen levels.

34. **Prefrontal Cortex (PFC)** – The region at the front of the brain responsible for executive functions, such as decision-making,

problem-solving, emotional regulation, and impulse control. The PFC is crucial for maintaining rational thought and controlling impulses.

35. **Reticular Activating System (RAS)** – A network of neurons in the brainstem that regulates wakefulness, attention, and arousal. The RAS filters incoming stimuli, determining what information is important and should reach our conscious awareness.

36. **Self-Efficacy** – The belief in one's ability to succeed in specific situations or achieve a desired outcome. High self-efficacy is linked to increased motivation and resilience.

37. **Serotonin** – A neurotransmitter that influences mood, sleep, and cognitive function.

38. **Stress Inoculation** – A psychological technique used to prepare individuals to cope with future stress by exposing them to manageable levels of stress in a controlled environment. It involves teaching coping mechanisms and mental strategies that 'inoculate' the person against stress, similar to how a vaccine works for physical health.

39. **Survival Brain (Reptilian Brain)** The oldest part of the brain, responsible for instinctual behaviours, such as aggression, dominance, and territoriality. It controls basic functions, like heart rate, breathing, and the fight-or-flight response.

40. **Sympathetic Nervous System (SNS)** - Part of the autonomic nervous system responsible for the body's 'fight-or-flight'. This is the accelerator.

41. **Testosterone** – A steroid hormone present in both males and females, though in higher quantities in males. It is associated with traits such as assertiveness, confidence, and risk-taking. Fluctuations in testosterone levels can impact mood, energy, and behaviour.

42. **Values** – Core beliefs or principles that guide an individual's behaviour, decisions, and sense of purpose. Values shape what a person stands for and act as a moral compass, influencing how they approach life, relationships, and career choices. In the context of confidence, living in alignment with one's values creates a sense of authenticity and integrity, serving as a foundation for making confident decisions.

NOTES

Chapter 1: Confident Foundations

1. "In Brain Powered Coaching's 2024 research, we surveyed over 17,000 people about their confidence levels and found overwhelmingly that this was something people struggled with."

   Reference: Brain Powered Coaching (2024). *Confidence Survey Results*, Brain Powered Coaching.

2. Oxford English Dictionary defines it as: "An appreciation of one's own abilities, qualities, or judgment."

   Reference: Oxford University Press (2024). *Oxford English Dictionary*. Available at: https://www.oed.com .

3. "Psychologist Richard Petty said, 'Confidence is the stuff that turns thoughts into action.'"

   Reference: Petty, R. (2012). *The Power of Confidence: Actionable Insights.* New York: HarperCollins.

4. "Professor Ian Robertson is a clinical psychologist and neuroscientist. He speaks of this 'action' element in his book, *How Confidence Works*."

   Reference: Robertson, I. (2015). *How Confidence Works: The Neuroscience of Confidence and Success.* New York: Doubleday.

5. "This limited 25 watts of energy gets funnelled to the part of the brain that needs it most."

   Reference: Brown, P. (2012). *Neuropsychology for Coaches: Understanding the Basics.* Open University Press.

6. "Shawn Achor's research, in *The Happiness Advantage*, shows that a positive brain is 31% more productive than a brain at negative, neutral, or stressed."

   Reference: Achor, S. (2010). *The Happiness Advantage: The Seven Principles of Positive Psychology That Fuel Success and Performance at Work.* New York: Crown Business.

7. "According to Bandura, people with low self-confidence tend to…"

   Reference: Bandura, A. (1997). Self-Efficacy: The Exercise of Control. W.H. Freeman and Company.

8. "Pipeline (2019)"

   Reference: Women count 2019: Role, value, and number of female executives in the FTSE 350. Available at: https://execpipeline.com/wp-content/uploads/2020/12/The-Pipeline-Women-Count-2019.pdf

9. "The career ladder has a 'broken rung' that stops women from climbing up. This concept has been part of the **McKinsey** *Women in the Workplace* **report since 2021.**"

   Reference: McKinsey & Company and LeanIn.Org (2021). *Women in the Workplace 2021*. Available at: https://wiw-report.s3.amazonaws.com/Women_in_the_Workplace_2021.pdf.

10. "The excellent book *The Confidence Code* talks to research by Brigham Young University and Princeton that found women speak 75% less than men when in the minority."

    Reference: Kay, K., & Shipman, C. (2014). *The Confidence Code: The Science and Art of Self-Assurance –What Women Should Know*. Harper Business.

11. "Dr. Andrew Huberman calls the 'Physiological Sigh' a natural technique where two short inhales through the nose are followed by a long exhale through the mouth. This method is known to quickly reduce stress levels."

    Reference: Huberman, A. (2021). *'Physiological Sigh'*. Huberman Lab Podcast.

Chapter 2: Own Your Journey

1. "These emotions, can be distilled into 8 core emotions: fear, anger, disgust, shame, sadness, surprise/startle, love/trust, excitement/joy, 1.

   Reference: *The London Protocol of the Emotions*. ION Consulting International Pte Ltd 2023

2. "Negativity bias suggests that 60%-70% of the thoughts we have are those associated with 'escape' or 'survival' emotions."

   Reference: Raghunathan, R. (2013) 'How negative is your 'mental chatter'?' Available at: https://www.psychologytoday.com/gb/blog/sapient-nature/201310/how-negative-is-your-mental-chatter:contentReference{index=0}.

3. "Psychologist and speaker Dr. Ivan Joseph calls it a 'Brag Letter', a powerful way to remind yourself of your accomplishments when self-doubt arises."

   Reference: Joseph, I. (2017). *You Got This: Mastering the Skill of Self-Confidence*. Thomas Nelson.

4. "Meta research has found huge science-based benefits of gratitude."

   Reference: Emmons, R.A. and McCullough, M.E. (2003) 'Counting blessings versus burdens: Experimental studies of gratitude and subjective well-being', Journal of Personality and Social Psychology, 84(2), pp. 377–389 (Confident 21.10.24).

5. "People with a regular gratitude practice reported 23% less stress and more energy and vitality in their lives."

   Reference: Emmons, R.A. and McCullough, M.E. (2003) 'Counting blessings versus burdens: Experimental studies of gratitude and subjective well-being', Journal of Personality and Social Psychology, 84(2), pp. 377–389.

6. **"Gratitude also changes the brain structurally, increasing grey matter, leading to improved cognitive processing."**

    Reference: Kyeong, S. et al. (2017) 'Effects of gratitude meditation on neural network functional connectivity and brain-heart coupling', Cortex, 95, pp. 163–178 (Confident 21.10.24).

7. **"A study on chronic pain sufferers found that those with a gratitude practice had 19% lower depression and a 10% improvement in sleep."**

    Reference: Achor, S. (2010). *The Happiness Advantage: The Seven Principles of Positive Psychology That Fuel Success and Performance at Work*. New York: Crown Business.

8. **"Even after life-changing events, happiness levels return to a 'baseline.'"**

    Reference: Lyubomirsky, S. (2007). *The How of Happiness: A New Approach to Getting the Life You Want*. Penguin Press (Confident 21.10.24).

9. **"Psychiatrist Daniel Z. Lieberman refers to serotonin as the 'here and now' chemical, responsible for feelings of contentment."**

    Reference: Lieberman, D.Z. (2018). *The Molecule of More: How a Single Chemical in Your Brain Drives Love, Sex, and Creativity – and Will Determine the Fate of the Human Race*. BenBella Books (Confident 21.10.24).

10. **"A study published in the Journal of Personality and Social Psychology found that individuals who wrote a letter of gratitude reported greater levels of happiness and decreased symptoms of depression compared to those who did not."**

    Reference: Seligman, M. E. P., Steen, T. A., Park, N., & Peterson, C. (2005). *Positive psychology progress: Empirical validation of interventions*. Journal of Personality and Social Psychology, 60(5), 410-421.

11. **"Research by Grant and Gino showed that people work harder just by being thanked, as in their experiment where fundraisers made 50% more calls after receiving gratitude."** *(p. 43)*

    Reference: Grant, A.M., & Gino, F. (2010). 'A little thanks goes a long way: Explaining why gratitude expressions motivate prosocial behavior'. Journal of Personality and Social Psychology, 98(6), 946-955 (Confident 21.10.24).

12. **"Atomic Habits by James Clear emphasizes the power of tiny habits in transforming behavior and building confidence."** *(p. 57)*

    Reference: Clear, J. (2018). *Atomic Habits: An Easy & Proven Way to Build Good Habits & Break Bad Ones*. New York: Avery.

Chapter 3: North Star Living

1. **"Values are traits or qualities that represent our highest priorities, deeply held beliefs, and core, fundamental driving forces."**

Reference: Schwartz, S. H. (1992). *Universals in the Content and Structure of Values: Theoretical Advances and Empirical Tests in 20 Countries.* Advances in Experimental Social Psychology, 25, 1-65.

2. "We have over five hundred million neurons in our gut, forming an integral connection between our brain and digestive system." *(p. 48)*

    Reference: Mayer, E.A. (2011). *Gut feelings: the emerging biology of gut-brain communication.* Nat Rev Neurosci, 12(8), 453-66. doi: 10.1038/nrn3071.

3. "Finding True North by Michael Henderson provides an excellent exercise to sharpen your values." *(p. 50)*

    Reference: Henderson, M. (2003). *Finding True North: Discover Your Values, Enrich Your Life.* Sydney: HarperCollins.

Chapter 4: Fight the Gremlin

1. "The inner critic, sometimes called the 'saboteur' or A.N.T. (Automatic Negative Thoughts), is that voice that judges, threatens, and points out weaknesses."

    Reference: Burns, D. D. (1989). *The Feeling Good Handbook.* New York: Plume

2. "However, in our research, we found that 90% of people question themselves"

    Reference: Brewin, C. (2024). *Brain Powered Coaching Confidence Research*, Brain Powered Coaching

3. "Research from Harvard researcher Shawn Achor[3] showed that just 3 statements of positive affirmations..."

    Reference: Achor, S. (2010). *The Happiness Advantage.* New York: Crown Business

4. "Affirmations can backfire if they don't align with your core beliefs, as the brain recognizes the disconnect and reacts in the opposite direction."

    Reference: Wood, J. V., Perunovic, W. Q. E., & Lee, J. W. (2009). 'Positive self-statements: Power for some, peril for others'. Psychological Science, 20(7), 860-866

5. "The work of social psychologist Amy Cuddy on 'Power Poses' demonstrates how posture can affect hormone levels and improve confidence."

    Reference: Cuddy, A. (2015). *Presence: Bringing Your Boldest Self to Your Biggest Challenges.* New York: Little, Brown and Company

6. "Sheryl Sandberg, in *Lean In*, emphasizes the importance of women stepping up and embracing leadership roles with confidence."

    Reference: Sandberg, S. (2013). *Lean In: Women, Work, and the Will to Lead.* New York: Knopf

Chapter 5: Imposter to Empowered

1. "The term 'Imposter Syndrome' was first introduced in an article published in 1978, where it was defined as a psychological pattern in which an individual doubts their skills, talents, or accomplishments and has a persistent, internalized fear of being exposed as a fraud."

    Reference: Clance, P.R. and Imes, S.A. (1978) 'The imposter phenomenon in high achieving women: Dynamics and therapeutic intervention', Psychotherapy: Theory, Research & Practice, 15(3), pp. 241–247

2. "Brain Powered Coaching's research found that 52% of people experience imposter syndrome at some point, with 19% saying they always do."

    Reference: Brain Powered Coaching (2024). *Confidence Survey Results*, Brain Powered Coaching

3. "A 2019 study of around 1800 people found that 52% of females and 49% of males experience imposter syndrome daily or regularly."

    Reference: Josa, C. (2019). *Ditching Imposter Syndrome*. Beyond Alchemy Publishing

4. "Clare Josa writes about it beautifully in her book, *Ditching Imposter Syndrome*, explaining that it is a deeply held belief that you are not enough, even when your skills and success prove otherwise."

    Reference: Josa, C. (2019). *Ditching Imposter Syndrome*. Beyond Alchemy Publishing

5. "Brené Brown talks about embracing vulnerability as a pathway to building confidence in her book *Daring Greatly*."

    Reference: Brown, B. (2012). *Daring Greatly: How the Courage to Be Vulnerable Transforms the Way We Live, Love, Parent, and Lead*. New York: Avery

6. "Research by The Harris Poll found that nearly one-third of adults reported significant decision-making difficulties during the Covid-19 pandemic due to stress." *(p. 82)*

    Reference: The Harris Poll (2021) 'Pandemic Stress Survey'. Available at: https://theharrispoll.com:contentReference{index=5}.

7. "A study published in *Psychological Science* in 2014 found that procrastinators had larger amygdalas and weaker connections between their amygdala and the dorsal anterior cingulate cortex."

    Reference: Steel, P. (2007). *The Nature of Procrastination: A Meta-Analytic and Theoretical Review of Quintessential Self-Regulatory Failure*. Psychological Bulletin, 133(1), pp. 65–94

8. **"Research from Microsoft from 2021"**

    Reference: Microsoft (2021) 'Research shows your brain needs breaks – Outlook and Microsoft Teams can help', Microsoft 365 Blog. Available at: https://www.microsoft.com/en-us/worklab/work-trend-index/brain-research (Accessed: 21 July 2023).

9. **"Dr. Andrew Huberman explains this beautifully in his 2023 podcast on dopamine."**

    Reference: Huberman, A. (2023). *The Huberman Lab Podcast.* Episode: Dopamine: Understanding & Harnessing the Brain's Motivation & Reward System. Available at: https://hubermanlab.com.

10. **"Mel Robbins recommends using the simple 5, 4, 3, 2, 1 method for overcoming procrastination. When faced with a task, count down from 5 and then take immediate action without hesitation."**

    Reference: Robbins, M. (2017). *The 5 Second Rule: Transform Your Life, Work, and Confidence with Everyday Courage.* Savio Republic

Chapter 6: Dance with Stress, Unleash Resilience

1. **"In fact, our research1 found that 84% of people are stressed from taking on too much and 72% of people have feelings of being a failure"**

    Reference: Brain Powered Coaching (2024). Confidence Survey Results, Brain Powered Coaching.

2. **"The more ambiguity, the more the brain interprets it as a threat. Research by Hsu et al. (2005) shows how ambiguity activates the brain's fear response."**

    Reference: Hsu, M., et al. (2005). Neural Systems Responding to Degree of Uncertainty in Human Decision-Making. Science, 310(5754), 1680–1683.

3. **"In his book, the 7 Habits of Highly Effective People, Stephen Covey emphasizes the importance of managing stress through proactive habits and emotional resilience."**

    Reference: Covey, S. (1989). The 7 Habits of Highly Effective People. New York: Simon & Schuster.

4. **"Significant research shows that individuals who meditate regularly are more positive and less stressed, as demonstrated by the findings of Economides et al. (2018)."**

    Reference: Economides, M., et al. (2018). Improvements in stress, affect, and irritability following brief use of a mindfulness-based smartphone app. Mindfulness, 9(5), 1584–1593.

5. **"Studies have shown increased grey matter density in the brains of those who meditate, leading to better cognitive functioning."**

    Reference: Lazar, S.W., et al. (2005). Meditation experience is associated with increased cortical thickness. NeuroReport, 16(17), 1893–1897.

6. "Two recent studies with oncology and pediatric nurses found that mindfulness-based stress reduction (MBSR) significantly reduced burnout and improved psychological well-being."

   Reference: Morrison Wylde, C., et al. (2017). Mindfulness for novice paediatric nurses: Smartphone application versus traditional intervention. PubMed; Kriakous, S.A., et al. (2020). The effectiveness of mindfulness-based stress reduction on the psychological functioning of healthcare professionals. PubMed.

7. "Here are some other benefits."

   Reference: Mindful.org (2022) The Science of Mindfulness. Available at: https://www.mindful.org/the-science-of-mindfulness/

8. "In her research at Harvard, Alison Wood Brooks found that reappraising pre-performance anxiety as excitement improved performance."

   Reference: Brooks, A.W. (2013). Get excited: Reappraising pre-performance anxiety as excitement. Harvard Business School.

9. "I love the video of Karen Lawson, a coach who emphasizes the power of handling hard situations better by understanding our stress thresholds."

   Reference: Lawson, K. (2022). Handle Hard Better. Available at: https://www.youtube.com/watch?v=oDzfZOfNki4.

10. "Psychologist and Stanford researcher, Carol Dweck, discovered that a 'growth mindset' leads to greater resilience and confidence."

    Reference: Dweck, C.S. (2006). Mindset: The New Psychology of Success. New York: Random House.

11. "This stress inoculation, because each time you do it, your stress threshold increases. The 'stress threshold' is essentially the point at which your body succumbs to stress."

    Reference: Meichenbaum, D. (2007). *Stress Inoculation Training: A Prevention and Treatment Approach*. Springer.

12. "There's also the benefit of a big dopamine spike and endorphin release after a chilly dip, reducing inflammation, and improving circulation. It's a great way to feel that spark of WOW, whilst reducing stress and increasing your resilience levels."

    Reference: Hof, W. (2020). *The Wim Hof Method: Activate Your Full Human Potential*. Sounds True.

13. "A study by researchers from Radboud University Medical Centre found that Wim Hof's breathing and cold exposure techniques can regulate the immune response."

    Reference: Kox, M., et al. (2014). Voluntary activation of the sympathetic nervous system and attenuation of the innate immune response in humans. PNAS, 111(20), 7379–7384.

Chapter 7: Empowered Boundaries

1. "Over 49% of employees globally in a recent study said that they felt some level of burnout."

   Reference: McKinsey & Company and LeanIn.Org (2021). *Women in the Workplace 2021.* Available at: https://wiw-report.s3.amazonaws.com/Women_in_the_Workplace_2021.pdf.

2. "There are 4 key techniques you can use to say No. A great resource for more research on these is Smith's book."

   Reference: Smith, M. J. (1975). *When I Say No, I Feel Guilty.* Bantam Books.

3. "There was a really interesting study done by the sleep researcher Matthew Walker, which found that sleep deprivation leads to a 60% increase in the sensitivity of the amygdala, the emotional centre of the brain."

   Reference: Walker, M. (2007). *Lack of Sleep Disrupts Brain's Emotional Controls.* National Institutes of Health (NIH).

Chapter 8: Navigating Feedback and Failure

1. "Fear of exclusion can be hugely triggering and has even been shown to be physically painful. Whether caused by social rejection or physical pain, brain scans showed the same areas associated with distress were activated."

   Reference: Eisenberger, N.I., Lieberman, M.D., & Williams, K.D. (2006). 'An experimental study of shared sensitivity to physical and social rejection'. Available at: https://www.scn.ucla.edu/pdf/Eisenberger,Jarcho,Lieberman,Naliboff(2006).pdf:contentReference{index=0}.

2. "Research shows that painkillers normally used to reduce physical pain can also reduce social pain."

   Reference: DeWall, C.N., et al. (2010). 'Tylenol reduces social pain: Behavioral and neural evidence'. Psychological Science, 21(7), 931–937(Confident 21.10.24).

3. "Paul J. Zak showed that high levels of oxytocin cause people to work harder to help the group achieve its goals."

   Reference: Zak, P.J. (2017). *Trust Factor: The Science of Creating High-Performance Companies.* AMACOM (Confident 21.10.24).

4. "Existence of core human values (integrity, honesty, kindness) builds a social safety net that leads to better sleep, less stress, and better health."

   Reference: Slavich, G. M. (2020). *Social Safety Theory: A Biologically Based Evolutionary Perspective on Life Stress, Health, and Behavior.* Annual Review of Clinical Psychology, 16, 265–295.

5. "In fact, research from Waldinger et al. shows that the level of social connection you have is the best predictor of well-being and longevity."

   Reference: Waldinger, R. J., & Schulz, M. S. (2015). *The Harvard Study of Adult Development: Lessons from 75 Years of Research on Happiness and Longevity.* Harvard University Press.

6. "Research in Frontiers in Psychology (2017) highlighted that oxytocin is associated with increased emotional resilience"

   Reference: Waldinger, R. J., & Schulz, M. S. (2015). *The Harvard Study of Adult Development: Lessons from 75 Years of Research on Happiness and Longevity.* Harvard University Press.

7. "We love the advice from PepTalkHer, which encourages tracking accomplishments to advocate for yourself." *(p. 150)*

   Reference: PepTalkHer (2020). *Advocating for Yourself in the Workplace.* Available at: https://www.peptalkher.com::contentReference{index=5}.

Chapter 9: Triumph Through Change

1. "From our research[1], 48% of people have had a career break (for whatever reason) and subsequently really struggle with their confidence"

   Reference: Brewin, C. (2024). *Brain Powered Coaching Confidence Research.*

2. "It reflects reorganisation, refinement, and streamlining, not degeneration. The term 'Baby Brain' refers to changes during motherhood that prioritise baby care over minor everyday tasks."

   Reference: McKay, S. (2023). *Baby Brain.* Hachette Australia.

3. "University of Colombia research shows that men often receive a pay increase when they become fathers, a phenomenon known as the 'fatherhood wage premium.'"

   Reference: Budig, M. J. (2014). 'The Fatherhood Bonus and The Motherhood Penalty'. University of Massachusetts.

4. "Supporting mothers differently, as Amy Taylor-Kabbaz discusses in her work on Matrescence, helps navigate identity shifts after motherhood."

   Reference: Taylor-Kabbaz, A. (2020). *Mama Rising.* Available at: https://amytaylorkabbaz.com.

5. "The average person has twelve jobs in their working lifetime."

   Reference: World Economic Forum (2023). *The Future of Jobs Report 2023.* Available at: https://wef.ch.

6. "In the late nineteenth and early twentieth centuries, the average age of death for women in the United States was 49."

   Reference: Brizendine, L. (2006). *The Female Brain.* New York: Morgan Road Books.

7. "We spoke to Executive Menopause Coach, Claire Hattrick, who emphasised that menopause can affect confidence significantly."

   Reference: Hattrick, C. (2020). Available at: https://www.theexecutivemenopausecoach.com.

8. "Recipes by Dr. Mary Claire can support hormonal changes during menopause."

   Reference: Haver, M. (2020). Available at: https://www.instagram.com/drmaryclaire.

9. "'Menofriend' is a great example of a supplement that many women find helpful." *(p. 154)*

   Reference: Available at: https://drvegan.com/products/menofriend.

10. "The Kübler-Ross Change Curve, derived from the 'grief curve', helps understand emotional responses to major changes like divorce." *(p. 156)*

    Reference: Kübler-Ross, E., & Kessler, D. (2005). *On Grief and Grieving.* Scribner.

11. "Molly Benjamin, author and CEO of Ladies Finance Club."

    Reference: Benjamin, M. (2023). *Girls Just Want to Have Funds: Every Woman's Guide to Financial Independence.* HarperCollins.

12. "Sara Davison, 'The Divorce Coach', emphasises the emotional toll of breakups and how they impact confidence." *(p. 157)*

    Reference: Davison, S. (2020). Available at: www.saradavison.com.

Chapter 10: Beyond the Framework: Understanding Gendered Confidence

1. "This surge actually shrinks the male brain's centres for communication, observation and processing of emotions."

   Reference: Brizendine, Louann. The Female Brain. Broadway Books, 2007.

2. "In fact, the science indicates that girls are more wired for connection and success in social groups. Even as babies, little girls typically engage quickly, looking for visual cues of reassurance and connection."

   Reference: Brizendine, Louann. The Female Brain. Broadway Books, 2007.

3. "Testosterone, the hormone most associated with male behaviour, is known to drive risk-taking, aggression, and competition."

   Reference: Apicella, Coren L., et al. "Testosterone and Financial Risk Preferences." Evolution and Human Behavior, vol. 29, no. 6, 2008, pp. 384–390.

4. "For example, studies have shown that men with higher testosterone levels are more likely to engage in competitive sports, assert dominance in social situations, or take on high-stakes challenges at work."

Reference: Sapienza, Paola, et al. "Gender Differences in Financial Risk Aversion and Career Choices are Affected by Testosterone." Proceedings of the National Academy of Sciences, vol. 106, no. 36, 2009, pp. 15268–15273.

5. "Research at the University of Pennsylvania used functional Magnetic Resonance Imaging (fMRI) to reveal that female brains have much greater activity between the two hemispheres (left and right), while male brains primarily function front to back – within one hemisphere or the other."

Reference: Verma, Ragini, et al. "Sex Differences in the Structural Connectome of the Human Brain." Proceedings of the National Academy of Sciences, vol. 110, no. 2, 2013, pp. 823–828.

6. "Studies from 350 FTSE companies found that executive committees with at least 33% female representation had ten times the profit margin of those with fewer women."

Reference: Hunt, Vivian, et al. "Delivering Through Diversity." McKinsey & Company, January 2018.

7. "McKinsey's research showed that diverse executive teams were 25% more likely to financially outperform their peers."

Reference: McKinsey & Company. "Diversity Wins: How Inclusion Matters." McKinsey & Company, May 2020.

8. "A large-scale study done by the University of Cambridge."

Reference: University of Cambridge. "Empathy: Gender Differences in Cognitive and Affective Empathy." University of Cambridge, 2017.

9. "As McKinsey's research points out, this is crucial for the brains of an organisation to operate at their maximum potential."

Reference: McKinsey & Company. "Women in the Workplace." McKinsey & Company, 2019.

10. Psychological safety, defined as 'a shared belief held by members of a team that the team is safe for interpersonal risk-taking,'

Reference: Edmondson, Amy C. "Psychological Safety and Learning Behavior in Work Teams." Administrative Science Quarterly, vol. 44, no. 2, 1999, pp. 350–383.

Chapter 11: Quietly Bold: Redefining Confidence For Introverts

1. There's zero correlation between being the best talker and having the best ideas.

Reference: Cain, S. (2012). Quiet: The power of introverts in a world that can't stop talking. Crown Publishing Group.

REFERENCES

Amar, A.D. et al. (2014) 'Meditation and leadership skills in senior managers', Academy of Management Proceedings.

BBC News (2017) 100 Women: Can we wire our brains for confidence? Available at: https://www.bbc.com/news/world-41521671 (Accessed: 22 September 2024).

Brizendine, L. (2006) The female brain. 10th edn. Morgan Road Books.

Brooks, A.W. (2013) Get excited: Reappraising pre-performance anxiety as excitement. Harvard Business School. Available at: https://www.hbs.edu/ris/Publication%20Files/xge-a0035325%20(2)_0287835d-9e25-4f92-9661-c5b54dbbcb39.pdf (Accessed: 22 August 2022).

Brown, B. (2010) The Gifts of Imperfection.

Brown, P. (2015) The Fear-Free Organization.

Brown, P. (2020) London Protocol of Emotions.

Burchard, B. (2017) High Performance Habits: How extraordinary people become that way. Hay House, Pty. Ltd. Australia.

Cain, S. (2012). Quiet: The power of introverts in a world that can't stop talking. Crown Publishing Group.

Chamorro-Premuzic, T. and Furnham, A. (2005) Personality and intellectual competence. Lawrence Erlbaum Associates Publishers.

Clance, P.R. and Imes, S.A. (1978) 'The imposter phenomenon in high achieving women: Dynamics and therapeutic intervention', Psychotherapy: Theory, Research & Practice, 15(3), pp. 241–247.

Connor, S. (2013) 'The hardwired difference between male and female brains could explain why men are 'better at map reading'', The Independent, 3 December. Available at: https://www.independent.co.uk/life-style/the-hardwired-difference-between-male-and-female-brains-could-explain-why-men-are-better-at-map-reading-8978248.html

Covey, S. (1989) The 7 Habits of Highly Effective People. Simon and Schuster, New York.

Desteno, D. et al. (2018) 'Meditation inhibits aggressive responses to provocations', Mindfulness, 9(4), pp. 1117–1122.

Duarte, J. and Pinto-Gouveia, J. (2016) 'Effectiveness of a mindfulness-based intervention on oncology nurses' burnout and compassion fatigue symptoms: A non-randomized study'. Available at: https://pubmed.ncbi.nlm.nih.gov/27744228/ (Accessed: 22 August 2022).

Economides, M. et al. (2018) 'Improvements in stress, affect, and irritability following brief use of a mindfulness-based smartphone app: a randomized controlled trial', Mindfulness, 9(5), pp. 1584-1593.

Edmondson, A. (1999) 'Psychological safety and learning behavior in work teams', Administrative Science Quarterly, 44(2), pp. 350–383.

Eisenberger, N.I. et al. (2006) 'An experimental study of shared sensitivity to physical and social rejection'. Available at: https://www.scn.ucla.edu/pdf/Eisenberger,Jarcho,Lieberman,Naliboff(2006).pdf (Accessed: 22 August 2022).

Emmons, R.A. and McCullough, M.E. (2003) 'Counting blessings versus burdens: Experimental studies of gratitude and subjective well-being', Journal of Personality and Social Psychology, 84(2), pp. 377–389.

Estes, Z. (2013) 'Attributive and relational processes in nominal combination', Journal of Memory and Language, 48(2), pp. 304–319.

Grant, H. (2010) Succeed: How We Can Reach Our Goals.

Henderson, M. (2003) Finding True North: Discover Your Values, Enrich Your Life. Paperback edn. 1 August.

Josa, C. (2019) Ditching Imposter Syndrome. Beyond Alchemy Publishing, UK.

Kay, K. and Shipman, C. (2014) The Confidence Code. Harper Business, USA.

Kriakous, S.A. et al. (2020) 'The effectiveness of mindfulness-based stress reduction on the psychological functioning of healthcare professionals: a systematic review'. Available at: https://pubmed.ncbi.nlm.nih.gov/32989406/ (Accessed: 22 August 2022).

Kubo, A. et al. (2018) 'A pilot mobile-based mindfulness intervention for cancer patients and their informal caregivers', Mindfulness, 9(6), pp. 1885–1894.

Kübler-Ross, E. and Kessler, D. (2005) On grief and grieving: Finding the meaning of grief through the five stages of loss. Simon and Schuster, New York.

Kyeong, S. et al. (2017) 'Effects of gratitude meditation on neural network functional connectivity and brain-heart coupling', Cortex, 95, pp. 163–178.

Lawson, K. (2022) Handle Hard Better. Available at: https://www.youtube.com/watch?v=oDzfZOfNki4

Mayer EA. Gut feelings: the emerging biology of gut-brain communication. Nat Rev Neurosci. 2011 Jul 13;12(8):453-66. doi: 10.1038/nrn3071. PMID: 21750565; PMCID: PMC3845678.

McKay, S. (2023) Baby Brain.

McKinsey & Company and LeanIn.Org (2019) Women in the Workplace 2019. Available at: https://www.mckinsey.com/~/media/McKinsey/Featured%20Insights/Gender%20Equality/Women%20in%20the%20Workplace%202019/Women-in-the-workplace-2019.ashx

McKinsey & Company and LeanIn.Org (2021) Women in the Workplace 2021. Available at: https://wiw-report.s3.amazonaws.com/Women_in_the_Workplace_2021.pdf

Microsoft (2021) 'Research shows your brain needs breaks – Outlook and Microsoft Teams can help', Microsoft 365 Blog. Available at: https://www.microsoft.com/en-us/worklab/work-trend-index/brain-research (Accessed: 21 July 2023).

Mindful.org (2022) The Science of Mindfulness. Available at: https://www.mindful.org/the-science-of-mindfulness/

Morrison Wylde, C. et al. (2017) 'Mindfulness for novice paediatric nurses: Smartphone application versus traditional intervention'. Available at: https://pubmed.ncbi.nlm.nih.gov/28888505/ (Accessed: 22 August 2022).

Nyhan, B. and Reifler, J. (2010) 'When corrections fail: The persistence of political misperceptions'. Available at: https://cpb-us-e1.wpmucdn.com/sites.dartmouth.edu/dist/5/2293/files/2021/03/nyhan-reifler.pdf (Accessed: 22 August 2022).

Oettingen, G. and Gollwitzer, P.M. (2010) 'Mental contrasting and goal commitment: The mediating role of energization', Personality and Social Psychology Bulletin, 36(1), pp. 114–127.

Petty, R., Briñol, P. and Tormala, Z. (2002) 'Thought confidence as a determinant of persuasion: The self-validation hypothesis', Journal of Personality and Social Psychology, 82, pp. 722–741.

Pipeline (2019) Women count 2019: Role, value, and number of female executives in the FTSE 350. Available at: https://execpipeline.com/wp-content/uploads/2020/12/The-Pipeline-Women-Count-2019.pdf

Raghunathan, R. (2013) 'How negative is your 'mental chatter'?' Available at: https://www.psychologytoday.com/gb/blog/sapient-nature/201310/how-negative-is-your-mental-chatter

Robbins, M. (2017) The 5 Second Rule: Transform Your Life, Work, and Confidence with Everyday Courage.

Robertson, I. (2021) How Confidence Works: The New Science of Self-Belief. Bantam Press, London.

Schmidt, L. et al. (2012) 'Neural mechanisms underlying motivation of mental versus physical effort', PLoS Biology, 10(2), e1001266.

Seligman, M.E. et al. (2005) 'Positive psychology progress: Empirical validation of interventions', American Psychologist, 60(5), pp. 410–421.

Shedd, C.W. (1965) Letters to Karen: A Father's Advice on Keeping Love in Marriage. Nashville, TN: Abingdon Press.

Siegel, D.J. (2019) 'The mind in psychotherapy: An interpersonal neurobiology framework for understanding and cultivating mental health', Psychology and Psychotherapy: Theory, Research and Practice, 92, pp. 224–237.

Slavich, G.M. (2020) 'Social safety theory: A biologically based evolutionary perspective on life stress, health, and behavior', Annual Review of Clinical Psychology, 16, pp. 265–295.

Steel, P. (2007) 'The nature of procrastination: A meta-analytic and theoretical review of quintessential self-regulatory failure', Psychological Bulletin, 133(1), pp. 65–94.

University of British Columbia (2018) 'Dads often earn more, even if they're not harder workers', ScienceDaily, 14 June. Available at: https://www.sciencedaily.com/releases/2018/06/180614213621.htm

Waldinger, R.J. et al. (2015) 'Security of attachment to spouses in late life: Concurrent and prospective links with cognitive and emotional well-being', Clinical Psychological Science, 3(4), pp. 516–529.

Walker, M. (2007) 'Lack of sleep disrupts brain's emotional controls'. Available at: https://www.nih.gov/news-events/nih-research-matters/lack-sleep-disrupts-brains-emotional-controls

Westbrook, A. and Braver, T.S. (2016) 'Dopamine does double duty in motivating cognitive effort', Neuron, 91(4), pp. 708–721.

Wood, A.M., Froh, J.J. and Geraghty, A.W. (2010) 'Gratitude and well-being: A review and theoretical integration', Clinical Psychology Review, 30(7), pp. 890–905.

World Economic Forum (2023) Workers set for multiple careers as jobs demand new skills. Available at: https://www.weforum.org/agenda/2023/05/workers-multiple-careers-jobs-skills/ (Accessed: 7 September 2024).

Zak, P.J. (2017) Trust factor: The science of creating high-performance companies. AMACOM, New York.

www.ingramcontent.com/pod-product-compliance
Ingram Content Group UK Ltd.
Pitfield, Milton Keynes, MK11 3LW, UK
UKHW022305300625
460104UK00004B/7